CINEMA AND SPECTATORSHIP

Cinema and Spectatorship is the first book to focus on the history and role of the spectator in contemporary film studies. Judith Mayne examines how spectatorship emerged in the 1970s as one of the major preoccupations of film theorists, particularly in relation to theories of the subject drawn from psychoanalysis and semiotics. She suggests that while 1970s film theory insisted on the separation between the cinematic subject and actual film viewers, interest in spectatorship in film studies has been characterized by a very real friction between "subjects" and "viewers". She evaluates challenges to and revisions of 1970s theory, from feminist analyses of female spectatorship to historical explorations of how the film–spectator relationship is shaped by particular cultural factors.

In the book's first section Mayne examines three theoretical models of spectatorship: the perceptual, the institutional and the historical, while the second section focuses on case studies which crystallize many of the issues already discussed, concentrating on textual analysis, genre, "star-gazing" and finally the audience itself. These include the place of the spectator in the textual analysis of individual films such as *The Picture of Dorian Gray*; the construction of Bette Davis's star persona; fantasies of race and film viewing in *Field of Dreams* and *Ghost*; and gay and lesbian audiences as "critical" audiences. *Cinema and Spectatorship* provides a thorough and accessible overview of this complex, fragmented and often controversial area of film theory.

Judith Mayne is Professor of French and Women's Studies at Ohio State University, where she has taught since 1976. She is the author of *The Woman at the Keyhole* (1990), *Kino and the Woman Question* (1989) and *Private Novels, Public Films* (1988).

SIGHTLINES

Edited by Edward Buscombe, The British Film Institute and Philip Rosen, Center for Modern Culture and Media, Brown University, USA

Cinema Studies has made extraordinary strides in the past two decades. Our capacity for understanding both how and what the cinema signifies has been developed through new methodologies, and hugely enriched in interaction with a wide variety of other disciplines, including literary studies, anthropology, linguistics, history, economics and psychology. As fertile and important as these new theoretical foundations are, their very complexity has made it increasingly difficult to track the main lines of conceptualization. Furthermore, they have made Cinema Studies an ever more daunting prospect for those coming new to the field.

This new series of books will map out the ground of major conceptual areas within Cinema Studies. Each volume is written by a recognized authority to provide a clear and detailed synopsis of current debates within a particular topic. Each will make an original contribution to advancing the state of knowledge within the area. Key arguments and terms will be clearly identified and explained, seminal thinkers will be assessed, and issues for further research will be laid out. Taken together the volumes in this series will constitute an indispensable chart of the terrain which Cinema Studies now occupies.

Books in the series include:

NARRATIVE COMPREHENSION AND FILM
Edward Branigan

NEW VOCABULARIES IN FILM SEMIOTICS
Structuralism, Post-structuralism and Beyond
Robert Stam, Robert Burgoyne and Sandy Flitterman-Lewis

CINEMA AND SPECTATORSHIP
Judith Mayne

Forthcoming:

UNTHINKING EUROCENTRISM
Towards a Multi-cultural Film Critique
Ella Shohat/Robert Stam

CINEMA AND SPECTATORSHIP

Judith Mayne

London & New York

First published 1993
by Routledge
11 New Fetter Lane, London EC4P 4EE

Simultaneously published in the USA and Canada
by Routledge
29 West 35th Street, New York, NY 10001

Phototypeset in 10/12 Palatino by Intype, London
Printed in Great Britain by
T. J. Press (Padstow) Ltd, Padstow, Cornwall

British Library Cataloguing in Publication Data
Mayne, Judith
Cinema and Spectatorship. – (Sightlines Series)
I. Title II. Series
791.43

Library of Congress Cataloging in Publication Data
Mayne, Judith.
Cinema and spectatorship/Judith Mayne.
p.   cm. – (Sightlines)
1. Motion picture audiences.   2. Film criticism.   I. Title.
II. Series: Sightlines (London, England)
PN1995.9.A8M28 1993
791.43'015–dc20   92–24927

ISBN 0–415–03415–9
ISBN 0–415–03416–7 (pbk)

For John Bush

CONTENTS

ILLUSTRATIONS

ACKNOWLEDGEMENTS

Thanks to John Bush for over thirty years of intellectual companionship; he influenced this book in ways that might surprise him. Thanks to series editors Philip Rosen and Ed Buscombe for their encouragement and patience. The College of Humanities, the Department of French and Italian, and the Center for Women's Studies at the Ohio State University have provided support for which I am grateful. Thanks also to Rebecca Thomas for research assistance; to Terry Geesken of the Museum of Modern Art Film Stills Archive for assistance in locating the stills for chapters 6, 7 and 8; to Anne Friedberg for conversations at crucial moments. I am particularly grateful to Terry Moore for her detailed comments on individual chapters and for her wicked sense of humor.

INTRODUCTION

In 1913 "Victor Appleton" – one of the fictitious authors' names created by the Stratemeyer Syndicate for an anonymous group of writers – introduced two new series of juvenile novels about the movies: the "Motion Picture Chums" and the "Moving Picture Boys." Both series detail the adventures of male friends who have entered the business of making and exhibiting movies – the Moving Picture Boys are filmmakers, and the Motion Picture Chums are exhibitors. One year later, under the equally fictitious name of Laura Lee Hope, a comparable series was introduced about young women, the "Moving Picture Girls." It will come as no surprise to those familiar with the history of motion pictures that the girls' adventures evolve from their position in front of the camera, as actresses, and not behind it.

These novels are interesting for more than the classic gender division they inscribe. For the series capitalize on the enormous interest that motion pictures had inspired in the two decades of their history, and in so doing function as early primers on spectatorship, the subject of this book. Spectatorship is not only the act of watching a film, but also the ways one takes pleasure in the experience, or not; the means by which watching movies becomes a passion, or a leisure-time activity like any other. Spectatorship refers to how film-going and the consumption of movies and their myths are symbolic activities, culturally significant events.

Clearly the series of novels by Appleton and Hope respond to a perceived need to justify the cinema in moral terms. The Motion Picture Chums, in Appleton's books, are models of middle-class respectability and ingenuity, and they are pitted against other less noble figures. In their second adventure, *The Motion Picture Chums at Seaside Park* (1913), for instance, the chums come to the rescue of a group of wealthy individuals whose motorboat has caught fire. Peter, one of the group, is foil to the Motion Picture Chums in that he embodies cowardice and narcissism and swims away from the others, while the chums assist them. That Peter represents the kind of

1

spectatorship to which the boys are the positive alternative is suggested more emphatically when he eavesdrops on a conversation, sneaking up on the friends unawares, all the while assuming that is his right. In contrast, Frank, Randy, and Pep are direct and forthright. One assumes not only that the books were designed to engage cinematic fantasies by offering behind-the-scenes views (in the Seaside Park adventure, the exhibition process is detailed), but also to encourage a kind of spectatorship that upheld the values of the chums while dismissing the spectatorship of one like Peter – voyeuristic, self-serving and immature.

The Moving Picture Girls – sisters Ruth and Alice DeVere – come to their cinematic adventures through a different route. Their father is a noted stage actor who has difficulty finding work. When at last he lands a part, he is stricken by a mysterious recurring throat ailment which leaves him unable to speak above a hoarse whisper. With the help of their neighbor, Russ, who is a projectionist and a camera operator, the girls convince their father that the movies provide an excellent outlet for his talents. The father's prejudices against the movies are soon overcome, and he becomes a regular actor in the Comet film company. Eventually the girls begin acting as well, and the series of novels details their adventures as the film company moves from one location to another. The Moving Picture Girls' adventures provide many opportunities to accentuate the positive moral side of motion pictures through the girls' reactions to the movies. After her first visit to the motion-picture studio, Alice describes to her sister her desire to act: "It's just lovely, I think. You don't have to act before a whole big audience that is staring at you. Just some nice men, in their shirt sleeves, turning cranks" (Hope 1914: 85).

The motion pictures as defined in these novels are not only embodiments of middle-class respectability, but also serve to demonstrate the superior pluck and courage of those drawn to the movies – with keen entrepreneurial skills thrown in for the boys, and domestic devotion for the girls. Now many films of the era were similarly concerned to demonstrate, in one way or another, the same kind of superior moral values, and a preoccupation with spectatorship has been evident in moving pictures virtually from the beginning, whether it be in a child looking gleefully through *Grandma's Reading Glass* (1900) or a country bumpkin visiting the cinema for the first time in *Uncle Josh at the Moving Picture Show* (1902). Unique to the adventures of the Moving Picture Girls and the Motion Picture Chums is that spectatorship has moved outside the movie theater, and that what the novels therefore promise is a reliving of filmic adventures and a re-creation of cinematic fantasies. For spectatorship is not just the relationship that occurs between the viewer and the screen, but also and especially how that relationship lives on once the spectator leaves the theater.

In my lifetime, there have been far more ways to extend the pleasure of the movies than the Moving Picture Girls or the Motion Picture chums ever dreamed of. I have a vague memory that when my parents took me to see my second film in a movie theater (I have no idea how old I was), I was astonished that you could see a *different* film every time you went to the movies, and the thought of how many movies must therefore exist was mind-boggling. I had the same thrill when I first discovered movie-fan magazines at the age of 10 or so, astonished that someone had thought of such a clever idea to supplement the enormously pleasureful but nonetheless limited two hours or so it took to watch a film. Thus, even though I grew up in the 1950s when more movie culture was available than in 1913 or 1914, my thrill at the possibilities of cinema spectatorship was not so unlike the Moving Picture Girls' discovery of the movies.

Since I am an academic who makes a living from studying film, I care about the quality of films as well as the myths surrounding their consumption. In that sense I perhaps share more with the Motion Picture Chums and the Moving Picture Girls than I would like, since the moral preoccupations of those novels are not so far removed from my assumption that "informed" spectatorship can only increase the desire for better-quality films. But it all depends, of course, on what kind of quality you are looking for. I may be an informed spectator, but that has not lessened my pleasure in what some consider inferior products, like Arnold Schwarzenegger films. Rather, the study of spectatorship has made me cognizant, in quite commonplace and everyday ways, of the kinds of contradictory impulses that comprise pleasure. For as much as feminism, for instance, is fully part of my everyday life, I have somewhat peculiar (peculiar, that is, to my friends and family; not to me) regressive fantasies about male adolescence which are given perfect expression by Schwarzenegger. Spectatorship is one of the few places in my life where the attractions to male adolescence and feminist avant-garde poetics exist side by side. For Chantal Akerman's particular approach to spectatorship, for instance, engages me in different but equally satisfying ways as Arnold Schwarzenegger's.

Film studies tells me that the difference between these two experiences of spectatorship is not so much that one is art and the other isn't, but rather that one kind of spectatorship is "critical" (Akerman's), engaged as it is with the relation between memory and duration, gender and address; while the other (Schwarzenegger's) is not. One kind of spectatorship makes me think and reflect, while the other makes me act out and forget. One kind of spectatorship

3

challenges cinematic conventions and attempts to create a new language of the cinema; the other perpetuates dominant cinematic and cultural practices.

When I became involved in film studies, this distinction between crude and sophisticated spectatorship was enormously seductive, and I embraced it wholeheartedly. As a graduate student in the early 1970s, the discovery, first, of the films of Jean-Luc Godard, and later, of Soviet films of the 1920s, was tantamount to a fundamental revision about everything I had assumed the cinema to be. The crucial dimension seemed to be the way these films addressed their viewers. I conveniently forgot the radical differences between Soviet audiences of the 1920s, struggling with the vicissitudes of socialist economic and cultural change; or a French, largely Parisian, intellectual crowd; and me, sitting in auditoriums in Buffalo, New York with mostly other students and the occasional local activist or film buff. Spectatorship became, to my mind, something a *film* or a *filmmaker* did, not something I necessarily brought to a film; it was there for me – or any cognizant viewer, whether a Russian peasant or Jean-Paul Sartre – to discover.

In retrospect, I am struck by how that perception of critical spectatorship is locked into a neat dualism with the view that was being elaborated in film studies at the time, concerning the "classical" or dominant cinema, which positioned spectators who were passive, or at the very least highly receptive to complicit, uncritical pleasures. Spectatorship was defined as an either/or proposition. At the same time, spectatorship was identified as purely a function of the individual film text, and presumably the critical spectatorship thus embodied would be identical whether you were in Paris or Buffalo or Leningrad.

It will be evident in the following chapters that I think spectatorship is at once the most valuable area of film studies, and the one that has been the most misunderstood, largely because of the obsessive preoccupation with dualistic categories of critique versus celebration, or "critical" versus "complacent" spectatorship. Many scholars working in the field share my reservations, but I am not so certain that the simple reversals that have taken place in recent years are necessarily improvements. While I do not think spectatorship of the classical Hollywood cinema is satisfactorily explained in terms of passivity and ideological indoctrination, for instance, the tendency to reverse the terms and to claim the site of viewing (clearly following the emphasis on reading in reader-response theory) as always active or contestatory is just as problematic.

While I am critical of this dualistic framework, this book is not intended as a demonstration of the error-filled ways of all of the different forms and evolutions spectatorship has taken in film studies.

I have limited the scope of my study in several ways. First, I discuss spectatorship and the cinema, without taking television spectatorship into account. While television watching is undoubtedly the most important spectating activity of the present time, film spectatorship nonetheless has a special quality given the important role motion pictures have played in the development of industries and institutions of the image and of narrative. And in any case, the way in which analyses of the spectator and spectatorship have evolved in television studies is quite different than in film. Second, I have limited my focus to mainstream, commercial film. While various independent and avant-garde cinemas take spectatorship as a major concern, film studies has nonetheless been preoccupied – and in some ways obsessed – with the "classical" models of dominant cinema. I question that preoccupation, but from within, as it were, by limiting my range of inquiry to mainstream, narrative films.

I have attempted both to summarize debates in film studies and to suggest ways they might continue more productively. When I point to limitations or blind spots in recent film theory, I have in mind a productive engagement, not a rejection from the exalted vantage point of theoretical purity or political righteousness. Theory and politics are two of the terms that have been uttered most frequently in film studies, as well as in contemporary critical theory in general. It is common, in genealogies of film studies (or contemporary critical theory), to trace their development to the political demonstrations and student-worker coalitions of May '68 in France, and to the general climate of contestation and protest that characterized the 1960s and 1970s in the US and Europe.

From the events of May '68 emerged a heightened awareness of both the ubiquity of images and commodities and the importance of understanding them critically. If the events of May '68 encouraged a rethinking of forms of political protest and an insistence on the importance of utopian thinking, the heritage of May '68 for film studies has far more to do with what was theorized as the problem – what Guy Debord in his famous book called *The Society of the Spectacle* (1967), a society, that is, in which the consumption and contemplation of images has replaced all forms of human communication – than with the various solutions that were proposed, from street theater to student/worker coalitions to a fusion of psychoanalysis and politics. Indeed, the psychoanalytic inflection of most contemporary film studies, rather than being a theory of emancipatory or radical practice, has been a reminder that no easy politics of the unconscious is possible. The theoretical legacy of 1968 for film studies was the recognition that the seemingly innocent activities of watching a movie or reading a magazine function to create a society of complicit individuals.

5

Citing May '68 has become a reflex, and too often such narratives of the development of a field make it seem as if there is an easy, direct link between politics and intellectual life. In fact the connections are more tenuous and therefore less amenable to easy cause-and-effect explanations. While theorists working in France in the 1960s and 1970s, like Christian Metz and Raymond Bellour, were central to the development of film theory, their interests need also to be seen within the development of film culture in France, where cinéphilia has had a respectable history and where the relationship between film theory and film practice has traditionally been close. However, one of the more striking features of recent film theory in France is that with few exceptions (video work by Raymond Bellour and Thierry Kuntzel), few of the theorists are themselves filmmakers. And whereas traditions of film theory in the past in France were linked to efforts to reinvent the cinema – film impressionism and the New Wave being the most prominent examples – theorists like Bellour and Metz had little interest in French cinema, but rather were more committed to analysis of the classical Hollywood cinema. Yet even this simultaneous attraction to and distance from the Hollywood model has a long history in French cinematic culture, in which Hollywood has always provided a model both to emulate and to reject.

To be sure, French film theory, while usually identified as the source of current thinking about film, is but one aspect of film studies. For there would have been no contemporary resurgence of film studies were it not for the British and the North American influence; the first, most present through figures like Laura Mulvey, Peter Wollen, and Stephen Heath and through institutions like the British Film Institute; the second, most apparent in the changes brought about in American universities after social and political movements of the 1960s and 1970s – the civil rights, anti-war, women's and gay/lesbian movements – whereby more opportunities were created for exploration of contemporary forms like the cinema. While the events of May '68 in France were particularly important for their concern with forms of representation, the political climate of contestation and change existed across Western Europe and in the US.

The particular interest in spectatorship parallels the shift toward the reader, in literary criticism, and toward the subject, in philosophy. The generation of film scholars who contributed to the growth of film studies in the 1970s had lived through various stages of the "society of the spectacle," from the rapid growth of consumer culture in the 1950s to the understanding of historical events, like the war in Vietnam, from the literal vantage point of a spectator watching television. Many found in the study of the cinema a way of understanding a shared past of images, myths, and narratives, and the particular focus

6

on the spectator foregrounded the importance of comprehending not just the cinema, but the cinema as it has shaped and defined the fantasies of generations of spectators.

This book is divided into two sections; the first, "Theories of Spectatorship," examines the major paradigms that shaped inquiry into spectatorship in the 1970s, as well as the models that have emerged as critiques and alternatives to those theories. Chapter 1, "The Subject of Spectatorship," sets out the major definitions that shaped the inquiry into spectatorship in 1970s film theory. In chapter 2, "Spectatorship as Institution," I examine the central notion of the cinematic *apparatus* as it developed in 1970s film theory. In chapter 3, "Spectatorship Reconsidered," I foreground three approaches to spectatorship which have evolved from criticisms of the apparatus model – empirical approaches, which focus on the need to displace the "subject" of apparatus theory and to study real people instead; historical approaches, which focus on specific forms spectatorship has taken rather than global definitions of the cinema as institution; and feminist approaches, which in foregrounding the female spectator examine the difference that gender makes. I suggest that what is most crucial to the critical understanding of spectatorship is the collision of and tension between seemingly opposing terms, and in chapter 4, "Paradoxes of Spectatorship," I examine particular modes of analysis that are fruitful for such an understanding, from the non-coincidence of address and reception, to the study of fantasy, to the negotiation of different discourses.

I have attempted, in Part I, to provide an overview of the field that is both comprehensive and critical. But it will become obvious by chapter 4 that I see some approaches to spectatorship as more useful than others. One of the controversies in film studies today concerns the value of cognitivism, the study of knowledge and perception, in relation to spectatorship. For many of the proponents of cognitivism, an entire redefinition of the field of film studies, away from psycho-analysis and toward psychology, away from interpretation and toward schemata, is at issue. While some of the criticisms made of film theory in the name of cognitivism are accurate, others seem to me to involve a classic case of apples and oranges, in that the "spectator" envisaged by cognitivism is entirely different than the one conceptualized by 1970s film theory. I discuss cognitivism only in chapter 3 (as one empirical model); in the remaining chapters of the book, I am more concerned with how the valuable insights of 1970s film theory might be revised, not rejected wholesale.

Part II, "Readings of Spectatorship," includes four case studies of spectatorship. In each of these chapters, I have brought together an approach to spectatorship with an area that has not been explored quite so extensively. In chapter 5, "Textual Analysis and Portraits of Spectatorship," I draw upon textual analysis, which in the 1970s was the preferred mode of analysis of the cinema, and the classical Hollywood cinema in particular. I discuss a film (*The Picture of Dorian Gray* [1945]) which is visibly preoccupied with spectatorship, but which does not follow the predictable patterns excavated by practitioners of textual analysis, particularly insofar as the figure of woman and heterosexual coupling are concerned. In chapter 6, I look at the construction of Bette Davis's star image across a range of texts, including magazines and star biographies as well as her films. My concern in this chapter is with how female spectators are addressed, not in relationship to the ubiquitous "male gaze," but through variations on the theme of female rivalry. In chapter 7, "White Spectatorship and Genre-Mixing," I consider how and to what extent the model of spectatorship in film studies has been concerned specifically with white spectators. I connect this exploration of white spectatorship with two recent films, *Field of Dreams* (1989) and *Ghost* (1990), both characterized simultaneously by a mixture of genres and a peculiar use of racist stereotypes.

In all three of these case studies, my focus is on how spectators are addressed, but I do not assume that spectatorship can be adequately analyzed in terms purely of individual films. Thus, I consider, in chapter 5, the influence of Oscar Wilde's persona on expectations about *The Picture of Dorian Gray*; the connection between different kinds of texts, in chapter 6; and the relationship between film reviews and films insofar as questions of race are concerned, in chapter 7. It will become apparent in these chapters that I do not think the study of spectatorship is well served by rejecting altogether the structure of individual film texts and the tools of textual analysis. What is needed, rather, is a recognition of the flexibility of different modes of address, as well as the hypothetical quality of any spectator imagined by film theory. In my last chapter, "The Critical Audience," I examine the concept of the audience, and I take as an example gay/lesbian viewers. As I have already mentioned, the notion of critical spectatorship has relied too much on a facile opposition of being "inside" dominant ideology and complacent, versus being "outside" ideology and critical. It is hard to imagine many US audiences of recent years more politically charged than gays and lesbians, so this particular example provides the opportunity to examine critically the notion of the "critical audience."

I stress throughout this book that the relationship between the "subject," the position supposedly assigned to the film viewer by the institutions of the cinema, and the "viewer," the real person who watches the movies, has never been resolved. For 1970s film theory,

8

the "viewer" was bracketed altogether, with attention concentrated rather on how discursive positions are established textually and ideologically. Revisions of 1970s film theory have tended to focus on the "viewer" as an active creator of meaning, thereby bracketing in turn many of the assumptions about the cinematic apparatus. The study of spectatorship in film theory has always involved some complicated negotiations of "subjects" and "viewers," despite claims that the two are incompatible terms. My aim in this book is to evaluate those complicated negotiations as the horizon of film spectatorship.

Part I

THEORIES OF SPECTATORSHIP

1

THE SUBJECT OF
SPECTATORSHIP

The notion of cinema as an *institution* is central both to spectatorship as defined in 1970s film theory and to more recent reformulations. In order to contextualize this discussion of spectatorship, it is important to understand what is meant by the idea of cinema as an "institution" and what it means to define the cinematic spectator as part of this institution. Two enormously influential works, both published in 1970 in France (and in English translation shortly thereafter), established a frame of reference for questions of the subject, representation, and discourse which would be taken up by film theorists in their exploration of cinema as an institution. Louis Althusser's essay "Ideology and Ideological State Apparatuses (Notes Toward an Investigation)" contains many of the assumptions about the nature of ideological representation which would be applied to film, while Roland Barthes's *S/Z*, a detailed reading of the novella *Sarrasine* by Honoré de Balzac, was perhaps the most influential single work to define the scope of textual analysis in 1970s film theory, that is, analysis of both the structures of film representation and of what exceeds, problematizes, or otherwise puts those structures into question.

Althusser's essay challenged the traditional Marxist notion of ideology as "false consciousness" or simple distortion of the economic realities of a given culture. Althusser draws a parallel between the traditional Marxist definition of ideology and the way dreams were understood prior to Freud: "the purely imaginary, i.e. null, result of 'day's residues,' presented in an arbitrary arrangement and order. . . . This is exactly the status of philosophy and ideology . . . in *The German Ideology*" (1971: 159–60). Freud insisted upon the complex function of dreams, and Althusser similarly argues that ideology cannot be dismissed as the simple distortion of the economic base. Althusser emphasizes, rather, that ideology, in his famous definition, "represents the imaginary relationship of individuals to their real conditions of existence" (162). This definition of ideology became one of the most basic working assumptions of all 1970s film theory. The key shift here

13

is the move away from ideology as false consciousness, and toward a concept of ideology that emphasizes not only its interpretive function, but its necessary function in any culture. At the same time, Althusser emphasizes that ideology "has a material existence" (165), and therefore needs to be understood and analyzed in similarly material terms. It is not enough, in other words, to demonstrate how ideologies of, for instance, religion, gender roles, and the arts "support" and "reflect" the capitalist mode of production; rather, the internal and "relatively autonomous" (to use Althusser's phrase) structures of these ideologies require analysis.

For the study of cinema, Althusser's intervention was taken as validation of the view that in order to understand how cinema functioned ideologically, it was not enough to submit films to a test to determine a political content distilled and rendered from the vehicle of the film. Rather, it was the "vehicle" itself – the situation of film viewing, the nature of film language – that required explanation. Even more important for the study of cinema was Althusser's insistence that "there is no ideology except by the subject and for subjects" (170). Ideology consists, then, of the very process of " 'constituting' concrete individuals as subjects" (171), of effects of recognition and identification, of structures of address. Althusser uses the term "interpellation" to define this process whereby individuals respond to ideologies by recognizing themselves as the subjects of ideology. Again, the importance of such a notion of ideological interpellation for the study of film cannot be overestimated, for what Althusser's analysis foregrounds is the need to understand just how and why ideological systems interpellate their subjects so effectively. Study of interpellation, or the *subject effect* in film, then, was designed to explore how film-goers become subjects, how the various devices and components of the cinema function to create ideological subjects.

The details of how the various ideological systems "interpellate" are not worked out in Althusser's essay (aside from a rather cursory exploration of Christian ideology). But in Roland Barthes's *S/Z*, film theorists found a literary model for analysis of the subject effect, one which became enormously important in the development of textual analysis in film studies. Indeed, many of the names recognized as most important to textual analysis in film had close affiliations with Barthes – Thierry Kuntzel and Stephen Heath were his students (Kuntzel's first contribution to film textual analysis was published in a special issue of *Communications* guest-edited by Barthes; Heath wrote a full-length study of Barthes in French), and Raymond Bellour was a longtime colleague. Now Barthes was not a Marxist, at least not at all in the same way as Althusser (who was a member of the French Communist Party), yet ideology also is at the core of his analysis of

14

how the narrative seduces the reader through the interaction of a variety of codes, formalized vehicles of meaning.

More specifically, Barthes's analysis of *Sarrasine*, his breakdown of the tale into 561 units of meaning, or "lexia," engages with the structure of narrative – with how, that is, a narrative text organizes meaning and addresses its readers in specific ways. Two procedures of Barthes's analysis in *S/Z* are particularly relevant to the development of film studies. First, the working distinction of the analysis is between the "readerly" (*le lisible*) and the "writerly" (*le scriptible*). The concept of discourse – of the conventions of language – is crucial; whereas "readerly" discourse presents the reader "with a world that is coherent, well-ordered and already meaningful," the writerly "does not assume the meaningfulness and coherence of discourse but rather challenges it, and in so doing challenges the reader as well, shaking his or her assumptions and conventions about literature and about one's very judgement of reality in the day-to-day world" (Mayne 1977: 42). The distinction between the readerly and the writerly appears to reflect the distinction between realist and experimental writing, but Barthes undoes any such easy opposition by proposing what he calls the "limited plurality" of the realist text, a plurality uncovered by the strategies of reading. This "limited plurality" challenges the order and coherence of realism, allowing for possibilities of multiple, shifting, and sometimes contradictory meanings.

Second, Barthes proposes five codes to organize his reading of the novella. While it could be said that the codes are defined somewhat arbitrarily, they offer a unique example of analysis that combines several points of reference – cultural and psychoanalytic as well as narrative. In other words, Barthes's reading refuses to foreground any one code as the ultimate determination of meaning. Rather, the very nature of reading occurs through the constant interplay of various codes. Three of these codes (the hermeneutic code, whereby a question is posed and answers delayed; the semic code, whereby characters are created and defined; and the proairetic code, or code of actions, whereby events are defined in a structured way) concern narrative devices, particularly insofar as realism is concerned. The remaining two codes – the referential code and the symbolic code – refer more to cultural knowledge and to the body as theorized in psychoanalysis, respectively. Of course these two codes are narrative codes as well, but with more specifically defined cultural and psychoanalytic contours.

Put another way, then, Barthes's analysis defines an approach to the study of textuality that "reads" in a "writerly" fashion, attentive not to any single determination but rather to how textuality is formed by the interplay of different discourses – political, narrative, psychoanalytic. While *S/Z* may appear to be far more engaged in the details of representational strategies than Althusser's account of ideology, it is important to understand the interplay between these approaches in order to situate the evolution of 1970s film theory. For both Althusser and Barthes, ideology – whether it be the ideology of Christianity or the ideology of realism – must be understood, first and foremost, as a *representational* system which addresses subjects. Furthermore, the very process of *reading* is foregrounded as a means of comprehending the complex ways in which subjects are addressed. Here, there *is* a significant divergence between Althusser's and Barthes's positions. In another context, Althusser coined the phrase "symptomatic reading," that is, a reading which is attentive not only to the apparent dominant structures of a text but also and especially to what is omitted, repressed, or otherwise marginalized (1968: 28–9). To read symptomatically is to read against the grain of the text, that is, to read critically. Barthes's notion of a "limited plurality" in realist discourse is just such a reading.

But whereas Barthes reads against the grain and discovers that the codes of realism are far less coherent than what immediately appears to be the case, Althusser makes a sharp distinction between the *recognition* of ideology and true *knowledge* of its functioning:

> you and I are *always already* subjects, and as such constantly practice the rituals of ideological recognition, which guarantee for us that we are indeed concrete, individual, distinguishable and (naturally) irreplaceable subjects. . . . But to recognize that we are subjects and that we function in the practical rituals of the most elementary everyday life (the hand-shake, the fact of calling you by your name . . .) – this recognition only gives us the "consciousness" of our incessant (eternal) practice of ideological recognition – its consciousness, i.e. its recognition – but in no sense does it give us the (scientific) *knowledge* of the mechanism of this recognition.

> (172–3)

In order to achieve this scientific knowledge, Althusser claims that "we have to outline a discourse which tries to break with ideology, in order to dare to be the beginning of a scientific (i.e. subjectless) discourse on ideology" (173). For the introductory purposes of this chapter, it is important to comprehend the different stakes attributed to analysis of the subject and ideology. The "subjectless" discourse on ideology would be virtually impossible in Barthes's account, in which there are multiple subject positions but never a discourse without a subject.

The difference in question is one of the most misunderstood aspects of 1970s critical theory, the difference between the "individual" and

16

the "subject." One is not a subject, although one responds to numerous subject positions; too often the claim, by 1970s theorists, that the "subject" is a discursive position and not a real person is taken to mean that the experiences of living, breathing communities comprised of individuals are not of interest to the loftier preoccupations of theorists. To be sure, some 1970s theorists were not in the least bit interested in the lives of real people, but more relevant to the present discussion is the critique that was made of the tendency in middle-class, Western cultures to understand the "real person" in terms of a universal "human nature" – that is, as an entity outside of history, outside of social constructions, yet available to common sense or consciousness. That the immediate association between subject positions and real people is nonetheless quite difficult to shake is amply demonstrated in Althusser's essay, where despite the initial distinction between subjects and individuals, the confusion persists (Heath 1979).

The very possibility of imagining a "discourse without a subject" points to another important distinction between Althusser's and Barthes's different accounts of ideology and the subject. The move from structuralism to post-structuralism is generally seen as one of the most significant shifts in contemporary critical theory (Lentricchia 1980). If structuralism assumed the ultimate readability of discourse and the attendant possibility of deciphering the meanings attributed to its codes, post-structuralism is less optimistic about any such finalizing knowledge of textuality. Rather, post-structuralists assume – and Barthes's analysis of *Sarrasine* has been a model for such investigation – that structures and codes are always provisional, and that a reading of what falls through the cracks of dominant structures is ultimately more productive. While I am putting Althusser in the "structuralist" camp and Barthes in the "post-structuralist" one, these divisions and shifts are never so clear-cut, since there are plenty of post-structuralist elements in Althusser's work, just as the 561 lexia in Barthes's analysis reveal the structuralist legacy. Indeed, Althusser's notion of symptomatic reading is post-structuralist, but his assumption that it is possible to move outside of ideology is not.

The examples of these influential works by Althusser and Barthes illustrate the importance of the subject, of discourse, of textual and ideological analysis. Methodologically, and following from the distinctions *and* similarities I have outlined between Althusser and Barthes, the contributions of 1970s film theory may be defined along two axes. First, the works of Jean-Louis Baudry and Christian Metz in France, and Laura Mulvey in Great Britain, have been most important to the definition of how the cinema functions as an institutional *apparatus*, a standardized arrangement of component parts, a machine with a variety of interlocking functions. The emphasis, in their analyses, is on the cinematic institution insofar as certain structures are virtually always part of what constitute the pleasures of film-going. For all three of these theorists, these pleasures are identified through the insights of psychoanalysis as they illuminate the study of ideology. Virtually all theorists of the apparatus assume a monolithic quality to the cinema, that is, the cinema works to acculturate individuals to structures of fantasy, desire, dream, and pleasure that are fully of a piece with dominant ideology.

This monolithic quality of the cinema is double-edged, referring simultaneously to large structures of the cinematic experience, at least insofar as mainstream film is concerned, as well as to the need to redefine those large structures so as to assure their continuing relevance. For Baudry, the cinema creates a regressive state in the spectator, a return to the sensations of infantile wholeness, and for Metz, that regressive state encourages the possibilities to reactivate the "imaginary signifier," that is, a host of traumas associated with the development of subjectivity – voyeurism, the primal scene. For Mulvey, the mainstream cinema is made to the measure of male desire, and the various devices central to the classical Hollywood cinema all serve to facilitate the identification of the male spectator with his like, the male protagonist on screen. In other words, then, theorists of the apparatus are concerned to demonstrate how the large structures of the cinema operate.

Second, while often informed by apparatus theory, the works of Raymond Bellour, Stephen Heath, and Thierry Kuntzel are more specifically concerned with how the cinematic institution functions in *textual* terms. Methodologically, then, this means that the concern is with detailed analysis of individual films insofar as they represent the cinematic institution. If theorists like Metz, Baudry, and Mulvey demonstrate the institutional qualities of spectatorship by examining the (classical) cinema in general, textual theorists take as their point of departure the micro-structures of the film text. All of these theorists, whether concerned with the apparatus or with the individual text, end up at the same point, the analysis of cinema as an institution; but in order to arrive at this understanding they take very different points of departure. The primary cinematic tool for textual theorists was a Steenbeck editing table or an analyst projector whereby the individual film is broken down into its smallest components in order to discern the structures central to classical film. Individual shots are timed, dialogue is transcribed and measured in relationship to image/sound relationships, editing patterns are recorded, systems of similarity and difference underpinning narrative and ideological meanings are constructed. For those preoccupied with the cinema as an apparatus, the primary tool is observation and analysis of the cinema in a situational sense – the nature of film viewing and the features common to all or most films.

I want to emphasize that my division of the most influential 1970s film theorists into the "apparatus" and "textual analysis" tendencies is provisional. I am aware, as well, that such a categorization of "important figures" does not entirely do justice to the actual historical development of film theory in the 1970s, particularly insofar as journals were concerned. Of course, the contributions to the journals most central to theoretical discussions were usually signed by individuals, although one important exception to the rule was *Cahiers du cinéma*, where jointly authored texts or texts signed only collectively were common. Individual journals also were affiliated with various positions concerning film spectatorship; in France, for instance, debates between *Cahiers du cinéma* and *Cinéthique* (where one of Baudry's most influential essays was published) were common. One such debate concerned the possibility of anything in film akin to Barthes's "limited plurality," and in essays that have been enormously influential in film studies, the *Cahiers*'s editors argued that some exceptional films contain an "internal criticism . . . which cracks the film apart at the seams. If one reads the film obliquely, looking for symptoms; if one looks beyond its apparent formal coherence, one can see that it is riddled with cracks: it is splitting under an internal tension which is simply not there in an ideologically innocuous film" (Comolli and Narboni 1969/ 1977: 7). The symptomatic status of this category of films is most worked out in the *Cahiers*'s collective analysis of John Ford's *Young Mr. Lincoln* (*Cahiers du cinéma* 1969/1972). Essays in *Cinéthique* were far less concerned with explorations of individual Hollywood films, and more concerned to demonstrate the homogeneity of the classical cinema.

Common to both apparatus and textual theorists was an emphasis on psychoanalysis far more pronounced than one finds in Althusser or Barthes, and many of the debates that occurred in film studies concerned precisely this emphasis. Indeed, in Britain the focus on psychoanalysis in *Screen* – arguably the most influential journal for film studies – initiated a conflict among the editors and an eventual departure of several of them (see *Screen* Editorial Board 1975; Buscombe, Gledhill, Lovell, and Williams 1975–6). In the US, *Screen* in particular and French theories of representation in general were often criticized in the pages of journals like *Film Quarterly* (where the English translation of an essay by Baudry appeared with something close to an apology) and *Jump Cut* for their uncritical use of psychoanalysis, particularly insofar as questions of gender and feminism were concerned (Lesage 1974).

Textual theorists used psychoanalysis in order to demonstrate how the most specific devices of the classical Hollywood cinema – like the use of close-ups, the relationship between sound and image, the use of shot-reverse shot – positioned spectators in such a way as to be defined within scenarios of desire theorized by psychoanalysis. Apparatus theorists explored parallels between film viewing – sitting still in a darkened theater before a screen – and situations central to psychoanalytic understanding of the subject – dreams and regression in particular. Indeed, if there is any single common denominator to all of 1970s film theory, it is the appeal to psychoanalysis as the privileged term for an understanding of how the cinema operates as an ideological medium. Now what is at stake here is not just the prominence of psychoanalysis, but more specifically of psychoanalysis as companion to ideological analysis. In other words, virtually all of the characteristics of the cinematic institution as defined by 1970s film theory are shaped, in one way or another, by the intersection of psychoanalysis and ideology. Let me move, then, to an overview of the most important aspects of the cinematic institution and spectatorship as defined by 1970s film theory, whether the emphasis was on the apparatus or on textual analysis.

THE *EMBLEMATIC* QUALITY OF THE CINEMA

Any discourse, any form of subject positioning, could be said to be of interest; what then, one might ask, makes the cinema worthy of special consideration? Althusser's insistence that various ideologies function in relatively autonomous ways was read as providing a theoretical basis for the argument that individual systems of representation needed to be understood in their own terms; hence, the notion of "materialism" was redefined, now not only as a constant reference to the organization of the means of production in a given culture (the classic Marxist sense of materialism), but also as "material" in the most literal sense, i.e., in the case of cinema, the organization of sounds and images. This need for autonomy in the understanding of individual sign systems could be applied, of course, to any ideological form. Theorists of the cinema went further in defining the particular interest of cinema by stressing its emblematic quality.

The cinema, it was argued, is a dense system of meaning, one that borrows from so many different discourses – of fashion, of narrative, of politics, of advertising, and so on – that it offers particularly rich possibilities for ideological understanding. The argument went still further; the cinema was not just any form of entertainment but rather one that embodied deep-seated myths and ideologies central to the functioning of modern, Western industrialized countries. Hence, many 1970s film theorists argued that the cinema is not just a product of a

20

particular culture, but rather a projection of its most fundamental needs, desires, and beliefs. These include a notion of narrative made to the measure of social needs, an extension of the nineteenth-century realist novel into the realm of the image and sound (Mayne 1988); a preoccupation with vision, with the eye as the center of knowledge (Comolli 1971/1986; Heath 1975); and a particular privilege given to witnessing, to being a spectator, as a position of unique understanding (Metz 1975/1982; Heath 1976).

Two caveats were generally implicit here – first, that the cinematic institution under investigation was the classical or mainstream cinema; second, that this classical cinema is emblematic of the modern cultures of Europe and North America, cultures, that is, which are predominantly white, industrialized, and Eurocentric, geared toward an ethos of consumption. Furthermore, in these cultures a number of divisions are in place – between private and public spheres, between socioeconomic classes, between races, between men and women, between work and family, between "normal" and marginal sexual identities. In the first case, the equation between the cinematic institution and the classical cinema, we confront one of the most profound conceptual oppositions in film studies, between the classical cinema and its supposed "alternatives." Only in understanding how the classical cinema functioned was it possible, according to 1970s film theorists, to create a genuinely oppositional counter-cinema. The classical cinema in question meant a number of things. Classical cinema meant, in terms of its form, standard realist narrative and codes (of character, genre, etc.). More historically, classical cinema referred to Hollywood cinema from the advent of sound in the late 1920s to the demise of the studio system in the 1950s in terms of its history. Nevertheless, while the history of the Hollywood studio system is the paradigm for classical cinema (see Bordwell, Staiger, and Thompson 1985), the term "classical cinema" is still often used to refer to a model of filmmaking rather than to a specific historical period, encompassing such recent films as *Fatal Attraction* or *Driving Miss Daisy*, for instance.

The emblematic quality of the cinema, once limited to modern Western cultures and to the classical, mainstream cinema, was further understood in two directions. First, cinema was assumed to possess a unique metaphoric quality. Going to the movies and seeking their pleasures were seen as activities that reflected deep-seated assumptions about what it means to be a subject in Western discourse. In later chapters I suggest that one of the characteristics of 1970s film theory was a tendency to take metaphors too literally; it is one thing to suggest the symbolic qualities of film-going, and another to read those qualities in such a literal way that the metaphoric quality is destroyed and becomes, rather, a mechanistic equation.

Second, one of the phrases most often used in film theory was "no accident" or "no coincidence." It was "no accident" that the cinema developed at the turn of the century, embodying as it did the myths and beliefs of a culture preoccupied with images of itself, with the perfect impression of reality. It was "no coincidence" that cinema was born at the same time as modern advertising, invested as both were in naturalizing the components of a society devoted to the production and consumption of goods (the relationship of cinema to consumerism is discussed further in chapter 2). Most of all, it was "no coincidence" that cinema developed at the same time as Freudian psychoanalysis. Now with the psychoanalytic connection, we enter into a somewhat different type of coincidence, for here the connection is more mediated, given that psychoanalysis was seen as providing unique tools for the analysis of film, of its subject effect. The basis of the connection was that cinema played upon the very desires central to psychoanalysis. As Jacqueline Rose puts it, the power of film as an "ideological apparatus rests on the mechanisms of identification and sexual fantasy which we all seem to participate in, but which – outside the cinema – are, for the most part, only ever admitted on the couch" (1986: 5).

One could also say that it is "no accident" that the non-coincidence that has received the most attention in contemporary film theory is the relationship between film and psychoanalysis. Indeed, one of the particular characteristics of recent film theory is its enormously strong connection to psychoanalytic language and methodology. While it is true that other forms of contemporary critical theory were influenced by psychoanalysis, film theorists found a reflection of their concerns in psychoanalysis that far surpassed any other area of inquiry.

DESIRE IN THE CINEMA

The strong connection between the preoccupations of both cinema and psychoanalysis takes as perhaps its most dominant term that of *desire*, that is, how individuals conceive of themselves in subjective terms, how relations between self and other are defined, and how pleasure is sought and satisfied. While Freudian psychoanalysis had plenty to offer the study of cinema, particularly insofar as desires that would appear to be inherently cinematic, like voyeurism and daydreaming, are concerned, the connection with Lacanian psychoanalysis was far more influential. Indeed, for many film theorists, Jacques Lacan – the most influential psychoanalyst in contemporary France – offered what appeared to be a theory of desire made to the measure of the cinema. Looking relations are central to Lacan's revision of Freud, with particular attention paid to the gaze as a primary structure of identity and its failures. The dual emphasis on identity and its failures is crucial to how Lacan was brought to bear on film theory, for central to the Lacanian notion of desire is a continuous process whereby desires are never satisfied, thus assuring an economy of desire which reinforces, in its turn, the wish to return to the cinema again and again. More specifically, Lacanian psychoanalysis has been adapted to film theory to explain precisely what cinematic address to the subject entails, an adaptation that follows – although more intensely – the parallel influence of Lacan's work on other areas similarly taken up with the place of the subject (see Silverman 1983).

Where Freud and Lacan both offer much to film theory is in the understanding of the kind of state the spectator enters when s/he begins watching a film. Laura Mulvey used Freud's theories of the instincts and ego identification to understand how the classical cinema encourages a re-enactment of psychic trauma with the subsequent reassurance that the threat – usually woman and/or castration in one form or another – has been dispelled. Raymond Bellour's account of cinematic identification is similar to Mulvey's in many important ways, even though her account is much more critical than his (see chapter 2 for a further discussion of the relationship between Mulvey and Bellour). Mulvey emphasizes how the spectator is encouraged to identify with the male protagonist of the classical cinema and thereby to act out a unique combination of voyeurism and fetishism, aligned with the spectacular and narrative strategies of the cinema. While the notion of oedipal desire appears throughout psychoanalytic theory of the cinema, its use is particularly pronounced in Bellour's writings. What does it mean to describe the classical cinema in terms of oedipal desire? In Freud's account, the oedipal scenario involves the process of maturation for the male child, the identification with the father as his like and simultaneous objectification of the mother as love object. In other words, oedipal desire is the desire to become like the father, to take his place in the heterosexual and familial economy of Western, industrialized culture.

The assumption of 1970s film theory was that the particular characteristics of the classical cinema encourage oedipal desire, through the looking structures that make the woman object of the look and man its subject, as well as through conventions of plot and characterization. It is said often enough – especially by Bellour – that the formation of the heterosexual couple is not just a banal plot resolution, but also and especially the resolution demanded by a form so wedded to oedipal desire as the cinema. Put another way, then, oedipal desire suggests that the subject of the classical cinema is male. The implications of that assumption have been far-reaching in analyses of feminism and sexual difference in film studies. Many 1970s film theorists were later

23

criticized for ignoring the difference that sexual difference makes, but it could be argued that what those theorists described was what is, not what might be (see Penley 1985; Rose 1980; Copjec 1982). Analysis of the oedipal structures of desire in classical film may well leave no place for the female spectator, but that may be precisely the point – that classical cinema "interpellates" by denying sexual difference. Whatever the actual gender of the audience, theories of the cinematic institution demonstrate how oedipal desire is naturalized, facilitated, or otherwise normalized.

Roland Barthes said, in *The Pleasure of the Text*, that there is virtually a cause-and-effect relationship between the Oedipus myth and story-telling. "Death of the Father would deprive literature of many of its pleasures," Barthes writes. "If there is no longer a Father, why tell stories? Doesn't every narrative lead back to Oedipus? Isn't storytelling always a way of searching for one's origins, speaking one's relation-ship to the Law, entering into the dialectic of tenderness and hatred?" (1975: 47). Barthes defines the common denominator between Oedipus and narrative as the desire for knowledge about one's self – one's masculine self, presumably. In the version of psychoanalysis which came to characterize 1970s film theory, the fusion of narrative and oedipal desire is complete; scenarios of castration anxiety and loss were identified as fundamental to the classical cinema (see Silverman 1983 and 1988). More recently in film theory, scholars have pursued the relationship between the subject and desire in another direction, exploring not the inevitablity of oedipal desire but rather the prolifer-ation of positions of desire in the classical cinema (see Bergstrom and Doane 1989; Rodowick 1991).

NARRATIVE IN THE CINEMA

If the classical cinema is a narrative institution, then this meant an obvious affiliation with the history of narrative in Western culture. That psychoanalysis has a very close connection to narrative, to the devices of storytelling, is central to its history; Freud often remarked, for instance, on the novelistic character of his published case histories ("it still strikes me myself as strange that the case histories I write should read like short stories" [Freud and Breuer 1893/1974: 231]). The common interface between narrative and psychoanalysis suggests that the act of storytelling needs to be understood as one of the most fundamental ways in which one constructs an identity, in both cultural and individual terms. Indeed, as we have seen, the psychoanalytic connection is one of the strongest in the theorizing of the cinematic institution. If one can speak of "oedipal narrative" in the cinema, then it consists of a series of structures whereby (male) infantile crises of

24

individuation, separation, and autonomy are rekindled in order to be smoothed over, naturalized.

The narrative dimensions of cinema as an institution also have important historical ramifications. Metz, Bellour, and Heath have described how the cinema carries on a tradition of realist narrative associated with the nineteenth-century novel in the West (Bergstrom 1979; Metz 1975/1982; Heath 1977). For some theorists, in fact, what was specific to the cinema was its ability not only to carry on that realist tradition but to perfect it, to produce an illusion of reality so complete that the cinema, and not the novel, becomes the dominant narrative form of the first half of the twentieth century. The distinction between the writerly and the readerly that Barthes makes in *S/Z* has also had a special function in terms of cinema's relationship to a narrative tradition. Raymond Bellour suggests that whereas Barthes could find a "limited plurality" in certain realist texts, the classical Hollywood cinema is a "machine of great homogeneity," i.e., a readerly institution from which all traces of the writerly have been banished (Bergstrom 1979: 89). This presumed homogeneity has been one of the most contested aspects of classical cinema in debates since the 1970s.

The dominant pattern of classical film narrative is crisis and resolution, i.e., a series of events into which disorder is introduced, the presentation of several possible resolutions before an ultimate resolution is possible. One of the basic tenets of structuralist analysis was that meaning is organized in terms of binary, or two-termed oppositions, and that narrative performs such operations on larger scales, with different systems of oppositions intersecting, provoking crises as well as the need for resolutions. Hence, much textual analysis of the classical cinema took as its point of departure the system of oppositions operative in classical film. Some oppositions tended to appear with great regularity – male/female, parent/child in particular – which of course emphasizes the oedipal quality of narrative, at least in a very broad sense.

The importance of the subject in narrative is that all of the meaningful oppositions, crises, and resolutions are addressed to a subject, i.e., positions of stability and coherence are assigned within the narrative. Put another way, narrative structures are not meaningful unless certain positions are taken up by the spectator, so the various narrative codes of film are meant to do precisely this – to give the spectator a privileged vantage point from which to understand, evaluate, and comprehend what occurs on screen. As Mary Ann Doane puts it, "in film there is a curious operation by means of which the 'I' and the 'you' of discourse are collapsed in the figure of the spectator" (1987: 10). If the classical cinema is first and foremost narrative cinema, then the subject becomes a narrative effect carried along by the force of the events represented on screen. More important, the subject of narrative is established through conventions that have a long history, conventions that position viewers to accept certain codes as "realist," others as "fantastic," and so on.

IDENTIFICATION IN THE CINEMA

One of the thorniest and most difficult questions raised by institutional theories of the cinema concerns identification. Given the close ties between cinema and the arts of realism, it is tempting to make a short-circuited argument about the nature of identification in the cinema, and to assume that the primary form it takes is identification with characters, with human figures on screen. Psychoanalytic theory does not always challenge this assumption; Laura Mulvey's theory of "visual pleasure," for instance, is based on the assumption that the male protagonist of a film provides a vehicle for identification on the part of the male spectator. Two further assumptions are implicit here – one, that identification in the cinema does proceed primarily in terms of individuals in the audience and characters projected on screen; two, that identification is literal, at least according to dominant cultural conventions, so that men identify with male characters, women with female characters, and so on.

Other theorists attempted to rethink the process of identification, and Christian Metz in particular distinguishes between primary and secondary cinematic identification. Anterior to any possible identification with characters (secondary identification) is identification with the projection situation itself, with "myself looking" (Metz 1975/1982). Similarly, Jean-Louis Baudry's contributions to a theory of the cinematic apparatus (discussed in detail in chapter 2) are concerned with how the projection situation operates, how the very conditions of representation in the cinema make it possible to speak of something like identification with characters, for instance (1970/1986; 1975/1986). For Baudry as for Metz, identification in the cinema needs to be understood in terms far more complex than characters, for the projection situation creates a *position* for the subject whereby myths of the transcendental subject, i.e., the unified, rational, coherent witness, as well as the regressive individual, are reactivated.

This notion of a subject position is crucial to the rethinking of cinematic identification – the notion, that is, that when I enter the movie theater and take my seat, I have already, on several levels (conscious as well as unconscious), engaged in an identificatory process. I have assumed a place within the cinematic apparatus, I have accepted its fictions, whether self-consciously or not. The cinematic institution positions me long before I have "identified" with a favorite

26

actor or character. Central, then, to the redefinition of identification that occurred in 1970s film theory was the importance of unconscious processes, and the attendant need to read critically the apparent processes at work in cinematic identification, like identification with characters. It is also important to understand that the notion of unconscious processes, while most clearly referring to Freudian discoveries concerning the residues of infantile sexuality in adult identities, was often used in a metaphoric way (although here again the metaphor often becomes mechanistic, which will be explored in more detail in chapter 2). While Christian Metz would speak in a fairly classical Freudian and Lacanian way about the function of cinema vis-à-vis the mirror stage (Lacan) or the primal scene (Freud), Jean-Louis Baudry would speak in more general terms about regressive fantasies having to do not only with psychoanalytic notions but also with philosophical and ideological notions about the transcendental self.

A further implication of the rethinking of identification in the cinema evolves from the notion of *position*. There is something too literal about a notion of identification whereby I, as a woman or a US citizen or a middle-class academic, necessarily and supposedly unproblematically "identify" with whatever I see on screen that most approximates my identity. To assume such identification, a stable notion of identity needs to be in place. But the theories to which 1970s film theorists were drawn, and the work of Lacan in particular, questioned any such evident stability. As a result, identification understood as a position – and more properly as a series of shifting positions – assumes that cinematic identification is as fragile and unstable as identity itself. Indeed, the possibilities opened up by this reconsideration of identification are enormous, challenging as they do both excessively literal assumptions about the pleasures taken in the cinema as well as any notion of identification as a simple one-way process from one individual to his or her like.

THE *SOCIALIZING* QUALITIES OF THE CINEMATIC INSTITUTION

Shifting and multiple positions notwithstanding, the positions available for "identification" were seen by 1970s film theorists as subjected to a set of constraints and limitations. Indeed, the very notion of the cinema as an institution conveys a sense of restraint and the attendant notion that the pleasures and joys of the cinema are ultimately defined by the social and cultural functions the cinema makes possible. For a number of 1970s film theorists, the cinema offered a remarkably bold demonstration – an emblematic quality, as I suggest above – of precisely what it means to be a subject in a Western, industrialized culture. The act of watching a film means subjecting one's self to the power of another vision, means assuming certain positions of viewing and hearing that have strong cultural ramifications. If – as Guy Debord argued in his influential study of the power of the image in Western capitalist countries – we live in a society of the spectacle, then the cinema is, quite literally, a training ground for acculturation to the spectacle form (Debord 1967/1970).

Perhaps the greatest contribution of 1970s film theory was the recognition and subsequent insistence that spectatorship is informed by deep and far-reaching structures that are simultaneously social and psychic, and which can only be understood by equally deep and far-reaching systematic analysis. Like much critical theory of the era, 1970s film theory was informed by the desire to join Marx and Freud, to understand political and cultural processes in relationship to unconscious processes, and therefore, in Barthes's words, to "change the economy of the relations of production and to change the economy of the subject" (1977a: 212). Yet recognition of the sheer enormity and influence of the cinematic institution, and by extension of virtually all institutions and practices, meant that the very nature of the "change" of which Barthes speaks was so ambitious as to appear impossible. Indeed, one of the charges often leveled against 1970s theory, and Althusser's work in particular, is the denial of resistance and agency as meaningful categories (Rancière 1974; Thompson 1978). If members of a given culture can only speak, communicate, and represent through the subject positions available to them, and if those positions are thoroughly saturated with ideological determinations, then how are any alternative positions even thinkable?

The paradox of 1970s film theory is precisely here. For in insisting upon the necessity to read and to comprehend the complex forms of interpellation in the cinema, the implication was that dominant ideology would be revealed as a construction, and once so revealed would be open to change. The down side of this process is that recognition of the complexity and the far reach of these forms of interpellation makes change itself seem more difficult. Two dilemmas have been particularly important in this context, particularly insofar as the legacy of 1970s film theory has been reconsidered by subsequent generations of researchers. First, the language of film theory is taken up with the imagery of domination and control (the apparatus, assigned positions, the institution), and the very notion of the subject implies "subjected to" as much as "subject of." With so much emphasis placed on how spectatorship affirms the dominant order, it becomes difficult to see how spectatorship could be anything else but such an affirmation. I have noted the opposition between the classical cinema and its alternatives that characterized 1970s film theory, but those alternatives tended

28

to be posed in a very abstract and utopian way, sometimes suggesting that the self-aware subject is the same as a radically new alternative one, and at other times displacing any genuinely new possibilities to some unspecified future date.

Second, 1970s film theory placed enormous emphasis on the representational strategies of film, resulting in a kind of textual idealism, or what Barbara Klinger has called a "textual-centric consideration of the cinema/ideology relation" (1984: 41). While the cinematic institution was described in 1970s film theory as complex, the tendency nonetheless was to focus on what happens inside the movie theater between spectator and screen, and (particularly in textual analysis) to analyze the components of cinematic signification. It is one thing to focus on particular aspects of the cinematic institution and another thing altogether to isolate and ultimately to fetishize certain of those aspects as more symptomatic, more significant than others; as a result, important features of the cinematic institution, such as advertising, or the relationship between film and other forms of representation, are marginalized. Similarly, it is one thing to call for a new, innovative cinematic practice and quite another to claim that such a practice will, by itself and on its own terms, create a new subject.

To some extent I have used Althusser and Barthes as imaginary opposing figures to give a sense of the issues and debates that informed the development of 1970s film theory. Barthes's emphasis on the reader and Althusser's on the subject are complementary to the extent that they foreground the importance of *discourse, address,* and *ideology* for the development of spectatorship in film studies. Yet my use of these two figures also recalls what has become a common practice in field summaries, i.e., to set up a series of easy dichotomies in establishing the frame of reference for contemporary critical theory. For example, in feminist film theory, the distinction between the "images of women" approach (sociological, looking for "positive role models") is regularly opposed to what was properly called "feminist film theory" (see Kaplan 1983b; Kuhn 1982; Mayne 1985). In the process, the former approach becomes theoretically insufficient, and while this may be an accurate assessment in the case of the "images of women" approach to film, the insistence upon a binary opposition can distill a simplistic dualism that does not do justice to the historical complexity of the era. Laura Mulvey, whose work has been so influential in defining the scope of institutional approaches to spectatorship, has also astutely evaluated the problems involved in assessing the historical contours of those approaches. Noting that her 1975 essay "Visual Pleasure and Narrative Cinema" has come to occupy a place in "film theoretical orthodoxy," Mulvey notes that the essay was "written in the polemical spirit that belongs properly to the early confrontational moments of a movement" (1989: 161). Mulvey describes the tendency, in the "Visual Pleasure" essay, to speak in dualistic terms of the active male gaze versus the female object of the gaze. She then goes on to say:

> There is a sense in which this argument, important as it is for analysing the existing state of things, hinders the possibility of change and remains caught ultimately within its own dualistic terms. The polarisation only allows an "either/or." As the two terms (masculine/feminine, voyeuristic/exhibitionist, active/passive) remain dependent on each other for meaning, their only possible movement is into inversion. They cannot be shifted easily into a new phase or new significance. There can be no space in between or space outside such a pairing.
>
> (1989: 162)

Mulvey is speaking here both of the need and the difficulty to move beyond dualisms in the relationship between film theory and film practice. Her recognition of the limits of dualism is also a useful reminder that, for a book like this one, concerned with spectatorship in both theoretical and historical terms, critics can often replicate the very terms under investigation, through a slash-and-burn approach to writing the history of a field. I think one of the most important projects for theory is to read critical activity historically, and this means trying to problematize some of the easy divisions that come quickly to mind. While I will have recourse to many qualifications that will strike some readers as too vacillating or too dualistic, I want to emphasize that this book is meant to be not only an introduction to the study of spectatorship in film studies, but also a rethinking of the history of the field.

2

SPECTATORSHIP AS INSTITUTION

James Stewart portrays a photographer who, incapacitated by a broken leg, becomes increasingly involved in the affairs of his neighbors across the apartment courtyard; Genevieve Bujold portrays a doctor who becomes suspicious about the mysterious deaths and medical goings-on at the hospital where she works. Whatever else one might say about these films (*Rear Window* [1954] and *Coma* [1978]), their appeal, both popular and scholarly, is due in large part to their preoccupation with spectatorship. For in these films, the act of watching is both pleasureful and dangerous, and if the characters of the male photographer and the female doctor are sources of identification, the identification is marked by a foregrounding of the cinema itself in its capacity to see, to hear, and to know (see Mulvey 1975; Wood 1982; Modleski 1988; Cowie 1979, 1980). To begin with, then, spectatorship refers not just to the acts of watching and listening, and not just to identification with human figures projected on the screen, but rather to the various values with which film viewing is invested. Hence, the pleasures and dangers affiliated with watching and listening, in *Rear Window* and *Coma*, are channeled into powerful cultural and narrative myths of man and woman, social class, private and public life.

There would be no such thing as spectatorship if the cinema did not function as a powerful form of pleasure, entertainment, and social-ization. Some films, like *Rear Window* (as well as virtually all of Hitchcock's films) and *Coma*, read easily as demonstrations – explicit or otherwise – of the lure of spectatorship. But spectatorship is more than individual film characters who embody spectator roles, by acting, as the characters portrayed by James Stewart and Genevieve Bujold do, as spectators within the film. Indeed, spectatorship entails much more than individual films or even the individual and collective view-ing experiences of audiences. Spectatorship involves the acts of looking and hearing inasmuch as the patterns of everyday life are dramatized, foregrounded, displaced, or otherwise inflected by the cinema.

Figures drawn from the cinema have been appropriated and utilized across a variety of forms, from advertising to literature, from music to magazines, from everyday conversation to dreams; these are all testimonies to the power of spectatorship. Here is another level of complexity, for spectatorship may find its most condensed forms in the cinema, but spectatorship is not reducible to the cinematic. For many scholars working in film studies, the study of spectatorship has provided a way to understand film in its cultural dimension, while avoiding the simple determinism of the reflection hypothesis, whereby films "show" or reflect in relatively static ways the preoccupations of a given society. Instead, the study of spectatorship involves an engagement with modes of seeing and telling, hearing and listening, not only in terms of how films are structured, but in terms of how audiences imagine themselves.

Spectatorship is one of a group of terms so closely affiliated with the development of film studies over the past twenty years that it has acquired almost a buzzword status. Along with terms and phrases like "apparatus," the "(male) gaze," and "suture," "spectatorship" denotes a preoccupation with the various ways in which responses to films are constructed by the institutions of the cinema and with the contexts – psychic as well as cultural, individual as well as social – that give those responses particular meanings. The term "spectatorship" also connotes allegiance to the various disciplines which contributed to the revitalization of film studies as a theoretical enterprise in the early to mid-1970s. As a term of theoretical affiliation, "spectatorship" signals attention to the role of the cinematic spectator and the attendant role of the viewer in the production of meaning, to be sure. But it also signals allegiance to a tradition of film studies marked by an interest in theory, and specifically in the intersections among Marxism, semiotics, feminism, and psychoanalysis, with the latter usually serving the predominant role, particularly since the mid-1970s.

The concept of spectatorship shares with those of the apparatus, the gaze, and suture an affinity with theories of the subject. Indeed, yet another keyword of contemporary film studies (as well as contemporary critical theory) is the "subject," and in film studies, attention paid to the "subject" of the cinema is virtually synonomous with the development of psychoanalytic film theory. As Kaja Silverman reads the history of the field in *The Subject of Semiotics*, the apparent shift in film theory from a semiotic model of inquiry to a psychoanalytic one results from the increasing recognition of the subject as the central issue. She writes that the term "subject" "helps us to conceive of human reality as a construction, as the product of signifying activities which are both culturally specific and generally unconscious" (Silverman 1983: 130). However, unlike the terms "apparatus," the "gaze," and "suture," spectatorship can be less absolutely defined within the

scope of psychoanalytic film theory. For these other terms take as
their point of departure the analogy between the mental apparatus as
theorized by Freud and the structure of cinematic representation, or
the gaze and suture as key components of desire as theorized by
Jacques Lacan and the structures of the look and of editing in film.
While the study of spectatorship has been shaped by psychoanalytic
terminology, it has also been a site for the contestation of the influence
of psychoanalysis.

Silverman's reference to "cultural specificity" and the "unconscious"
in the above quotation suggests that the "subject" in film studies is
understood as simultaneously a social and a psychic entity. It has been
an observation of long standing in film studies that the cinematic
subject refers not to real people who attend movies and who may
respond in a number of complex and compelling ways to the spectacle
on screen, but rather to positions constructed by the various and
interconnecting institutions of the cinema. To be sure, this notion of
a *position* is social and cultural in that all institutions are social and
cultural. But film theorists have insisted that the subject should not
be confused with the individual.

Referring specifically to the female spectator, Mary Ann Doane says
she "is a concept, not a person," and notes that the preferred mode
for investigating the cinematic subject, textual analysis, "strive[s] to
delineate *conditions of readability* (which involves an understanding of
psychic investments in texts) and not the ways in which texts are
appropriated and used" (Doane 1990: 143). While Doane is using the
term "spectator" here as synonomous with the "subject," I would
argue that the term "spectatorship" carries with it some distrust of
the separation of subjects and "real people." At the same time, spectatorship marks the necessity of the distinction in order to understand
the functioning of film as discourse. While studies of spectatorship in
the cinema have drawn from psychoanalytic explorations of the subject, the "spectator" located in the term spectatorship in fact rubs
against the "subject" of psychoanalytic film theory. I noted in chapter
1 that in Althusser's work the "subject" and the "individual" may be
distinguished but they are also confused. In film theory's preoccupation with the subject and spectatorship, I am less concerned to argue
that the confusion is a "mistake," and more concerned to read the
confusion as symptomatic of unresolved and insufficiently theorized
complications.

Arguably the insistence upon the cinematic subject as non-
synonymous with the film viewer marks one of the most important
insights of contemporary film studies. While theories of the subject
associated with Althusserian Marxism and Lacanian psychoanalysis
met with resistance in the field of literary criticism and theory, they

were also welcome to the extent that the complexities of discourse were assumed. But 1970s film theory – the foundation of contemporary film studies – developed at the same time that theories of representation and difference associated primarily with the French were becoming increasingly influential in Anglo-American intellectual and cultural life. Many disciplines, like literature, the law, and history, could write their contemporary histories as narratives of "us" versus "them," of the forces of stodgy humanist tradition besieged by the young radicals of the deconstructed subject. But film studies was nonetheless somewhat unique.

Indeed, much of the enthusiasm with which film scholars welcomed the demise of the humanist self can be attributed to the perception that tedious scholarship comprised most of what was called "film studies" prior to the early 1970s. Paradigm shifts and changes in intellectual disciplines are frequently characterized by a wholesale dismissal of virtually all preceding work as tainted by error, and film studies was no exception. On the one hand, contemporary film theorists saw earlier film studies as having been defined by a notion of the audience which tended toward homogeneity, of the sociological/mass-communications model. The very notion of a "response" – not to mention a viewer, or a relationship between a text and a viewer – had been postulated in a totally self-evident, unproblematized way. Scholarly responses to the cinema were often indistinguishable from "market research" studies done by film studios, and in fact many studies served precisely that purpose (see Handel 1950; Jowett 1985; Turner 1988: 24–41). On the other hand, despite a venerable history of film theory dating from Hugo Munsterberg and Vachel Lindsay, previous approaches to the study of film were seen to have defined theory in aesthetic or sociological terms exclusively, with film criticism tending toward the impressionistic. Some theoretical figures from the past, like Dziga Vertov or Sergei Eisenstein, were resurrected, but usually with the assumption that their theoretical contributions were only capable of being truly comprehended in the enlightened intellectual context of the present.

As I noted in chapter 1, it is common to cite the events of May '68 in France as the privileged source for so much of the rethinking of subject positions and the intersections of social and psychic forces that informed the growth of contemporary critical theory. The combined forces of workers and students during the 1968 uprisings in France consolidated a critique of politics that indicted the traditional left as well as the right. The events of May '68 are often remembered more for their innovative slogans and striking visual images (in posters, costume, and graffiti) than for more classically political issues like student strikes and workplace conditions. While contemporary critical

34

theory was in the process of development long before May '68, the political events of that era in France captured a sense of political crisis, of an urgent need to rethink the very nature of politics and political representation.

Now the use of political moments as datelines for theories often seems, at best, like simplistic cause-and-effect thinking, and at worst, like an attempt to convince one's self and the world of the political efficacy of theoretical work. In the case of film studies, however, one particularly influential concept associated with the events of May '68 did have particular influence, and that is the "society of the spectacle," the title of Guy Debord's much quoted book (Debord 1967/1970). In Debord's account, the spectacle is reification on a universal scale; "the principle of commodity fetishism . . . reaches its absolute fulfillment in the spectacle, where the tangible world is replaced by a selection of images" (Debord 1970: 16). It does not require too much imagination to see the cinema as a particularly concrete representation of the "society of the spectacle," and the development of recent film theory relies on the assumption that the cinema is not just any complex representational form, but rather one that has strategic importance, the "emblematic quality" referred to in chapter 1, in that it embodies the fantasies and fears of a society of the spectacle.

As with any emerging field, there was a tendency in the 1970s to read all prior film theory with arrogant self-assuredness. There is no question that 1970s film theory brought a new sophistication to the study of film, but it was a sophistication bought at the price of large dichotomies (the classical versus the alternative text; idealist versus materialist film theory) and sweeping generalizations. The trend in more recent years has been to reconsider those dichotomies and generalizations; whether this move is a function of intellectual growth or institutional retrenchment (or both) remains to be seen. In any case, what also needs to be recognized is the importance of the university setting in the development of film studies. In the US in particular, film studies means first and foremost the growth of college and university programs, whether film studies programs *per se*, or interdisciplinary programs like Women's Studies or American Studies which would include courses representing the "new" discipline of film studies.

Film studies looked toward the spectator at the same time that literary studies looked toward the reader, and contemporary theories of representation examined the subject effect produced in discourse. Contemporary film studies grew in the wake of the much heralded "death of the author" proclaimed by Roland Barthes in 1968. The displacement of the author as the privileged source of a text's meaning was accompanied, in Barthes's terms, by the emergence of the reader, not as a new source of unity but as a dismantling of the very notion of unity:

> The reader is the space on which all the quotations that make up a writing are inscribed without any of them being lost; a text's unity lies not in its origin but in its destination. Yet this destination cannot any longer be personal: the reader is without history, biography, psychology; he is simply that *someone* who holds together in a single field all the traces by which the written text is constituted.
>
> (Barthes 1977b: 148)

I've suggested that despite the insistence on "real viewers" as distinct from the "subject," the place of the "spectator" in film studies is not easily or readily defined as "either" a real person "or" a position, a construction. Let me elaborate, then, on the distinctions I am using among "viewers," "subjects," and "spectators." I deliberately speak of the film *viewer* as the "real person," whether myself or the object of my fantasies. I am not so naive as to think that these real viewers are available to the researcher in any unmediated way, but I do not find it particularly useful to insist, over and over again as some theorists of the subject do, that the category of a "real person" (or viewer) is a purely "discursive" one. Yet while I think it crucial to acknowledge that real people do exist outside of the categories of theory, it is equally crucial to acknowledge that those real people are always the function of my or my culture's notion of what a real person is. I am opposing, in other words, the cinematic *subject* and the film *viewer* so as better to situate the *spectator* as a viewer who is and is not the cinematic subject, and as a subject who is and is not a film viewer. However crucial it was to contemporary film studies to distinguish between the "subject" and the "viewer," and however much film theorists have stressed that the cinematic subject is not identical to the film viewer, the two categories are not and have not been so easily separable.

In his provocative account of contemporary theories of the subject, Paul Smith argues that the term "subject" has been summoned to explain a range of effects that are quite different. Smith distinguishes, therefore, between the *individual* ("the illusion of whole and coherent personal organization"), the human *agent* ("the place from which resistance to the ideological is produced or played out"), and the *subject* ("the series or the conglomeration of positions, subject-positions, provisional and not necessarily indefeasible, into which a person is called momentarily by the discourses and the world that he/she inhabits") (Smith 1988: xxxv). As long as no distinction is made among these three terms, then fantasies of the "individual" are played out across their disavowal in theories of the "subject," and the possibility of any agency is conflated with fictions of the individual. In film theory, this failure to explore the various components of what Smith appropriately calls (citing Jean-Louis Schefer) a "fiction of the subject" has erected false dualities between the institution and its alternatives, between subjectivity and agency (Smith 1988: xxix).

Spectatorship occurs at precisely those spaces where "subjects" and "viewers" rub against each other. In other words, I believe that the interest in spectatorship in film studies attests to a discomfort with either a too easy separation *or* a too easy collapse of the subject and the viewer. I am not convinced that the crucial division which some theorists have assumed to preside over the gap between subjects and "real people" is firm. Indeed, I think that the interest in spectatorship in film studies attests to simultaneous commitment to, yet frustration with, that division. Put another way, the significance of spectatorship in film studies is critical, rather than symptomatic, for implicit in much of the more recent work on spectatorship is the sneaking suspicion that theorists of the subject have left aside the problem of the relationship between constructions and contradictory people by discarding the people altogether. This is not to say that the baby of psychoanalytic film theory has gotten thrown out with the bathwater. Rather, more recent studies of spectatorship have foregrounded what I think is a healthy skepticism about a theory of the subject that would dismiss prematurely the possibility of a relationship between itself and the various models that shape how film viewers are constructed and how those viewers shape the cinematic institution.

Spectatorship offers a unique vantage point on a series of inter-related questions concerning the very nature of the critical and theoretical enterprise. Just because theorists of the cinematic subject bracket the immediate connection between subjects and viewers does not, of course, mean a lack of interest on their part in the various and often contradictory ways in which people view films. "The subject" and "the viewer" are not commensurate terms, and in the eyes of some I may have already fallen into theoretical error by suggesting that, even after nearly two decades of recent film theory, there is a slippage between the two presumably incompatible categories. One can understand the historical necessity for bracketing "real people" when the only available way to talk about such viewers was in the language of sociological or mass-communications research – a language, that is, totally drenched in the assumptions of a white, male, heterosexual norm and a belief in conscious, rational responses presumably untainted by contradiction or unconscious desires. Now I am definitely *not* suggesting that now that those assumptions have been deconstructed, problematized, or otherwise put into question, we can go back and analyze those real people as decentered entities! However, I do think that it is possible to approach the study of the cinema in such a way that would account for the difficulties as well as the limitations of both viewer- and subject-oriented studies.

Too often, the limitations of a psychoanalytic view of spectatorship – i.e., of the cinematic subject – are claimed in the name of the "social," as if the psychic were in sharp opposition to cultural forces. Some psychoanalytic critics have dismissed too easily criticisms of their methods as obvious sociologizing, thus assuming that *any* discussion of "viewers" is hopelessly caught up in the limitations of positivism. At the same time, some objections to psychoanalysis treat the unconscious as a threatening irrationality, thus merely confirming the claims by psychoanalytic critics that the unconscious threatens the stability of the supposedly conscious, rational self. In suggesting that spectatorship is located at a point of tension between the subject and the viewer, I am not proposing a renewal of the desire to "combine" in a happy integration theories of the social and theories of the psychic. Rather, spectatorship offers one of the most challenging arenas for the recognition that tension and conflict need to be better theorized.

At such a point of tension, it is no longer possible to adhere to the strict dichotomies of unconscious/conscious desires, of the psychic versus the ideological, of the individual self versus the social or collective self. The problem with such dichotomies is that by simplifying complex issues into bold oppositions, they too often lead to a simplistic model of "integration," whereby it is assumed that all one needs to do is take what is most attractive from supposedly opposing theoretical claims and mix them together. I want to emphasize the points of *tension* so as to stress spectatorship's role in the complex and difficult negotiation of a series of determinations – political and ideological as well as historical and theoretical. Some work on spectatorship may seem indistinguishable from explorations into the cinematic subject, and other work may seem to bracket entirely the psychoanalytic claims that have been made for the processes that comprise the pleasure of watching films. But I think that on the whole, spectatorship is defined by the competing yet simultaneous claims of the cinematic institution and what exceeds or problematizes it.

I certainly do not want to suggest that the conflicting and often antagonistic positions articulated in the name of spectatorship are only apparent, or that they are all united by a transcendent unifying project. But many of those conflicts and antagonisms stem from a false opposition that underscores many aspects of recent film theory. One of the worst hold-overs of Althusserian Marxism is the opposition between science and ideology, between the assumption that one either lives ideology and is contained by it, or succeeds in analyzing and laying bare its workings and is therefore outside it. In film studies, this opposition took a related form: either the cinema is not only thoroughly saturated with bourgeois ideology but is its greatest fantasy machine, or the cinema is a theoretical demonstration of its own ideological "work." That the only truly alternative films were supposedly those that demonstrated the ideological workings of the medium is the most characteristic position of the science/ideology dichotomy (for an extended discussion of these assumptions see Rodowick 1988). An either/or of this magnitude does not offer many possibilities for more mediated, not to mention historically specific, positions about how the cinema functions. To be sure, film theorists have explored categories of films which perform an "internal criticism" (Comolli and Narboni 1969/1977), which critique the very values they appear to celebrate. But such exceptional films do not necessarily challenge the fundamentally dualistic view that films can, for the most part, be easily categorized as "within" ideology or "critical" of it.

To criticize 1970s film theory for its excessive dualism or its lack of attention to history is in part the privilege of hindsight. Christian Metz, for instance, is recognized as perhaps the most important single figure in the development of contemporary film studies, in part because his own intellectual shifts, from classical semiotics to psychoanalysis, so closely mirror the larger developments of the field. While much of Metz's earlier work on, say, the "grande syntagmatique" of classical film or the peculiar status of film as a language with no language system ("un langage sans langue"), was characterized by the dry expressions of scientific proof, I can remember vividly the sense of challenge and discovery that I and others of my generation experienced in reading and discussing his work. For Metz's enormous erudition in the history of film theory, combined with the analytic methods of semiotics he developed, promised a new way of approaching the film as text, one that would comprehend the very conditions of representation and reception of the cinema. To be sure, these were grand claims, but at the same time Metz's work was so grounded in detailed, exhaustive examination of both film and film theory that they did not seem so excessive. Put another way, Metz's work at the time seemed very historically aware within a specific context, that of film theory and semiotics.

The intersection of semiotics and psychoanalysis is largely assumed to be characteristic of the development of recent film theory, and to be as typical of film theory as of other forms of post-structuralist thought similarly preoccupied with the subject, its desires, and its excesses. As Bertrand Augst has pointed out, however, there is nonetheless a unique quality in the way the intersection has occurred in film theory, and this is largely because of Metz's intervention: "what is different about the assimilation of psychoanalysis into film theory is that this assimilation has been entirely determined by the internal logic of the field's evolution" (Augst 1980: 415). Augst assumes, like Metz, that the intersection of semiotics and psychoanalysis does indeed provide the fullest theoretical account possible of the cinema.

If I am not so convinced of the explanatory power of semiotics and psychoanalysis, this has less to do with mistrust of either method *per se* than of any theory that presumes to explain everything. My point, however, is that recent film theory evolves from the assumption that theory *does* have the capacity to engage fully and comprehensively with signification and representation. Such theoretical claims are usually accompanied by the assumption that the cinema, because it taps so many myths of seeing and believing, fantasy and desire, has a uniquely symptomatic status in Western culture, the emblematic quality to which I referred in the previous chapter. Augst writes, for instance:

> The emergence of cinema as a social institution and its stabilization in the classic Hollywood model is not an accident. The Cinema was invented at a crucial point in the development of the systems of representation which since the Renaissance have sought to secure their ascendancy over the "subject's" freedom. Among all the instruments of power, cinema is undoubtedly the most finely tooled for ideology to secure and perpetuate its control.
>
> (Augst 1980: 436)

This assumption of the unique ideological status of film characterizes virtually all film theory of the 1970s to varying degrees. While Metz's development of semiotic and psychoanalytic film theory emerged from his own work in film theory, writers like Raymond Bellour and Jean-Louis Baudry brought extensive backgrounds in literary theory and philosophy to the study of the cinema. Indeed, what the cinema offered, as an object of analysis, was a foregrounding of the myths of oedipal narrative in nineteenth-century literature (Bellour) or sight and perception in Western philosophy (Baudry).

The theoretical work of the 1970s was enormously important in demonstrating the systematic ways in which cinema was ideological. But despite the usual qualifier that the object of inquiry was the classical, narrative cinema, it was difficult to see how *any* cinema could be conceived outside of those paradigms, particularly since the arguments were based on the technological organization of the medium. Laura Mulvey, in her classic essay, "Visual Pleasure and Narrative Cinema," shares the assumptions of theory's explanatory power and the particular symbolic status of the cinema that characterize 1970s film theory (1975). Mulvey also offers perhaps the most succinct argument for the necessity of an avant-garde practice that departs from classical cinema. But by introducing in an unprecedented way the question of sexual difference into the discussion of film theory, Mulvey also initiated a series of challenges to 1970s film theory. In the years since the publication of work by Metz, Bellour, Baudry, Mulvey, and others, dialogues have continued to take place, dialogues which have productively extended and revised many of the assumptions of 1970s film theory in some cases, but which in others seem locked into the rigid opposition of a monolithic institution, on the one hand, and possible openings, mediations, or reformulations, on the other.

In this and the following chapters, I propose several large groupings for the analysis of spectatorship as they have emerged in film studies of the past two decades. Chronologically the "first," in terms of contemporary film studies, and the subject of this chapter, is what I will call *institutional models* of spectatorship, which include the groundbreaking work of the early and mid–1970s. The term "apparatus" in Jean-Louis Baudry's essays ("Ideological Effects of the Basic Cinematographic Apparatus" and "The Apparatus: Metapsychological Approaches to the Impression of Reality in Cinema") refers both to Freud and to Althusser. The cinematic apparatus as theorized in France in particular was conceived as a psychic and ideological mechanism simultaneously. More importantly, perhaps, the foregrounding of the apparatus repositioned the notion of identification as the central mechanism for spectators' investment in the film experience. For, as noted in chapter 1, the term "identification" usually presumes identification with fictional characters, and Metz, following Baudry, would argue that far more fundamental to the subject's pleasure is the very mechanism of projection. In other words, what is commonly referred to as identification in the cinema is, in Metz's formulation, more properly called secondary cinematic identification (Metz 1975/1982: 47). Logically and psychically prior is "primary cinematic identification": the spectator "identifies with himself, with himself as a pure act of perception" (Metz 1975: 49). Hence, the apparatus is the most basic condition of identification in the cinema:

> it is true that as he identifies with himself as look, the spectator can do no other than identify with the camera, too, which has looked before him at what he is now looking at and whose stationing (=framing) determines the vanishing point. During the projection this camera is absent, but it has a representative consisting of another apparatus, called precisely a "projector."

An apparatus the spectator has behind him, *at the back of his head,*
that is, precisely where phantasy locates the "focus" of all vision.

(Metz 1975: 49)

While institutional models fall more squarely on the side of the "subject" than the viewer, they nonetheless are constructed on the basis
of some notion of a film audience. I will take as my primary example
of the "institutional model" of spectatorship the significance of the
term "apparatus," which is foregrounded in Baudry's work, but
implicit in the work of Mulvey, Metz, and Bellour as well. These are
all examples of psychoanalytic explorations of the cinema, to which
the social dimension suggested by the adjective "institutional" was
central. But since it is still common to criticize psychoanalysis for being
insufficiently attentive to social concerns, I will examine one particular
version of the institutional model which problematizes any dichotomy
between the psychoanalytic and the social: the analogy between
cinema and consumerist culture, and the specific intersections between
cinema and the desire to buy.

Spectatorship studies of the past ten to fifteen years have revised,
challenged, or otherwise extended the implications of the institutional
model. In chapter 3, I evaluate three directions that this work has
taken. Dissatisfaction with the perceived implications of institutional
theory – that the spectator is fully a function of dominant ideology –
has inspired the rethinking of other models of spectatorship. The first
of the three such "revisions" I will discuss is "empirical models"
which stress the need to examine how film viewers actually respond
to the cinema. In some cases this renewed interest in empirical study
involves a rejection of the examination of the cinematic subject, and
in others a testing of that examination against the experiences of real
people. Two variations of empirical models have been crucial in film
studies: cognitivism and ethnography.

The cognitive variation is perhaps most antagonistic to the claims
of 1970s film theory. In the early 1970s, the very perception of cinematic images was assumed by some to require a position not unlike
that of the ideal spectator for Renaissance painting. In other words,
the force of the cinematic institution was so great that even perception
itself assumed ideological form. The cognitive model attempts to
account for the spectator's activity by re-evaluating claims that the
consumption of and identification with cinematic images is necessarily
ideologically overdetermined. The ethnographic variation of empirical
models is also critical of 1970s film theory, specifically of the passive
subject it supposedly presumed – i.e., a subject made to the measure
of dominant ideology does not have the capacity for any kind of
resistance. But in this case, ideological determinations have been not

42

so much bracketed (as is the case with cognitivism) as revised, so as to identify film viewers as resistant agents. Both of these variations of empirical models have entailed explorations of other areas of research – cognitive psychology in the first, cultural studies in the second.

The second "revisionist" category includes "historical models." Historical models of spectatorship share the conviction that models of spectatorship defined institutionally are accurate only to a point, since they perpetuate the notion of a cinematic subject/viewer/spectator who can only be always already (to borrow Derrida's famous phrase) equivalent to the dominant subject of Western society. What is required, rather, is an understanding of *how* the notion of a "dominant" subject may change according to historical circumstance, and how, therefore, what is "dominant" in one set of circumstances may not be in another. Historical models of spectatorship assume, then, that spectatorship must be defined as historically and culturally specific.

The final category is feminism, which includes feminist work on the female spectator as she is largely excluded by 1970s film theory. By defining feminist approaches to spectatorship as a separate category, I am taking the risk of suggesting that the empirical and historical responses to institutional models of spectatorship are separate from feminist concerns. This is far from the case. But feminist approaches to spectatorship nonetheless demand specific consideration, since the very development of feminist film studies has been centrally concerned with theorizing the female spectator. In addition, feminist approaches to spectatorship have critiqued what is an all too common elision in institutional models of spectatorship, the difference that gender makes.

As will become obvious, these are not mutually exclusive categories, and my goal in these two chapters is to account for the directions the investigation of spectatorship has taken rather than pigeonhole work into one category versus another. For instance, much feminist work on the female spectator shares the assumptions of the historical model. But since feminist film theory and criticism have foregrounded so consistently issues of spectatorship, and most important, since the paradigm of gender has been a perspective from which other assumptions of both the empirical and the historical models have been questioned, then much of the work done in the name of feminism is irreducible to my other two categories. In any case, these categories are meant to be understood as points of emphasis in the study and definition of spectatorship, and not definitive categories to divide up the field.

THE INSTITUTIONAL MODEL

Virtually every major figure associated with the development of film theory in the 1970s – Christian Metz, Laura Mulvey, Stephen Heath, Jean-Louis Baudry, Raymond Bellour, and Thierry Kuntzel – takes as a point of departure the institutional quality of the cinema. The institutional approaches to cinematic spectatorship assume the simultaneity of psychic and social factors; indeed, the very term "apparatus" signifies the dual imprint of the psychoanalytic (Freud used the term "apparatus" to describe the architecture of the mind) and the ideological (the title of Althusser's famous essay is "Ideology and Ideological State Apparatuses"). As Metz puts it, "the cinematic institution is not just the cinema industry (which works to fill cinemas, not to empty them), it is also the mental machinery – another industry – which spectators 'accustomed to the cinema' have internalised historically and which has adapted them to the consumption of films" (1975/ 1982: 2). The apparatus which thus emerges as so central to institutional models of spectatorship is a technological system with psychic ramifications, concerning fantasies of regression and affirmations of the imaginary order. In Metz's terms, cinema is governed by the "imaginary signifier," that is, the constant assurance that the imaginary unity of the mirror stage remains intact in face of the division and lack inscribed in the symbolic order.

Film theory of the 1970s, influenced by theories of the subject, stressed that any separation of the social from the psychic is false inasmuch as ideology, the cement that makes any kind of social interraction and communication possible, works in psychic terms. Because a separation is artificial does not necessarily mean it is irrelevant, however. It seems to me more accurate to say that in revisions of these institutional models, different meanings of the social and the psychic have become confused. Hence, when some critics take recent film theory to task for being "inattentive" to social concerns, it is usually different conceptions of the social that are in conflict, particularly insofar as the unconscious is concerned. Just because the unconscious is not accessible to the same kind of quantifiable analysis as directly observable social phenomena are, does not make it any less social, but rather social in a different way. In addition, another division underscores the apparent split of social/psychic structures – the split, that is, between monolithic and heterogeneous forms of organization.

The opposition between the social and the psychic, when used as a critique of contemporary theory, often conceals the assumption that the psychic is unchangeable while the social is permeable, historical, and therefore open to change. Indeed, one of the most persistent criticisms of contemporary film theory in political terms is that it has

44

sacrificed the possibility of any genuinely alternative cinema, particularly since phenomena like MTV and post-modern commercial cinema have made it abundantly clear that there is no necessary link between "foregrounding" the work of cinematic production and criticizing it. Even though the work of Michel Foucault is less often cited in contemporary film studies than Althusser's work was in the 1970s, and than Lacan's was and continues to be at present, its specter is quite ominously – or productively, depending upon your point of view – present.

Central to Foucault's analyses of power and discourse is the assumption that modern systems of power function by instigating a series of ruptures which are then reincorporated into the dominant order. As Theodore B. Leinwand puts it, responses to Foucault's work suggest that there are the proverbial "two Foucaults." According to the first, "not only subversion but the very dialectic of subversion and containment is misguided. . . . A totalizing, perhaps totalitarian, vision emerges from the Foucauldian pun on the word *discipline*." The second is "more optimistic," arguing that "since all relations [of power] are contingent, each is vulnerable" (1990: 478). If the first version of Foucault is more typical of 1970s apparatus theory, the second (which "directs our attention to microencounters, sites at which power is not so much possessed as exercised") is more characteristic of the revisionist responses to it. As with most oppositions, however, this distinction between two readings of Foucault suggests a duality which is in fact not always so clear-cut. For it may not be the possibilities of social change and alternative cinemas that are challenged by contemporary film theory, but rather the too easy assumption that change exists in any simple, voluntaristic way. Only by understanding the tenacity of the cinema as an ideological institution is it possible to explore the possibilities of genuine alternatives. From these considerations emerged the 1970s attack on the assumption that "positive images" – e.g., images which cast women, blacks, gays and other non-dominant groups in strong, powerful roles – are politically and socially effective alternatives.

This brings us to the term "apparatus," which suggests perhaps more than any other key word of contemporary film studies the institutional quality of cinema in a monolithic, deterministic sense. Two essays by Jean-Louis Baudry, one published in 1970 and the second in 1975, introduced and defined the cinematic apparatus in ways that would remain influential. In both essays, Baudry argues that the cinema produces an ideological position through its very mechanics of representation – i.e., the camera, editing, the immobile spectator situated before a screen. Ideology is not imposed upon the cinema, it is always already implicated in it. However, while it has been common to refer to Baudry's two essays as arguing basically the same position, there are in fact significant differences between them.

For in the 1970 essay, Baudry's emphasis is far more heavily on the side of ideology, on a metaphoric quality of the cinema so overdetermined that it is practically impossible to imagine a relationship to the cinema that is *not* fully implicated by dominant ideology. I have already alluded to the split between science and ideology that contemporary film theory inherited from Althusser, and that split is evident in Baudry's article. The implication is that one is either contained by the mechanisms of cinema/ideology and impervious to them, or critically aware of them and therefore outside of them. It is crucial, according to Baudry, that the "work" of production be concealed in dominant cinema, so as not to reveal that the "impression of reality" central to the cinema is a construction. The subject thus constructed by the cinema is fully consonant with the transcendental subject of Western philosophical idealism. Baudry says of the cinematic apparatus that it is "destined to obtain a precise ideological effect, necessary to the dominant ideology: creating a phantasmatization of the subject, it collaborates with a marked efficacy in the maintenance of idealism" (1970: 295). In the 1975 essay, the stakes of the transcendental subject have shifted somewhat. Despite its references to Plato, it is less the collaboration with idealism that is stressed, and more the capacity of the cinema to embody a psychic desire.

While historical specificity was never a strong suit in any of the work produced in France in the 1970s, the assumptions made by Baudry in the 1975 essay are nonetheless striking for their disregard of any historical specificity whatsoever. For by means of a dizzying array of analogies between the cinema, Plato's cave, Freud's analysis of dreams, and various art forms (like painting and theater) preoccupied with the "impression of reality," Baudry ascribes to the cinema a "psychical source" (307), and says that the cinema "brings about a state of artificial regression. It artificially leads back to an anterior phase of his development – a phase which is barely hidden, as dream and certain pathological forms of our mental life have shown. It is the desire, unrecognized as such by the subject, to return to this phase, an early state of development with its own forms of satisfaction which may play a determining role in his desire for cinema and the pleasure he finds in it" (313). The desire for regression would be equated with the recapturing by the cinema of the (Lacanian) imaginary, particularly influential in Metz's better-known hypothesis of the "imaginary signifier" of the cinema.

The most obvious difference between Baudry's two essays is the increasing importance of psychoanalysis in the second. The second essay appeared in the 1975 issue of *Communications* devoted to psychoanalysis and the cinema, arguably one of the landmark texts of recent film theory, including the first publication of portions of Metz's *The Imaginary Signifier* and frequently cited essays by Thierry Kuntzel (on *The Most Dangerous Game*) and Raymond Bellour (on *North by Northwest*). The 1970 essay was published in *Cinéthique*, a journal committed to a rather peculiar mix of Marxist-Leninist cultural politics and theories of the subject, as well as to insistent battles with *Cahiers du cinéma* (battles which echo those that engaged the two theoretical and literary journals *Tel Quel* and *Change*). Psychoanalysis is already as present in the first essay as it was in the theoretical agendas that defined Baudry's work and those of other *Cinéthique* writers in the 1970s. The crucial difference, rather, is the determinism embodied in the second essay, the definition of the cinematic apparatus as so imbricated in psychic desire for regression that it can only replicate itself over and over again. As has been pointed out on more than one occasion, Baudry's work, like Metz's, demonstrates a desire for psychic origin and more problematically for psychic homogeneity (Doane 1980).

It is perhaps unfortunate that the identical English word, "apparatus," is used to translate what are two distinct terms in the French – "appareil" in the 1970 essay, and "dispositif" in the 1975 essay (see Copjec 1982; Penley 1985). Curiously, the word "appareil" is used in French as "apparatus" is in English to translate Freud's *Apparat*; but in the second essay – more indebted to psychoanalysis than the first – the word "dispositif" is used in contrast with "appareil." Unlike "appareil," "dispositif" signifies an arrangement as much as it does a mechanism, and early on in the essay, Baudry opens up an interesting space between the possibly competing notions of "appareil" and "dispositif" when he notes that "we are dealing here with an apparatus [*un dispositif*], with a metaphorical relationship between places or a relationship between metaphorical places, with a topography" (300). In a footnote, Baudry explains that in the previous essay, "appareil" refers to all of the components necessary both to the production and the projection of a film, whereas "dispositif" is more limited, referring solely to "projection and which includes the subject to whom the projection is addressed" (317). The distinction is somewhat deceptive, to the extent that the more limited scope of *dispositif* results in claims that are much broader.

Baudry claims that his analyses are materialist, but his is a mechanistic notion of materialism, with economy and production defined as the actual means by which one produces a film. In a remarkably literal extension, *any* demonstration of technological means becomes a potentially radical act. The shift in the two essays from one dimension of the apparatus to another leaves aside the possibility that other organizations of cinematic production might situate differently the desire embodied in the cinema. It is interesting, in this respect, to read Baudry's work next to Laura Mulvey's essay "Visual Pleasure and Narrative Cinema," perhaps the most frequently cited essay in contemporary film studies. For while Mulvey too assumes that cinema "works" by its appeal to psychic desires ("the cinema satisfies a primordial wish for pleasurable looking" [1975: 9]), there is more a sense of a metaphoric distance in Mulvey's essay, in distinction to Baudry's metaphoric collapse of the cinema and psychic desire. Mulvey says, for instance, that the cinema – always specified in her account as the classical narrative cinema – "has played on" scopophilic desire and ego libido, not "is reducible to" or "is equivalent to." Indeed, at the very beginning of her essay Mulvey defines the context of her intervention as shaped by other production possibilities. The "formal preoccupations" of the classical narrative cinema "reflect the psychical obsessions of the society which produced it." While the term "reflect" is not unproblematic, the apparatus thus designated by Mulvey is defined in a way more historically specific than in Baudry's essays.

The difference here is instructive, for while Mulvey too is concerned with the institutional function of spectatorship, it is already an institution from which some distance – metaphoric as well as critical and ideological – has been attained. Mulvey's essay has been criticized for assuming a monolithic definition of both male and female positions, and for assuming that the classical Hollywood cinema is totally of a piece with patriarchy itself (Bergstrom and Doane 1989; Rodowick 1991). But when read in comparison to Baudry's insistence upon the conflation of cinema, ideology, and psychic desire, Mulvey's intervention seems much less categorical in its delineation of the hierarchies of masculinity/femininity, activity/passivity. Particularly crucial is the distinction made between narrative and spectacle in Mulvey's account. To be sure, she defines the various components of the cinema as working together to produce a reassuring effect for the male or male-identified spectator, but the very understanding of interwoven components is quite different from the relationship between "dispositif" and "appareil" in Baudry's essays, wherein the one is always a mirror reflection of the other.

Put another way, Mulvey analyzes the interlocking systems of narrative and spectacle, and thereby gives narrative a function it does not have in Baudry's account of the apparatus. This is not to say that a focus on narrative is any assurance of a more complex model of spectatorship; Raymond Bellour's analyses of the classical Hollywood cinema are also concerned with the primacy of the oedipal narrative, and narrative is given every bit as much of a monolithic inflection as the apparatus is in Baudry's account. Mulvey foregrounds what is only implicit in virtually every other theory of the cinematic apparatus

– that the ideal spectator of the classical cinema is male. Instructive in this regard are the different ways in which Bellour and Mulvey therefore address the position of the female spectator.

In an interview with Janet Bergstrom, Bellour responds to a question about women's love for the Hollywood cinema with what has become something of a notorious dismissal: "I think that a woman can love, accept and give a positive value to these films only from her own masochism, and from a certain sadism that she can exercise in return on the masculine subject, within a system loaded with traps" (Bergstrom 1979: 97). The dialectic of masochism and sadism from which the female spectator of the classical cinema can presumably never flee has received extensive critical attention, and I will return to the issue of the female spectator in chapter 3. What I want to draw attention to here is the way in which Bellour and Mulvey have addressed their *own* investment in the institution of the classical cinema.

In the same interview, Bellour describes himself as one who is "caught within" the classical cinema: "It was as the subject whose desire is the prisoner of this machinery that I tried to demonstrate its functioning. In this sense the desire to analyze cannot help but manifest a certain ambiguity, since the analysis repeats the movement of the film in order to understand it" (Bergstrom 1979: 95). In the introduction to her follow-up essay to "Visual Pleasure and Narrative Cinema," in which Mulvey considers the implications of female spectatorship, she writes about her use of the "masculine third person" in the 1975 essay: "the persistent question 'what about the women in the audience?' and my own love of Hollywood melodrama (equally shelved as an issue in 'Visual Pleasure') combined to convince me that, *however ironically it had been intended originally*, the male third person closed off avenues of inquiry that should be followed up" (1989: 29) (my emphasis). "Ironic" is not a term one would ever use to describe the kind of analysis pursued in any of the musings about the cinematic apparatus one finds in Metz's or Baudry's writings, and while there are shades of irony in Bellour's own analysis of his imprisonment in the oedipal plot, they foreclose on the impossible pleasure of the female spectator.

If there is no room for irony in most apparatus theory, it is precisely because there is no metaphoric distance between the cinema and the psychic desires it supposedly embodies so fully. The apparatus model is literal; it is as mimetic as the classical cinema claims itself to be. In this sense, much apparatus theory replicates, in psychoanalytic terms, the reductive notion of homology in Lucien Goldmann's account of the relationship between the novel and capitalist society. Goldmann defines the special status of the middle-class novel in these terms:

"The novel form seems to me, in effect, to be *the transposition on the literary plane of everyday life in the individualistic society created by market production*. There is a *rigorous homology* between the literary form of the novel . . . and the everyday relation between man and commodities in general, and by extension between man and other men, in a market society" (1975: 71). In Goldmann's desire to claim identity and relationship, any sense of specificity, and in particular any sense of what might exceed, problematize, or otherwise escape the homology, is marginalized or ignored altogether. Despite Baudry's claims for a "metaphorical relationship" between places in the motif of the apparatus, the relationship of the cinema, psychic desire, and ideology in his account is homological, not metaphoric.

The difference that irony makes is significant, to the extent that it opens up a space for alternatives – even though those alternatives are located firmly in what is perhaps an equally problematic assumption in Mulvey's account, that only a radical avant-garde cinema creates the possibility for the articulation of other modes of spectatorship. In contrast, there is a sollipsistic quality in most theories of the cinematic apparatus. A literal homology is drawn between the cinema and the angst of the castrated male in such a way that any questions of difference or historical specificity are bracketed.

Yet the ease with which the cinematic apparatus fits into the broad lines of the culture of consumption and consumerism suggests that the problem is not a *lack* of historical specificity per se, but rather the *kind* of historical specificity that is implied. The emergence of motion pictures occurred at the same time as the development of the modern culture of consumption (e.g., where economic organization is focussed more on markets for consumption than on sites for production), and in particular at the same time as the birth of modern advertising. This historical coincidence is quite suggestive if one assumes that the relationship between film and consumerism is no more of an "accident" than the coincidence of the births of cinema and psychoanalysis. While it is true that apparatus theorists were not generally inclined to make historical determinations, except to equate the cinema with the "Western subject," few steps are required to see immediately the direct links between the cinematic apparatus and the kind of argument elaborated by many scholars about the equation between cinema and consumerist culture.

Noting the ways in which the consumer is identified as "taken in by the lure of advertising, the seduction of the image," Mary Ann Doane says: "In other words, the phenomenon of consumerism is conceptualized in terms which are not far from those used to delineate spectatorship in the cinema" (1987: 24). A number of recent studies have postulated specific forms of the analogies between film-going and consumption, from the practice of tie-ins between commercial products and films (Eckert 1978; Gaines 1989), to the relationship between clothing and the cinema (Gaines and Herzog 1990), to implications of the analogy between the consumer and the spectator (Allen 1980; Doane 1987: 22–33). These studies have the historical advantage of specifying the analogy between cinema and consumerism within the development of Western industrial capitalism, and so in that sense they avoid such ahistorical, transcendant categories as Baudry's "Western idealist subject." And in some cases, such as Anne Friedberg's recent study of film spectatorship and postmodernism, the connection between cinema and the culture of consumption demonstrates the weak links in apparatus theory, particularly insofar as gender and the supposed immobility of the spectator are concerned (Friedberg 1993).

I am not convinced that historicization alone is sufficient grounds for challenging the key element in apparatus theory, the appeal to mechanistic homologies. It is one thing to say that the cinema is metonymically linked to the institutions of consumerism, and another thing altogether to conflate the cinema with consumerism. When the latter conflation occurs, it becomes impossible to distinguish between the image the industry and the institutions of cinema create of its spectators, and the ways in which viewers actually respond to the cinema, since such a top-down view cannot imagine viewers except as the constructions of the industry. But the risk in downplaying the totalizing effects of consumerism is in underestimating the extent to which cinema *is* a part of a larger system of domination and manipulation of needs and desires.

It may well be that the problem with all versions of apparatus theory is the appeal to a master discourse, to large and sweeping historical moments, to a definition of theory capable of explaining everything. Consumerism has been summoned to explain or otherwise rationalize so many twentieth-century phenomena that one might begin to suspect that it explains everything and nothing simultaneously, just as appeals to the transcendantal subject of idealism provide such overarching categorizations that potentially significant details or variations are lost. The problem with theories-that-explain-everything is not so much that they are "wrong" (even though they often are). These theories involve projection and desire just as all discourses do, and the failure to examine those mechanisms leads to a notion of subjectivity with no possibility of contradiction or significant variation from the norm. Convincing feminist arguments about Baudry's work, for instance, have suggested that the critique of the cinematic apparatus involves an idealization of the very subject supposedly under investigation (Copjec 1982; Rose 1980; Penley 1985). In Charles Eckert's account of cinema and consumerism, an ideal female spectator/buyer is described in terms that oscillate between the symptomatic and the voyeuristic. As a result, when Eckert's essay concludes with an appeal to "we," one senses the evocation of a golden age prior to the invention of advertising: "Were we, as consumers, such skilled and habituated perceivers of libidinal cues, such receptive audiences for associational complexes, such romanticizers of homes, stores, and highways before Hollywood gave us *Dinner at Eight, The Big Store* and *The Speed that Kills*? I would suggest that we were not" (1978: 21).

I suggested that Laura Mulvey's account of the cinematic institution differs sharply from Baudry's because of the attention paid to the different and intertwining elements – narrative and spectacle – as well as to the kind of metaphoric status male oedipal desire acquires in relation to the cinema. Since Mulvey brings a feminist perspective to bear on questions of film and spectatorship that is totally lacking in Baudry's, Metz's, or Bellour's work, it is thus tempting to argue that questions of gender and sexual difference are as crucial to film theory as they have been to the historical construction of the cinema's appeal. While I think this is true, I do not want to suggest that feminism is a necessary guarantee against the overly literal and deterministic readings of the cinematic institution that have characterized much apparatus theory. Indeed, some feminist work which takes Mulvey's essay as an inspiration puts forth just as rigidly a master plot of men looking at women from which any possibility of the female subject has been evacuated.

Since the publication of work devoted to various aspects of the cinematic apparatus in the early to mid–1970s, film theorists have responded to the implications of these arguments in a variety of ways. The most common criticisms of the institutional model are first, that the spectator postulated is a totally passive one; second, that no allowance is made for the difference that difference makes – sexual difference, certainly, but also differences of race and culture; third, that history is given no place in the argument; and finally, that psychoanalysis is used in an abstracted, almost deterministic way. Before moving on to a specific examination of these responses to the institutional model, let me say that whatever criticisms I share of the institutional model, I think it crucial to recognize how significant these works were in redefining the general field of film studies, and specifically in bringing the subject of spectatorship to the foreground. The homological quality of the institutional model is the risk one takes in attempting to understand any kind of parallel or relationship, and often a bold demonstration of the homology is required before it is possible to rethink the relationship between films and spectators.

3

SPECTATORSHIP RECONSIDERED

One of the most frequent criticisms made of the apparatus models is that they presume a homogeneous spectator – totally a function of Western idealism in the case of Baudry, totally male or male-identified in the case of Mulvey. Even though passivity is traditionally affiliated with femininity, the two criticisms are compatible to the extent that Mulvey's active male protagonist nonetheless presumes a fairly passive male spectator, and Baudry's passive spectator is fully consonant with myths of male subjectivity. What is not altogether clear is the critical and theoretical difference that a heterogeneous, as opposed to a homogeneous concept of spectatorship, would make.

It is possible, in other words, to imagine a more heterogeneous spectator who remains male or male-identified, just in different ways; indeed, much of the work that has been done in feminist film studies as a response to Mulvey can be interrogated on just these grounds. Respondents imagine that they are conceptualizing a radically different spectator, but there is no guarantee that the "female spectator" thus theorized is any less male-identified. As Mary Ann Doane has shown, for instance, the very films that inspire strong female spectatorial investment may only confirm, rather than challenge, the institutional qualities that Mulvey identified (1987). Similarly, Baudry's spectator can be criticized as participating too fully in the very myth of the cinema that is supposedly being dismantled, or as presuming an institution so powerful that it incorporates all spectators in an identical way. But even if that institution were defined with more variables, identified as susceptible to various differences and specificities, this is no guarantee that the fantasies of regression and fusion will be equally dismantled.

EMPIRICAL MODELS

One of the problems with theoretical abstraction, of course, is that arguments occur in areas that are not subject to the kind of "proof" that can make clear and visible the difference between valid and invalid claims. Indeed, the theoretical agendas that defined 1970s film theory – semiotics, Althusserian Marxism, psychoanalysis and feminism – are grounded in a refusal of the equation between the apparent and the self-evident. Central to each are strategies of reading which are designed to make visible what is transformed, displaced, or otherwise disguised by ideology. One of the most mistrusted arenas for scholarship in the 1970s was empirical research; indeed, empiricism as an approach grounded on the finality of perception is a word virtually synonomous with what those theoretical agendas were rejecting. Part of the move to reject empiricism needs to be seen, of course, in the context of what film studies was reacting to, particularly insofar as traditions of mass communications or sociological research were concerned, traditions within which theoretical sophistication was the exception rather than the rule.

Given this distrust of empiricism which so informed the development of the field of film studies, it is interesting to see in recent years a return to empirically oriented research. In terms of spectatorship, such studies are meant to correct, challenge, and revise what has been perceived as the monolithic and homogeneous spectator theorized in film studies. The two major directions that the re-evaluation of empirical research has taken are quite different. On the one hand, contemporary film theorists such as David Bordwell, Edward Branigan, and Noël Carroll have found in the areas of cognitive psychology and linguistics the possibility for a much more dynamic and complex – and in their view scientifically grounded – view of film spectatorship (Bordwell 1985, 1989; Branigan 1984, 1986; Carroll 1988). Implicit in the interest in cognitivism is the assumption that film theorists have assumed too quickly an ideological status for film viewing, one less reliant on the specific films and film-going practices themselves than on the nature of film viewing in general. Others have incorporated cognitive perspectives into the project of rethinking, but not necessarily rejecting, the implications of the institutional model (Butzel 1992; De Lauretis 1984; Nichols 1989).

On the other hand, there has been a renewed interest in ethnography in film studies, on observations of audience responses to and reception of different types of films. While researchers like Bruce A. Austin (1989) have done extensive and detailed studies on film audiences, the new turn toward ethnography has been largely inspired by the work associated originally with the University of Birmingham Centre for Contemporary Cultural Studies. Whereas much of the interest in cognitivism as a basis for understanding film spectatorship has entailed a bracketing of the polarity of complicity versus subversion of dominant ideology, the ethnographic approach has renewed it, particularly by arguing that the ways in which specific audiences "use" mass culture involve some degree of subversion and resistance. In other words, then, the stakes of empiricism in these two undertakings are radically different, involving a challenge to the very notion of *ideological* complicity in the case of cognitivism, and a challenge to the necessary pairing of ideology and *complicity* in the case of ethnography.

Near the conclusion of the 1975 essay "The Apparatus," Baudry makes one of many sweeping statements concerning the desires embodied in the cinema. A wish prepares, says Baudry, the "long history of cinema: the wish to construct a simulation machine capable of offering the subject perceptions which are really representations mistaken for perceptions" (315). If the cinematic apparatus holds its subject in a state of hypnotized fascination, of subjugated fantasy, then surely one of the most decisive markers of the power of the cinematic institution is precisely this confusion of perception and representation. This supposed equation points not only to a powerful system of representation, but to a spectator so caught up in the illusions of this system that all perceptual activity is, if not suspended, then at the very least subjugated to the regressive desires instigated by the machine.

The appeal to cognitive perspectives takes cinematic *perception* as its key point of departure. David Bordwell writes in *Narration in the Fiction Film* that many theories of film narration ignore the spectator or define the subject as "the victim or dupe of narrational illusion-making." Bordwell continues that "the passivity of the spectator . . . generally is suggested . . . by the use of terms like the 'position' or the 'place' of the subject. Such metaphors lead us to conceive of the perceiver as backed into a corner by conventions of perspective, editing, narrative point of view, and psychic unity. A film, I shall suggest, does not 'position' anybody. A film cues the spectator to execute a definable variety of *operations*" (1985: 29). Particularly important in this context is the notion of a *schema* in cognitive psychology, a set of familiar elements which "acts as a structured set of expectations in which the data of a given text can be factored" (1989: 26). Bordwell's stress on operations and schemata is accompanied by two other crucial moves. First, the need, in his view, to move away from psychoanalytic explorations toward psychological ones; and second, the need for more empirical studies of how the perception and understanding of motion pictures actually work.

In Bordwell's account, spectating is an activity undertaken by individuals of wide range, perhaps, but united by their capacity for active perception. The "spectator" as defined in apparatus theory is the ideal spectator of motion pictures, a horizon – indeed, as Bordwell says, a

55

position – and not a real person. I have already suggested that despite the insistence of film theorists that the "subject" of the cinema is not the same as the "viewer," some relationship between the two supposedly incommensurate terms nonetheless exists. Bordwell's criticisms are to some extent on target, since the theories in question lend themselves to the very confusion which they presumably set out to correct. By bracketing the "real viewers" altogether, such theories undertake what is ultimately an impossible task. However much one can insist upon the theoretical need for separating the ideal spectator from the real viewers of motion pictures, the two categories are not so easily separated. Instead of theorizing the difficulty, the slippage between the two supposed incommensurate terms, much film theory has ignored the problem altogether by dismissing one or the other as irrelevant or secondary. Yet Bordwell's critique of film theory in the name of cognitivism ignores the attempt to separate the subject and the viewer, and proceeds as if psychoanalytic theories of the subject and cognitive theories of perception, mapping, and knowledge start from the same point of departure (see also Carroll 1988).

When perception is at issue in many theories of the 1970s, it is understood as something imposed, perception as ideology. The suspicion of any kinds of arguments rooted in human biological capacities might have been well founded, but as Bordwell suggests, engaging with human perceptual capacities is not necessarily the same thing as re-erecting a "norm" (needless to say, one shaped by cultural demands) against which anything departing even slightly from its standards will be defined as deviant. One of the most common refrains in 1970s film theory was that the perceiving subject of the motion pictures was the heir to the subject of perspective in Renaissance painting (Pleynet 1969). The ideal spectator of the motion pictures, in other words, was the culmination of the eye as the center of human subjectivity and meaning, the receptacle of truth. While this was rarely spelled out in any detail, the tendency was to treat perception as if it were totally acculturated, totally imposed.

Bordwell argues that contemporary film theory is both "constructivist" ("the spectator-as-subject is assumed to partly collude in his or her subjection by contributing expectations and desires that the text requires") and "conventionalist" ("meaning is held to be constructed according to conventions; it arises from the contingencies of the given social formation") (1989: 19). The problem, Bordwell says, is that "without prior factors, construction . . . is impossible" (19), and film theorists have had precious little to say about those prior factors – for example, the neuro-biological factors that determine film perception, the extent to which such perception is a complex activity, and the overlap that may well exist across cultures.

It is not altogether clear whether cognitivism provides a necessary corrective which is fully compatible with the psychoanalytically inspired project of recent film theory, or a completely different agenda altogether. In any case, Bordwell's picture of the field of film studies seems to me somewhat inaccurate. Bill Nichols has noted, for instance, that while it is undoubtedly true that much recent film theory has paid insufficient attention to cognitive processing, it has not rejected cognitive activity but has "associated that activity with the social ends it served" (1989: 509). In other words, one can define perception as an active process without necessarily discarding the notion of the cinematic institution. However, Bordwell's challenge does not consist in discarding the notion of the cinema as an institution, but rather in displacing it from the exclusive role it had in 1970s film theory.

Teresa de Lauretis emphasizes the dynamic, complex role of perception in a way that problematizes Bordwell's description of the field and the attendant place of cognitive research. In *Alice Doesn't*, for example, de Lauretis draws upon the relationship between perception and signification in order to draw implications that challenge those of Baudry, but which are quite different from Bordwell's appeal to cognitivism. Noting that the term "mapping" applies both to theories of perception (Colin Blakemore) and theories of signification (Umberto Eco), de Lauretis suggests that in both instances, we are talking about complex processes mutually implicating each other. De Lauretis says: "If, then, subjectivity is engaged in semiosis at all levels, not just in visual pleasure but in all cognitive processes, in turn semiosis (coded expectations, patterns of response, assumptions, inferences, predictions, and, I would add, fantasy) is at work in sensory perception, inscribed in the body – the human body and the film body" (1984: 56).

That de Lauretis's appeal to the perceptual apparatus is a somewhat unexpected move in the context of feminist film theory has been noted by several critics, so it would be mistaken to extrapolate too much of a trend from this one example (Radstone 1985). But this example does serve the purpose of illustrating that the appeal to perception studies and cognitivism is not *necessarily* in radical contradistinction from the theories of the apparatus (as is the case with Bordwell and others), but can be instead a revision of them. Marcia Butzel has suggested the stakes of the revision in an example drawn from the opening images of *His Girl Friday* (1940), particularly insofar as the representation of movement – that of characters and the camera – is concerned. Noting that "figural movement articulates sexual difference (males huddle in seats, vainly seeking to exchange or complete stories; females move through space but only to relay the stories of others)," Butzel adds to this narrative analysis a discussion of perceptual

57

analysis, where the latter "interestingly complicates" the narrative implications. Butzel describes the "luminous balding head" of a male character who passes by and evokes similar perceptual cues as a blonde female had previously. Butzel asks:

> Could this be a cue for us to repeat our perceptual response to the similarly shifting luminosity of the blonde female's head? Could the shot at this point work to overcome the evidence of sexual difference at a very fundamental level? As a matter of perceptual orientation, the opening mobile shot could indeed provide cues for viewers to "manage" differently the conventional scenario of gender division.
>
> (1992: 44–5 [manu.])

The far more decisive implications of Bordwell's appeal to cognitivism have to do with the status of empirical research. More specifically, what separates the differing ways in which de Lauretis, Butzel, and Nichols, on the one hand, and Bordwell on the other, read cognitivism is the role of psychoanalysis and desire. Bordwell notes that one of the advantages of cognitivism is its engagement with the norm rather than with what deviates from the norm, as is (presumably) the case in psychoanalysis. While this may be true as far as it goes, what is left unarticulated in this account of psychoanalysis is the extent to which psychoanalysis puts radically into question the very notion of a norm. One could say also that it is through the exceptional, the extreme case, that psychoanalysis reads the norm, from the assumption that it is only in so-called deviance that anything resembling the "norm" – which is a concept that is meaningless *without* deviance – is readable. For the insight central to the most radical forms of psychoanalysis is that any notion of the norm is fragile indeed.

I am tempted to say that Bordwell's direction points then quite naturally toward the validity of empirical research, while the work of those who engage simultaneously with cognitivism and institutional theories of spectatorship points just as naturally away from it. But I think it is erroneous to assume that theory informed by a notion of psychoanalytically inspired desire is necessarily *opposed* to any form of empirical evidence. It is, rather, a question of how that empirical evidence is read, and of the status of the findings. The validity of any kind of empirical research has been under suspicion in film studies for so long that there is something refreshing about the renewed claim for its value. Yet what threatens to get lost completely in the move toward perception studies and cognitivism is the unconscious. Some might argue that this is no great loss, particularly since the unconscious that has emerged from much psychoanalytic criticism is indistinguishable from a master plot of male oedipal desire. But as I suggest above, there is a far more radical possibility for psychoanalysis, and while contemporary film theory has leaned more toward the master plot, a significant direction in film theory has been undertaken by those who resist such easy definitions of the unconscious (Rose 1986). Bordwell's reading of cognitivism against psychoanalysis is interesting in this respect, since the unconscious seems to be identified as having only to do with deviance and neurosis. "The vicissitudes of the Rat Man's desire are bizarre enough to attract anybody's interest," he writes, "but there is something quietly awesome in the creative resourcefulness exhibited by ordinary people practicing a well-learned skill" (1989: 30).

Interest in the unconscious cannot really take the particular kind of empirical route that Bordwell proposes. However much film theorists may think otherwise, the therapeutic analytic situation is not identical or even analogous to the film analytic one, unless of course one wants to practice the kind of psychoanalyzing of authors or characters that has been discredited for some time. Yet psychoanalysis has just as much of a stake in exploring "creative resourcefulness" as cognitive studies have. Indeed, some directions in psychoanalytic theory (discussed more in detail in chapter 4) have explored the analogy between cinema and fantasy in ways that seem to avoid some of the homological problems of the institutional model. Criticisms of the apparatus model are certainly well taken, but while the trick is to account for a spectator who is active, this activity nonetheless needs to be read in relationship to unconscious processes.

The supposed passivity of the film spectator has been challenged in another appeal to empirical research, based not on "scientific" studies of perception and understanding, but on critical and qualitative observations of how individuals actually respond to the cinema. Inspired by Stuart Hall's work (1980) on "encoding" and "decoding" – e.g., on the relationship between the ideology contained within texts and the various ways in which individuals "decode" or interpret that ideology based on their own social positioning – as well as by audience studies like Janice Radway's analysis of women's responses to romance fiction (1984), some film scholars have turned to ethnographic studies as a way of restoring complexity and contradiction in flesh-and-blood people in contrast to the abstract and often politically dismal pronouncements of apparatus theory.

The ethnographic approach to the audience has been more of a horizon of research in film studies than an actual practice. Perhaps because television watching is the most representative, typical, and common spectating activity in contemporary industrial societies, the ethnographic approach has been more visible in television studies than in film studies. As a horizon, the cultural studies approach is nonetheless influential, and some recently-published textual or theoretical analyses find it necessary to explain their lack of audience-response investigation. The enthusiasm which has greeted ethnographic studies may seem curious in a field that has been so concerned with studying the subject effect. Indeed, there is something in the current popularity of ethnography and cultural studies that suggests the return of the repressed. One particularly striking manifestation of this is an issue of *Camera Obscura* devoted to the female spectator (Bergstrom and Doane 1989). In a series of responses sollicited to a questionnaire on female spectatorship, one critic after another voices frustration with or at the very least acknowledgement of the difficulty with which theories of the subject remain separate from real viewers. Given that *Camera Obscura* has been one of the most significant sources in the US for the publication of work (translations as well as original work) devoted to theories of the subject, it is a bit of a surprise to see such testimony to the limitations of those theories.

In the context of the UK, the development of cultural studies was in part a response to the journal *Screen*, where many of the most influential texts of apparatus theory first appeared, including Mulvey's 1975 essay as well as translations of Metz and Bellour. As Tania Modleski puts it in a critique of feminism's attraction to ethnographic criticism, "[i]n the dissenters' view, *Screen*'s psychoanalytically informed theory, concerned largely with describing the way subjects are 'constructed' by popular film texts, tended to ignore actual social subjects, who by virtue of their complex histories and multiple cultural affiliations (educational, religious, vocational, political, etc.) always, it is argued, exceed the subject implied by the text" (1989: 4). If cognitivism displaces the already tenuous relationship between the "subject" and "real people" in order to redefine substantially the very notion of response to film, the cultural studies/ethnographic approach may be said to do the same, since the "subject" is also presumed to represent a problematic abstraction, albeit problematic in different ways than it is for the cognitive model.

Thus, there is a difference between the cognitive and the ethnographic approach to "real people." The cognitive approach as defined by Bordwell and Carroll has the value of consistency, to the extent that (successfully or not) the psychoanalytic approach to the subject is rejected or bracketed. In ethnographic studies of the audience, it is not entirely clear *what* has happened to psychoanalysis or to the subject as a construction, particularly given the emphasis on literal audience response. Yet despite their extreme differences in other ways, the cognitive and the ethnographic perspectives share a turn to empiricism characterized by a refusal or reluctance to engage with unconscious processes.

In the case of ethnography specifically and cultural studies in general, however, there is more caution in dismissing altogether the force of the unconscious. Rather, the unconscious seems to be largely synonomous with the dominant ideology contained within the text. In other words, the notion of the unconscious seems to have become purely instrumental, referring to how individuals unconsciously assume the attributes of subjectivity and ideology in a given culture. At the same time, proponents of ethnographic studies suggest that researchers themselves make visible what may not be visible to the audiences under investigation, i.e., that their responses to mass culture are in fact composed of various resistances to the meanings of the text as they might be uncovered by a "purely" textual reading. In other words, ethnography becomes a means to situate in the realm of real readers and viewers the possibility of "reading against the grain" as a strategy not limited to textual analysis, but rather part of the reception context itself.

While the move toward cognitivism suggests a more clear-cut "scientific" agenda for film studies, one that would displace what Bordwell sees as the unrigorous and mechanical emphasis placed on "interpretation," the move toward ethnography is informed by a desire to make scholarship more politically and ideologically involved, rather than less so. But if cognitive studies foreground the overly schematic ways in which the unconscious has been understood in apparatus theory, cultural studies and ethnography foreground yet another problem, and that is the tendency for the researcher to construct an image of the "spectator" or the "real viewer" every bit as monolithic as the "subject" of dominant ideology. Now, however, the monolithic quality works in another direction, constituting a viewer who is always resisting, always struggling, always seemingly just on the verge of becoming the embodiment of the researcher's own political ideal.

Tania Modleski has described this problem as follows:

> It seemed important at one historical moment to emphasize the way "the people" resist mass culture's manipulations. Today, we are in danger of forgetting the crucial fact that, like everyone else, even the cultural analyst may sometimes be a "cultural dupe" – which is, after all, only an ugly way of saying that we exist inside ideology, that we are all victims, down to the very depths of our psyches, of political and cultural domination (even though we are never only victims).
>
> (1989: 12)

Indeed, the current interest in cultural studies and ethnography raises important questions about the degree of abstraction present in theories of the subject, but raises even more insistently the question of the

61

position of the researcher. In an examination of both how a working-class family watches a video of the film *Rocky II* and how the scene of observation activates her own fantasies and desires, Valerie Walkerdine notes that what is missing in much ethnographic work is "any account of the ethnographer's own position in the web of power/knowledge/desire." She continues:

> Another problem with much ethnographic work (my own included) has been the way it takes discourse at face value. In working with a transcript, for example, of what can we take it as evidence? Ethnographic interviews with adolescent working-class girls are often used to justify theories of girls' resistance, as is their anti-school behaviour and taking on of femininity (through using make-up or subverting uniform). Yet could these discourses and actions not equally well hide pain and anxiety in relation to academic failure? The problem of ethnographic work is how to take adequate account of the psychical reality of both observer and observed.
>
> (1986: 192)

As a model for spectatorship studies, ethnography can serve as an important reminder that the bracketing of the referent in contemporary theories of signification does not mean that the responses of real, historical beings are irrelevant; only a simplistic, mechanical textuality could claim such a disregard for history. Yet a desire for unproblematized and romanticized agency ultimately characterizes much of the work done in the name of ethnography. If the "subject" as theorized by apparatus studies is "passive" and "constructed," the argument seems to go, then the "audience" will be just the opposite – active sites of agency and struggle. Psychoanalysis is more or less evacuated from this account, except in one important (and, as Walkerdine suggests, largely unacknowledged) dimension – projection.

HISTORICAL MODELS

Empirical evidence means, of course, many things, and the cognitive and ethnographic approaches interpret the significance of such evidence in different ways. Bordwell is referring to verifiable, experimental evidence which would provide the foundations for a presumably new theoretical sophistication in film studies, while researchers in cultural studies challenge the overly abstract definition of reception that characterizes theories of the apparatus. For other studies of spectatorship in the cinema, the major limitation of apparatus studies has been their lack of any kind of historical precision. By and large, studies of the cinematic apparatus seem caught in the paradox which has been so central to feminist inquiry – that is, by describing an institution that is defined monolithically in its effects and domination by the white, male subject of "Western" civilization, you end up giving that institution more stability than it ever had in the first place. The problem, in other words, is in, if not celebrating, then at the very least reifying the monolithic quality you set out to critique.

While there have been many studies of national cinemas that fall far outside the purview of Hollywood, these tend to be done independently of the kind of apparatus concerns that characterize 1970s film theory, as if to reinforce the sense that the apparatus is a peculiarity of classical filmmaking (one notable exception is Noël Burch's study of Japanese cinema [1979]). Even within the limited body of classical cinema, however, it has been questioned whether the apparatus can account for the historical and cultural variation in the cinema. For example, of what usefulness is Baudry's claim that cinema always inspires a regressive state, when that regression might mean something radically different in the context of rural 1930s US society and the post-Vietnam 1970s, for instance? Or, to put this another way, are the differences between one oedipal narrative and another not potentially as significant as their similarities?

In fact, there are many spectatorship studies that assume it is crucial to understand how spectatorship is defined within specific cultural and historical periods. This involves a number of questions which the apparatus model – concerned as it is with the larger instance of the "cinema" as such – is insufficient to address on its own terms. Some of these questions include: What did film going represent for historically different audiences? Do different film genres address spectators in radically different ways? How are the cinema and individual films contextualized in a given culture? What are the different texts and institutions that define how individual films, groups of films, audiences, and film-going patterns are defined? In short, the central question raised is two-fold: what are the histories of spectatorship, and what is historical about spectatorship?

Not all historical accounts of film and spectatorship are necessarily opposed to the institutional models. Mary Ann Doane's analysis of the "woman's film" of the 1940s, for instance, affirms the somewhat dismal view of the restrictions of the cinematic apparatus insofar as any possibility of a female point of view is concerned, for the sample of films analyzed in her study emphasize in a variety of ways the equation between classical cinema (at least in this particular version of it) and patriarchal desires. While Doane's study shares the assumptions of the institutional model, it nonetheless affords a more precise historical perspective on the characteristics of the dominant cinema described so universally in 1970s film theory. Doane limits her study to the "woman's film," that is, films presumably addressed to female spectators and preoccupied with relationships that are evocative of women's position in patriarchal culture – as patients and mothers, for instance. Her study does not presume to account for all instances of classical cinema, even though her examples are strategically chosen in that they foreground devices which may well appear in other films.

While Doane's study illustrates that a historical model need not always mean a rejection of the key assumptions of theories of the cinematic apparatus, the move away from theory and toward history that has characterized film studies in the past several years has been accompanied by a frustration with large pronouncements about the cinema, and an attendant interest in the specific, local ways in which films work and engage their viewers. The term "history" threatens to become a buzzword with some of the same problems that the "subject" acquired in the 1970s. For while in many cases the historical perspective reminds us that theories can become as monolithic and rigid as the institutions they describe, in other cases "history" has acquired the status of unquestionable evidence, a secure vantage point from which to reject theoretical interrogation.

Several distinct directions characterize the present concern with historicizing spectatorship. Four of these directions have emerged as particularly influential, and offer the possibility of examining spectatorship as a complex and often contradictory historical – and theoretical – phenomenon. First, the notion of *intertextuality* has been revised from its 1970s connotations (as, in Julia Kristeva's words, the recognition that every text is a "mosaic of citations" [1969: 139]) to refer less to the discursive and self-referential quality of all signification, and more to the ways in which film addresses its viewers across a wide range of texts. Some critics have sustained the primacy of textual analysis in film studies of the 1970s, but have enlarged its scope considerably, by examining the textual strategies of address in a group of films defined generically and historically, as in Doane's account, or by extending textual analysis from the individual films to the various texts that accompany them. The assumption here is that spectatorship is structured not just by the experience of going to the movies and being seduced by the spectacle on screen, but by the influence of a whole range of texts that seek, in one way or another, to spark interest in films and keep movie theaters full.

Magazines have proven to be a particularly rich source of documentation. Patrice Petro (1989) examines Weimar melodramas in relationship to magazines addressed specifically to female readers, and hypothesizes on the relationship between these different forms of gendered spectatorship. The crisis situation engendered by World War II, and the changing dimensions of private and public life, particularly insofar as women (as workers and spectators) were concerned, gives American film of the 1940s an almost emblematic status for the mutual influence of film and magazines. Studies by Susan Ohmer, Dana Polan, and Michael Renov have examined how spectatorship is constructed across a wide range of positions, in which the codes of advertising and magazine journalism intersect with those of the cinema in complex ways (Ohmer 1990; Polan 1986; Renov 1988, 1989). While these works examine some of the same ground as studies of the analogy between cinema and the culture of consumerism, the emphasis is nonetheless different, since the revision of intertextuality assumes a shifting ground of representation and address rather than a seamless, homogeneous institution.

Perhaps the most obvious way that film circulates outside of the movie theater is through the personae of stars. The visibility of fan magazines, and features in women's magazines and lifestyle magazines (as well as magazine-style television in the past ten years), create a complex network of address which also challenges the notion of a cinematic institution located exclusively in film-specific textual properties. Critics like Maria LaPlace (writing on Bette Davis), Andrew Britton (on Katharine Hepburn), and Richard Dyer (on Marilyn Monroe, Paul Robeson, and Judy Garland) have examined the ways in which star images are produced and circulated through various kinds of address, including the films as well as fan magazines and the popular press (LaPlace 1987; Britton 1984; Dyer 1986). Indeed, the study of stars has been the arena where the revision of intertextuality has been most influential. If one has considered the star persona of a figure like Marlene Dietrich exclusively in terms of how she appears on screen, then one has a very different perception when that image is read across the different texts that constructed it. Fan-magazine profiles of Dietrich in the 1930s focussed regularly on her off-screen role as devoted *hausfrau* and mother, as if to suggest that the androgynous sexual figure projected on screen required some form of counterpoint. In other words, then, this revision of intertextuality draws attention toward the process of construction of the cinematic image (see chapter 6 for a more extended discussion of stars and spectatorship).

A second important direction in the historicizing of spectatorship concerns film exhibition. Like many film scholars, I remember with considerable nostalgia the neighborhood theaters where I saw virtually all of the films that remain the privileged texts in my own history as a film spectator, and I bemoan the growth of multiplex, shopping-mall cinemas and the domination of "film" exhibition by the remarkable development of home VCRs that characterize contemporary film reception. While studies of the exhibition contexts for motion pictures have been a major development in film history, due in particular to the work of historians like Douglas Gomery and Robert Allen, there has been considerable reluctance on the part of film scholars to examine the extent to which their own memories and fantasies of the exhibition context shape their theoretical enterprise (for a significant exception see Rosenbaum 1980). Part of the appeal of textual analysis may well be the "fixing" on the film text, a way of committing to permanence an artifact which can no longer mean what it did for audiences of the 1940s, for instance.

In their book on film history, Robert Allen and Douglas Gomery distinguish between four traditional approaches to film history, and in a survey of recent scholarship on film exhibition, Douglas Gomery identifies those same four approaches: the economic, the technological, the social, and the aesthetic (Allen and Gomery 1985; Gomery 1990). What Gomery refers to as the "social" has the most relevance to spectatorship, not just in the obvious sense of audience study, but in the ways that the "new" social histories, particularly those that focus on the patterns of everyday life and on the experiences of those once dismissed as "marginal" to historiography, define film exhibition as a play between empowerment and control of spectators. Studies of the exhibition contexts for early motion pictures provide some of the most interesting and provocative analyses of how spectatorship is defined in historical terms. It is an observation of long-standing that immigrants in urban settings were drawn to motion pictures as a form of acculturation into American life. But recent scholarship on the early cinema goes far beyond the romanticized notion of immigrants finding idealized identification figures in the movies. The exhibition context for immigrant and working-class audiences and early motion pictures emphasizes, rather, the complex relationship between private and public life in which movies played such a crucial role, as well as the structure of neighborhoods and the changing role of leisure in the development of motion pictures (Mayne 1988: 68–81; Allen 1979, 1980; Merritt 1976; Ewen 1985; Peiss 1986).

Related to the focus on the exhibition context is a third important direction in historical studies of spectatorship, and that is the examination of cinema as a particular public sphere, that is, a space where viewing communities are constructed in a way that involves both acculturation to social ideals and the affirmation of marginality. From the earliest years of motion pictures, the experience of film viewing has involved a unique and specific combination of individual fantasy and social ritual. Examination of the cinema as a public sphere offers the opportunity to examine how that combination of individual fantasy and social ritual contributes to the development of communities of individuals for whom the cinema serves as a crucial component.

Immigrant audiences for early films demonstrate the increasingly important role of cinema as a unique public sphere where the sense of a viewing community functioned in contradictory ways, as an affirmation of neighborhood defined in ethnic terms, but also as a showcase for the values to which immigrant populations were expected to adapt (Ewen 1985; Mayne 1988). Miriam Hansen's study of early American film examines how the cinema functioned, particularly for women, as an "alternative" public sphere, that is, a space where women were free to enjoy the pleasures of voyeurism and active spectatorship otherwise denied them (1991). The growth of cinema as a popular form of entertainment corresponds to radical changes in the relationship between private and public spheres, with attendant changes in the very nature of film spectatorship (see Friedberg 1993). The relationship between specific social groups and how they identify themselves as participants in the public sphere of the cinema offers the opportunity to examine how cinema has played a crucial role in the very notion of community. Examination of cinema and the public sphere has tended to focus on early film and on the difference gender and class make. In chapter 8 I examine in more detail how contemporary notions of the gay and lesbian community connect with the status of film spectatorship insofar as the notion of a cinematic public sphere is concerned.

The fourth significant direction in historical studies of spectatorship is the analysis of reception. Here film studies shares some ground with contemporary literary criticism that uses reception theory as a means of exploring the ways in which the meanings of a text are always shaped by the historical circumstances of reading or viewing at a particular moment (Rentschler 1981). Janet Staiger, for instance, has borrowed from Hans Robert Jauss's notion of the "horizons of expectation" for any single text. She reads various responses to a single film inasmuch as they shape and determine to some extent the range of meanings (Jauss 1982; Staiger 1986, 1992). As Staiger puts it, "What we are interested in, then, is not a so-called correct reading of a particular film but the range of possible readings and reading processes at historical moments and their relation or lack of relation to groups of historical spectators" (1986: 20). Staiger's approach is defined by the particular function and institution of film reviewing, and other studies of reception have examined how "marginal" practices of film reviewing define and are defined in their turn by the responses of particular audiences to films – like the reception of *Personal Best* by feminist and lesbian feminist journalists examined by Elizabeth Ellsworth (1986). Other critics have defined reception in a way more immediately compatible with the cultural-studies approach, by interviewing particular groups of spectators and situating their responses at specific cultural and historical intersections, as Jacqueline Bobo does with the responses of black women viewers to the film version of *The Color Purple*, particularly insofar as they contradict or otherwise mediate the published and televised commentary on the film (1988).

The four approaches to the historical model of spectatorship I've outlined are quite different, but there is an interesting methodological common denominator. Textual analysis, the detailed reading of the individual film text in order to uncover the patterns of opposition, crisis, and resolution, is one of the legacies of 1970s film theory. While much of the work on spectatorship done in the name of history is extremely critical of that theory, textual analysis has not been rejected but rather revised. For a common point of agreement in studies of intertextuality, exhibition, the cinematic public sphere, and reception is the need not to reject textual analysis, but rather to expand its parameters beyond the individual film text. Textual analysis thus becomes attentive to the intersecting and sometimes contradictory ways in which different forms of address function across different textual registers.

What is not altogether clear, however, is what happens to the psychoanalytic dimension so central to textual analysis in the 1970s – to the assumption, that is, that texts can be read as symptoms, and that patterns of crisis and resolution connect to psychic structures of desire, investment, and repression. A common refrain in historical studies of spectatorship is that 1970s film theory sacrificed a knowledge of the social for the psychic. Indeed, one of the problems with histori-cal models of spectatorship is a persistent dualism. Theories of the subject are assumed to be "psychoanalytic," not "social," thereby implicitly equating the "social" with the sociological, which is not the same thing. At the same time, of course, those very theorists of the subject have usually ignored attempts to account for the historical constitution of the film audience, which only perpetuates the dualism. To put this in the baldest – and admittedly just as dualistic – terms, the question which underscores the drive toward historicizing spec-tatorship is whether those theories of the cinematic institution can have any compatibility whatsoever with specific, local studies of spec-tatorship. And beneath that question is another, which has preoccu-pied film studies from the outset – whether and how psychoanalysis can function in relationship to ideological (to use the terminology of the 1970s) or cultural (to use the terminology of the 1980s) determi-nations.

The problem may have less to do with psychoanalytic approaches to film study and spectatorship in general, and more with the specific kind of psychoanalytic inquiry that has characterized contemporary film studies, where there is such a desire to understand the psychic foundation of culture that oftentimes the two are conflated. How many times does one need to be told that individual film *x*, or film genre *y*, articulates the law of the father, assigns the spectator a position of male oedipal desire, marshals castration anxiety in the form of voyeurism and fetishism, before psychoanalysis begins to sound less like the exploration of the unconscious, and more like a master plot? Put another way, historical studies of spectatorship may find it necessary, if not to reject psychoanalysis altogether, then to revise substantially the particular view of psychoanalysis that has characterized institutional theories of spectatorship.

Critics like Philip Rosen and Thomas Elsaesser have approached the historical dimensions of spectatorship in somewhat different terms from those I have outlined thus far, asking what *is* historical about the cinema and the cinematic apparatus? Rosen notes that while the fact that cinema and psychoanalysis emerged at the same time is considered "no coincidence" in film studies, little attention has been paid to an equally compelling coincidence, that the cinema emerged at a moment of historiographical change as well: "the appearance of the machine for ideal looking, cinema, was coincident with a crisis in the security of history's meaning and knowledge" (1984: 22). Rosen suggests that a recognition of the relationship between cinema and history would mean at the very least that "each classical film offers in its ideological interpellation a version of and attitude toward history, whether or not the film is explicitly historical" (1984: 26).

In his studies both of Weimar cinema and of the New German Cinema, Thomas Elsaesser has spoken of the social imaginary – that is, of the ways in which those devices of positioning, binding and visual pleasure defined in apparatus theory find a particularly insistent match with certain historical conditions. In the case of Weimar cinema, Elsaesser notes a preoccupation with those very figures that define certain dominant effects of the cinematic apparatus; thus, "what makes Weimar cinema historical . . . is the prominence it gives to this mise-en-scène of the (cinematic) imaginary" (1984: 80). In the case of Fassbinder's cinema – so preoccupied with the relationship of seeing and being seen – the social imaginary invites a historicizing, not just of visual pleasure and the cinematic apparatus, but of those very theories that have thus conceptualized the cinema. For Elsaesser suggests that those structures that have "habitually been interpreted as coinciding with the construction of the basic cinematic apparatus" might be "equally amenable to a historical reading" (1980; rpt. 1986: 545).

Hence, Elsaesser suggests that fascism be understood as a form of spectatorship: "Might not the pleasure of fascism, its fascination have been less the sadism and brutality of SS officers than the pleasure of being seen, of placing oneself in view of the all-seeing eye of the

69

State?" (ibid.). Crucial to Elsaesser's references to a social imaginary are, first, the conviction that the very components that have been described as central to the cinematic apparatus need to be seen, themselves, as historically determined. Hence, says Elsaesser, Lacan's constant return to the specular demonstrates a reading of Freud "in the light of concrete historical and social changes," while Metz's notion of primary cinematic identification also partakes of a historical development, "the specularization of consciousness and social production – which his categories do not adequately reflect" (ibid., 548). Second, those crises of male oedipal identity, scopophilia and voyeurism, that have been identified as central to the cinematic apparatus offer particular vantage points on the social construction of spectatorship, for what may well characterize spectatorship in historical terms is the excessive foregrounding of one particular aspect of the cinematic apparatus, for instance, or an overlap between particular pleasures validated by the cinema and the social crises of a given era.

What remains something of a problem, however, is the extent to which, in historicizing the cinematic apparatus, one confirms rather than challenges some of the more deeply problematic aspects of apparatus theory. Patrice Petro has criticized Elsaesser precisely in these terms, for in assuming an apparatus which provides visual pleasure and spectatorial investment in (basically) the terms articulated by Metz and Baudry (but "correcting" them by insisting on the social and historical dimensions to their arguments), the spectator thus theorized remains male (1989). In other words, Elsaesser's historicizing of the apparatus may not be quite historically differentiated enough.

FEMINIST MODELS

Without voyeurism, fetishism, and the apparatus there would be no cinema, and within that array of components there is nothing but rigid duality – such is the dilemma of feminist institutional film theory in attempting to account for the *female* spectator. To be sure, there are different kinds of voyeurism, and even different kinds of fetishism, and therefore different ways to understand cinematic pleasure. Or are there? A pessimism about *any* alternative pleasures has characterized many feminist discussions of the cinema. It has been said frequently enough that Mulvey's analysis posits a monolithic object, the classical Hollywood cinema, in relationship to which the female spectator can occupy only an alienated, and ultimately impossible position. Hence, much feminist criticism has been concerned to open up the dualities of the classical cinema, frequently in the name of female spectatorship.

From this perspective, one of the most important theoretical contributions to the analysis of female spectatorship is de Lauretis's definition of the feminist enterprise, in *Alice Doesn't*, as evolving from the contradiction between "woman" – the configuration of patriarchal ideology – and women, historical subjects who live in a tangential relationship to those configurations. De Lauretis writes: "woman is constituted as the ground of representation, the looking-glass held up to man. But, as historical individual, the female viewer is also positioned in the films of classical cinema as spectator-subject; she is thus doubly bound to that very representation which calls on her directly, engages her desire, elicits her pleasure, frames her identification, and makes her complicit in the production of (her) woman-ness" (1984: 15). Of the strategies designed to articulate that contradiction between "woman" and "women," perhaps the best known is the reading against the grain of the classical Hollywood cinema, an attempt to demonstrate the precariousness of narrative and ideological hierarchy. Frequently such resistances within the text are understood as the basis, not only for a feminist reading of the classical cinema, but for a theory of female spectatorship. While counter-readings are a central part of feminist criticism, there are obvious limitations to the designation of female spectatorship as what falls through the cracks of patriarchal discourse.

Alternatively, it has been suggested that if the voyeurism/fetishism model, with its attendant implications of castration anxiety and male oedipal scenarios, is problematic vis-à-vis female spectators, it is equally incapable of theorizing the complex range of desires inspired by the cinema. Hence Gaylyn Studlar has postulated, in opposition to the sadistic model of voyeurism and fetishism, a masochistic model of spectatorship which takes as its point of departure the desire to fuse and be dominated rather than the desire to control and to dominate (1988). Other recent explorations of alternative models of spectatorship have moved away from Lacan, and toward Freud, and in particular toward the postulation of bisexuality, of the vacillation between masculine and feminine positions as a key component in sexual identity (Hansen 1986; Rodowick 1982, 1991). In cinematic terms, this would suggest that cinematic identification is never masculine or feminine, but rather a movement between the two. From this vantage point, positions may well be defined as masculine and feminine (or both), but they are taken up by spectators regardless of their gender or sexuality. As de Lauretis writes, "The analogy that links identification-with-the-look to masculinity and identification-with-the-image to femininity breaks down precisely when we think of a spectator alternating between the two" (1984: 142–3).

Indeed, many classical films do not fit neatly into the parameters of the male look. Miriam Hansen's analysis of Rudolf Valentino and his appeal to female spectators demonstrates the fluidity and

71

interchangeability of categories of activity and passivity, the look and the object of the look (1986: 15). In an essay on the 1937 film, *Stella Dallas*, Linda Williams argues that, in the "woman's film" – addressed to a female audience and taken up with traditionally female concerns – a multiplicity of subject positions are produced, standing in sharp contrast to what 1970s theory treated as the single narrational perspective of the classical Hollywood cinema. Hence, for Williams, "the female spectator tends to identify with contradiction itself – with contradictions located at the heart of the socially constructed roles of daughter, wife, *and* mother – rather than with the single person of the mother" (1984: 17). Williams's essay responds to an earlier piece on the film by Ann Kaplan, which is predicated on the repression of contradiction and the attendant implications of socializing women toward their appropriate roles (1983a). Williams's essay also makes for an interesting conversation with Mary Ann Doane's work on the woman's film, which emphasizes that contradiction is less than emancipatory.

Williams's essay on *Stella Dallas* inspired a debate in the pages of *Cinema Journal* in which a number of problems in the theorizing of female spectatorship emerged, problems that affect virtually all discussions of feminist film theory. First, to what extent are the contradictions central to Williams's analysis recuperated by the movement toward closure so integral to the classical realist text? And are such moments of closure totally successful, particularly when the "ideal spectator" of the cinematic apparatus is no longer assumed to be such a coherent entity? Second, is the position of a feminist film critic necessarily identical to, or even analogous to, the female spectator? And finally, are discussions of female spectatorship symptoms of creeping essentialism, of a desire to resurrect patriarchal definitions of femininity in the name of feminist alternatives?

These tensions – between the controlling apparatus of the cinema and spectatorship understood as the engagement with a multiplicity of positions, and between the feminist critic and the female spectator – define the "female spectator" of feminist film theory. If feminist work on the cinema has a particularly distinct role to play in the mapping out of the tension between "woman" and "women," it is because of the status of cinema as spectacle and narrative, as the acting out of patriarchy's most pervasive notions of the woman as other, whether as object of the look or as proof of narrative resolution; and as the site of multiple positions of desire. For in attempting to understand how and why women like the movies, and how the cinema might function otherwise than as the projection of patriarchal configurations, feminist theorists encounter constantly, and with a vengeance, that tension between "woman" and "women," where it is not always clear just where the image of woman as contained by patriarchal ideology leaves off and where the woman as historical subject begins. As de Lauretis puts it, "the feminist critique is a critique of culture from within and from without, in the same way in which women are both *in* the cinema as representation and *outside* the cinema as subjects of practices" (1984: 15). The "both/and" of "woman" and "women" is a far more productive situating of the feminist enterprise, and, I would argue, of the study of spectatorship, than the "either/ or" of "subjects" versus "real viewers."

An apt demonstration of the challenge of this "both/and" for the subject of spectatorship is a figure who could almost serve as a screen upon which to chart the ebb and flow of feminist definitions of cinematic pleasure (not to mention non-feminist ones) – Marilyn Monroe. A book on Monroe, with photographs by George Barris and text by Gloria Steinem, raises issues central to the study of spectatorship. The cover of the book features a photograph of the actress, with the title *Marilyn* in bold block letters. On the name "Marilyn" is superimposed, in script, the equally familiar name "Norma Jeane," yet "Norma Jeane" is legible only at close view. That the purpose of this book is to uncover the "real" Marilyn Monroe – Norma Jeane – is suggested by Steinem's dedication: "This book is dedicated to the real Marilyn. And to the reality in us all" (Steinem 1986: v). For a feminist film theorist, Steinem's intentions evoke a sense of history repeating itself, or, more pessimistically, the persistence of the myth of the female screen image. That image may be resituated in feminist terms, perhaps, but it is mythic nonetheless. Speculating on the significance of recent analyses of the films of Alfred Hitchcock, Robin Wood asked the question, "Can Hitchcock be saved for feminism?" (1983: 30). A similar question haunts Steinem's book – can Marilyn Monroe be saved for feminism?

In feminist film theory, it is a given that there is no easy fit between "real" women and cinematic images of the female body, and, in some cases, that there is no fit at all. Yet whatever the stated intentions of Steinem's text, *Marilyn* is a fascinating exploration of the difficult and complex connection between the discourse of feminism and the most famous female icon of the screen. Steinem seems to resist the function of direct commentary on the many photographs in the volume, and speaks in her introduction of her desire to "find a way to give words some of the nonlinear pleasure that images have always had" (1986: 1). Linear or not, however, text and image here form a narrative, one from which there emerges a curious irony. In a chapter entitled "Work and Money, Sex and Politics," for instance, Steinem writes sympathetically of how Monroe, as part of her "unguided self-education," began reading *The Autobiography of Lincoln Steffens*, and was chastised by her producers for her choice of subversive reading material. Steinem says

73

that Monroe continued to read the autobiography in secret, and kept both volumes hidden beneath her bed. On the pages following this text are a series of full-length photographs of Monroe ostensibly "reading," in which the activity of reading serves only to highlight the familiar seductive poses for which Monroe is so famous (1986: 71–3).

From the standpoint of almost any recent film theory, the overt claims of *Marilyn* are at best problematic and at worst naive. However, within this text there is a tension between two positions of desire, a tension that sets out remarkably well the terms of spectatorship. In her introduction, Steinem describes an exceptional scene at the movies: "For me, this book began when, in 1953, as a teenager who loved all movies, I still walked out of *Gentlemen Prefer Blondes* in embarrassment at seeing this whispering, simpering, big-breasted child woman who was simply hoping her way into total vulnerability. How dare she be just as vulnerable and unconfident as I felt?" (1986: 3). Later in the book, Steinem discusses how Monroe – then Norma Jeane – discovered the movies: "Soon the movies were Norma Jeane's passion: a day-dreaming refuge from her past, from the shy inferiority she still felt with other children at school, and from her mother's occasional moodiness. . . . She discovered Clark Gable and Jean Harlow, Fred Astaire and Ginger Rogers, Claudette Colbert, Joan Crawford, and all the shimmering giants of the fantastic screen" (48). Steinem notes that Monroe had a particular fondness for Jean Harlow, to whom she would later be compared.

These two accounts of women who loved the movies reflect the excessive identification of women with the screen image that has been central both to the film industry's image of its female audiences and to contemporary feminist film theory. One assumes that it was Steinem's feminism, however nascent, that motivated her to walk out of the movie theater in embarrassment, while Marilyn Monroe, as she is described in this book, did not have such a choice. Monroe's love of the movies evokes what Mary Ann Doane calls the "over-presence of the image – she *is* the image" (1982: 78). Monroe's position as a female spectator suggests as well Mulvey's polarity of man as "bearer of the look," woman as its object. Steinem's position as a more ambivalent film viewer evokes another, seemingly opposed definition of the female spectator as, in B. Ruby Rich's words, the "ultimate dialectician." Rich writes:

> the cinematic codes have structured our absence to such an extent that the only choice allowed to us is to identify either with Marilyn Monroe or with the man behind me hitting the back of my seat with his knees. How does one formulate an understanding of a structure that insists on our absence even in the face of

our presence? What is there in a film with which a woman viewer identifies? How can the contradictions be used as a critique?

(Rich in Citron et al. 1978: 87)

It is, of course, "no coincidence" that it should be Marilyn Monroe who so well represents the absence of women from the film-going experience. Steinem ends her text on a utopian note:

It is the lost possibilities of Marilyn Monroe that capture our imaginations. It was the lost Norma Jeane, looking out of Marilyn's eyes, who captured our hearts. Now that more women are declaring our full humanity – now that we are more likely to be valued for our heads and hearts, not just the bodies that house them – we also wonder: Could we have helped Marilyn survive?

(1986: 180)

To her credit, Steinem responds to the implicit question of whether feminism could have "saved" Monroe by asserting that there can be no answer. Indeed, for all of her rescue fantasies, Steinem points in her text to another kind of utopian desire, one that acknowledges, however tentatively, the difficulty of contradictory desires. Feminist film theorists who examine female spectatorship explore and expand an understanding of the contradiction that is at the very core of utopian thought – a desire that wavers between a celebration of woman's status as "other" within patriarchy, and a critique of the very structures that define women as marginal.

An essay by feminist historian Linda Gordon on the status of women's history offers a mapping of these questions with remarkable relevance to issues and problems at stake in the study of spectatorship. Gordon notes that contemporary women's history has moved in two different directions: the one, empirical in scope, seeking to uncover the truth of women's lives that have been obscured by the falsehoods of previous generations of historians; the other, "rejecting the possibility of objectivity," defining history as myth-making and storytelling (1986: 22). Although the two poles are not identical, there has been a similar divergence in the work of feminist film theory, between explorations of how and why women have found, in the cinema, a form of representation of their desires; and analyses of how representations of woman tend to upset and disrupt patriarchal forms of representation. More specifically, there is a divergence, in feminist film theory, between woman as object – to which considerable theoretical attention has been paid – and women as subjects, which has received much less attention.

Describing the two poles of philosophical assumption, the two different purposes of women's history, Gordon writes of her desire to find a "method in between." She says:

> This inbetween would not imply resolution, careful balance of fact and myth, or synthesis of fact and interpretation. My sense of a liminal method is rather a condition of being constantly pulled, usually off balance, sometimes teetering wildly, almost always tense. The tension cannot be released. Indeed, the very desire to find a way to relax the tension is a temptation that must be avoided. Neither goal can be surrendered.
>
> (22)

Gordon's emphasis on tension, and her refusal of easy "synthesis," speaks crucially to the study of spectatorship. The cinematic apparatus has been described as a machine which tells the same story again and again, and which situates its subjects in fixed positions. Frustration with the totalizing and homogeneous implications of such a model has led some critics to reject it along with the bathwater of psychoanalysis. Such rejection may lead to more attractive and less pessimistic models of how the cinema works, but such models may well elide questions of sexuality and the unconscious in the name of deceptively neutral (and neutered) and rational notions of representation. But it is equally problematic to reject every challenge to the cinematic apparatus as mere wishful thinking on the part of theorists. What is needed is precisely that tension of which Gordon speaks, between the competing claims of homogeneity and heterogeneity, domination and resistance.

As I suggested earlier in this chapter, institutional theories of spectatorship have been criticized for being too homogeneous, too monolithic. Too frequently it is assumed that if homogeneity is monolithic, then heterogeneity must be at the very least a potential site for resistance. The most significant challenge for the study of spectatorship is to attend to the tension of which Gordon speaks, a recognition that the cinema functions in contradictory ways, and that in order to understand how institutions are open to change, there must be simultaneous attention to their resistance to change. The competing claims of domination and resistance, of structure and agency, of homogeneity and heterogeneity, have resulted in the foregrounding of a series of concepts meant to understand spectatorship as comprising "both" the cinematic institution "and" possible excesses and resistances. In the next chapter I turn to an exploration of how concepts like address and reception, fantasy, and negotiation ground spectatorship in an understanding of contradiction.

4

PARADOXES OF SPECTATORSHIP

No matter how controversial and contested theories of the cinematic institution have been, few would argue with their basic premise that the capacity of the cinema to seduce, entertain, or otherwise appeal to its audiences needs to be understood in ideological and psychic terms. The trick, however, is not only in understanding the relationship between the two realms of psychic and social life – a rather large undertaking in any case – but in defining with precision the ways in which the cinema is describable in terms of ideological and psychoanalytic theory, and the extent to which different types of cinema and varied contexts articulate spectatorship in different ways. Even the cognitive approach, which departs most sharply from the assumptions of 1970s film theory, is concerned with conditions of coherence and intelligibility which relate to the kind of ideological analysis central to 1970s film theory.

Does the analysis of the cinematic institution as a staging and restaging of the crises of male oedipal desire, as a regressive plenitude, apply only to a specific historical mode of the cinema – i.e., the classical, narrative Hollywood film? Or, rather, given that the emergence of the cinema is so closely linked to the fictions of Western patriarchal culture, is the cinematic apparatus as theorized in film theory bound to be the condition of *all* cinematic representation? Even within the classical Hollywood cinema, are female spectators thus bound by the Scylla of male spectatorial desire and the Charybdis of exclusion from cinematic fantasies? Given the extent to which analysis of spectatorship has focussed on sexual difference (whether foregrounded or so blatantly ignored as to function as a symptom, as in Baudry's case), are other forms of spectator identity – race, class, sexual identity other than gendered identity, age, etc. – always built upon the model of sexual difference, or are they potentially formative in their own right? And to what extent is identity a misleading route toward understanding spectatorship, particularly if it is limited by literalist assumptions, i.e., that black audiences can only "identify" with black characters, female audiences with female ones, etc.? If apparatus theory displaced character identification as the central dynamic in understanding spectatorship, this does not mean that questions of identity have been in any way resolved. For the displacement of identification, however necessary and valuable to the project of 1970s film theory, was nonetheless accomplished at a price – a too easy equation between the "subject" and the attributes of dominance.

Perhaps one of the greatest ironies of contemporary film studies is that the obsessive attention devoted to the cinematic institution occured at a time when there has perhaps existed more diversity than ever before insofar as modes of cinematic representation and address are concerned. In the US alone, independent film and video, specifically addressed to a variety of markets – gay and lesbian, feminist, black, hispanic – continues to grow. One of the largest problems confronting spectatorship studies is the simultaneous affirmation of diversity and the recognition that "diversity" can easily function as a ploy, a way of perpeptuating the illusions of mainstream cinema rather than challenging them. Put another way, there is no simple division between the cinema which functions as an instrument of dominant ideology, and the cinema which facilitates challenges to it. Now if you assume, as some theorists of the 1970s did, that there is nothing about cinema that is not saturated with ideology, then the radical or contestatory powers of the cinema were limited to those films which functioned to demonstrate the ideological complicity of film.

The most promising and influential work on spectatorship assumes the necessity for understanding cinema as ideologically influenced, but not necessarily monolithically so. Linda Gordon speaks of the necessity to hold competing claims of domination and resistance in unwavering tension, refusing to collapse one into the other (1986). In spectatorship studies, several concepts have emerged to engage with the tension between cinema as monolithic institution and cinema as heterogeneous diversity. The competing claims of homogeneity (of the cinematic apparatus) and heterogeneity (of the spectator and therefore of the different ways in which the an apparatus can be understood) frame this chapter.

If the cinematic apparatus is as fully saturated with the ideology of idealism and oedipal desire as 1970s film theory would suggest, then there can be no real history of the cinema, except as variations on a common theme. Or rather, there can be no history within the cinema, if all cinema is ideological in the same way. We have already encountered criticisms of models of the cinematic apparatus for establishing a monolithic role for the spectator, and for literalizing whatever analogy was articulated, from Plato's cave to the Lacanian imaginary. An opposition between homogeneity and heterogeneity underscores these criticisms, since most alternatives to 1970s film theory take the spectator, not as the effect of the cinema institution, but as a point of departure; and not the ideal spectator as theorized by the cinematic apparatus, but the socially defined spectator who is necessarily heterogeneous – i.e., addressed through a variety of discourses. In other words, responses to apparatus theory are founded on a gap between the ideal subject postulated by the apparatus and the spectator who is always in an imperfect relation to that ideal.

In this chapter, I will examine three terms which have emerged in spectatorship studies to conceptualize the competing claims of the homogeneous cinematic institution and heterogeneous responses to it: the gap between "address" and "reception;" fantasy; and negotiation. Linda Gordon speaks of the need to find a method "in between" the claims of domination and resistance, and the terms I will examine in this chapter are precisely that, concepts meant to convey the contradictory ways in which spectatorship functions. First, the relationship between cinematic address and cinematic reception opens up a space between the "ideal" viewer and the "real" viewer. Address refers to the ways in which a text assumes certain responses, which may or may not be operative in different reception conditions. Central to this apparent paradox is the role of the cinematic "text," whether defined as the individual film or as a set of operations which situate the spectator in certain ways. If spectators can and do respond to films in ways that contradict, reject, or otherwise problematize the presumably "ideal" spectator structured into the text, then the value of textual analysis – arguably the most significant methodological direction undertaken by 1970s film theory – needs to be seriously rethought or re-evaluated.

In the previous chapter I noted that the version of psychoanalysis promoted within theories of the cinematic subject tends toward a uniform and totalizing version of the unconscious, almost always understood as the resurgence of various crises of (male) oedipal identity. The advantage of such a view, of course, is that the psychic foundations of the cultural order are open to investigation, but the disadvantages far outnumber such advantages. For the unconscious thus defined becomes one more totalizing system, and the work of the psychoanalytically inspired critic becomes just as framed by a master code as any other application of a method. In the context of these problems with psychoanalytic theory and criticism, the notion of *fantasy* has received increasing attention and is the second concept to be discussed in this chapter. An exploration of fantasy allows a far more radical exploration of psychic investment in the cinema, and suggests, as well, intersections between the psychic and the political. Yet it is not altogether clear whether the implications of fantasy for the cinema allow for an understanding of the social in terms that exceed the family romance so central to any psychoanalytic understanding of culture.

It is one thing to compare the claims that can be made for cinema as a homogeneous and homogenizing, versus a heterogeneous institution, and another thing to valorize heterogeneity as necessarily contestatory. The third concept I will discuss is the term "negotiation," which is used frequently to suggest that different texts can be "used," "interpreted," or "appropriated" in a variety of ways. Sometimes the diversity thus postulated by "negotiated" readings or viewings is assumed to challenge the power of the institution. The sheer fact that a spectator or group of spectators makes unauthorized uses of the cinema is no guarantee that such uses are contestatory. Here, the central question has less to do with the status of the text, than with the value one assigns to differing modes of response – how those responses are assessed, and how film-going is "read" in relationship to other social, cultural, and psychic formations. Indeed, the emphasis on "negotiation" de-emphasizes the primacy of the cinematic text, focussing rather on how different responses can be read, whether critically, symptomatically, or otherwise.

ADDRESS AND RECEPTION

A common characteristic of textual theories of the spectator was the assumption that the cinematic apparatus "situates," "positions," or otherwise assigns a position of coherence to the implied spectator. Now however much this implied spectator position functioned as something of a phantom, and not a person to be confused with real viewers, it nonetheless managed to marginalize any consideration of how real viewers might view films in ways considerably more various than any monolithic conception of the cinematic apparatus could imply. It is one thing to assume that cinema is determined in ideological ways, to assume that cinema is a discourse (or a variety of discourses), to assume, that is, that the various institutions of the cinema *do* project an ideal viewer, and another thing to assume that those projections *work*. One of the most significant directions in spectatorship studies has investigated the gap opened up between the ways in which texts construct viewers, and how those texts may be read or used in ways that depart from what the institution valorizes.

The operative assumption here is that apparatus theories are not completely wrong, but rather incomplete. The issue is one of flexibility, of recognizing that an apparatus can have unexpected effects, and that no apparatus can function quite so smoothly and efficiently as most film theory of the 1970s would suggest. That theory was most obviously lacking and problematic in the kinds of hypotheses it led to concerning any kind of alternative cinematic practice, particularly insofar as a deconstruction of so-called dominant modes and a presumable re-positioning of the spectator are concerned. Both assume a fairly stable, fixed, one-way, top-down model of agent and object, with a spectator still locked into a programme of representation defined romantically and mechanistically according to the agenda of the filmmaker or the institution – an "active" viewer is still one "positioned" to be so by textual constructs.

Yet to go to the other extreme, and to define texts as only offering the positions that viewers create for them, and thereby to mediate *any* notion of the cinematic institution out of existence, substitutes one monolithic political notion for another. The challenge, then, is to understand the complicated ways in which meanings are both assigned and created. If apparatus theorists were overly zealous in defining all meanings as assigned ones, there has been considerable zeal at the other end of the spectrum as well, by virtually disavowing any power of institutions and conceptualizing readers/viewers as completely free and autonomous agents – a tendency that has been particularly marked, for instance, in some versions of reader-response theory and cultural studies (especially in the US) (see Budd, Entman, and Steinman 1990). Since dominant ideology is neither a person nor a one-dimensional set of concepts, it is virtually impossible to say with certainty that a particular effect is complicit with or resistant to the force of an institution. But one can assess the different effects of cinema in relationship to other discourses in order to assess the complicated ways in which the cinema functions, for instance.

One of the great difficulties here is a fairly obvious one. Individual films lend themselves to far neater and easier hypotheses about structure and excess than individual viewers or groups of viewers do. A mistrust of sociological surveys has been one of the most ingrained features of contemporary theoretical work, and so it is perhaps something of a surprise to see the analysis of "real viewers" return, in recent years, as a theoretically credible exercise. The influence of cultural studies, specifically as defined through the work of Stuart Hall and the Centre for Contemporary Cultural Studies at the University of Birmingham, and more generally by analyses of the ways different specific audiences respond to instances of mass culture, has been enormous.

In a series of interviews with teenage girls, for instance, Angela McRobbie concluded that their passion for a film like *Flashdance* had far more to do with their own desire for physical autonomy than with any simple notion of acculturation to a patriarchal definition of feminine desirability (1984). Now it seems to me that one can only be stunned by these tentative conclusions if the model of the cinematic institution one had in the first place corresponded to the "conspiracy theory" view of capitalism popular in some New Left circles in the 1960s. While I find McRobbie's study intriguing, and will turn to it in more detail later in this chapter, I am not convinced that her hypotheses lead necessarily to a dismissal of the power of the cinematic institution. Unfortunately, this type of work has led to a peculiar reading of the reception of mass culture, whereby any and all responses are critical ones. Some sort of understanding of the non-coincidence of address and reception is required in which power is analyzed rather than taken for granted.

One of the most influential studies along these lines is Janice Radway's *Reading the Romance*, an analysis of romance novels as they are read by a group of devoted women fans (1984). Because many of the issues that Radway raises have equal relevance to film studies, and in particular because her book has been cited many times as a model of how film researchers might rethink many of the theoretical assumptions that have been seen increasingly as limitations, her book merits examination for the questions it raises for film spectatorship (Bergstrom and Doane 1989). While Radway examines the structural and ideological features of the romance novel as a genre, she situates that analysis alongside of what is perhaps the most noteworthy achievement of the book, a complex profile of a group of eager and committed romance readers. The advantage of Radway's analysis is that she acknowledges the persuasive power of the romance novel as a genre, at the same time that she refuses to reduce the genre to a series of ideological complicities. Put another way, one senses throughout *Reading the Romance* that the textual evidence is put to the test of Radway's sample audience, and vice versa.

Radway's study focuses on a group of women fictitiously referred to as the "Smithton women," all of whom bought the majority of their romance-reading material from a salesclerk named Dorothy Evans ("Dot"), an expert on romance fiction. Radway's study of this group of women took the form of group and individual interviews (with sixteen women), as well as a lengthy questionnaire distributed to forty-two women. Radway describes her sample as consisting for the most part of "married, middle-class mothers," and she notes that while "not representative of all women who read romances, the group appears to be demographically similar to a sizable segment of that audience as it has been mapped by several very secretive publishing houses" (12). Much of the force of Radway's analysis comes from a variety of juxtapositions of differing notions of the "ideal" – from the ideal reader as posited in much narrative analysis, to the "ideal romance" as postulated by the Smithton women, to a feminist ideal which seems to characterize much of how Radway approaches the women's responses to romance fiction.

Radway echoes much feminist analysis of mass cultural forms when she argues that romance novels function as "compensatory fiction," that is, "the act of reading them fulfills certain basic psychological needs for women that have been induced by the culture and its social structures but that often remain unmet in day-to-day existence as the result of concomitant restrictions on female activity" (112–13). Like Vladimir Propp in his famous analysis of the Russian folktale, Radway notes that romance fiction is composed of certain unchanging elements – notably patriarchy, heterosexuality, and male personality (143). But within those unchanging rules, romances offer the possibility of fantasizing solutions that are otherwise unavailable. Throughout *Reading the Romance*, the reading of romance fiction is portrayed as emblematic of the ambivalence which these particular women feel about themselves, not just in relationship to patriarchy, but in relationship to feminism as well. Indeed, the emphasis on female autonomy within a passionate relationship and the simultaneity of dependence and independence suggest that – to reiterate a phrase that appears frequently in Radway's analysis – romance readers want to have it both ways.

That Radway herself is ambivalent about how to read the results of her analysis is evident, especially in her conclusion. She says, "the question of whether the activity of romance reading does, in reality, deflect such change [i.e., the restructuring of sexual relations] by successfully defusing or recontaining this protest must remain unanswered for the moment" (213). I find it curious that such a dualistic political framework should be erected in this book, but in some ways this either/or – the either/or, that is, of a conservative status quo versus radical change, of celebration versus critique – remains as a stubborn reminder that the theoretical problem raised by the apparatus (cinematic or otherwise) has not been wished away. For the very notion of a cinematic apparatus suggests a rigid distinction between what is contaminated by dominant ideology and what is not, suggests the possibility of knowing with certainty whether an activity is contestatory or conservative. What always seems to happen with such dualisms is the hardening of one abstraction or another – only a deconstruction of the apparatus is genuinely revolutionary! Readers and viewers are always active producers of meaning! – before it has been possible to consider in more depth the complexity of the issues at hand.

The major problem in Radway's analysis is that for all of the criticism offered of theoretical modes which ignore real readers in favor of the critic's own projections, there is a fair share of projection and idealization going on here, as well. For the white, heterosexual, middle-class women that Radway discusses may well be complex agents who live the contradictions of middle-class patriarchal culture in equally complex ways, but they are also projections of American, middle-class, academic feminism. This is not meant in any way as a condemnation; far from it. But the desire to name "real readers" is neither transparent nor innocent, for the women readers who appear in Radway's analysis are mediated by her questions, her analyses, and her narrative. It is inevitable that such projections exist in this kind of analysis, and unless those projections are analyzed, then we are left with an ideal reader who seems more real because she is quoted and referred to, but who is every bit as problematic as the ideal reader constructed by abstract theories of an apparatus positioning passive vessels.

It would, of course, be presumptuous of me to hypothesize what function the Smithton women have in Radway's imagination, but I can say what her analysis suggests quite strongly to me – a desire, on the part of feminists like myself, to see my mother and by extension members of my mother's generation as not so invested in patriarchy, as pre-feminist or proto-feminist, as a figure who nurtured feminism even while she argued otherwise, as someone who was really a feminist but didn't know it yet. Lest a particularly literal-minded soul wants to remind me that not all mothers of middle-class feminists fit this bill, I would say that this is precisely the point. For regardless of whether we are talking about literal mothers (as I am here), or mothers in the sense of a generation of women from whom the contemporary feminist movement developed and against whom it reacted, or a group of women who function as a horizon against which much feminist activity operates, we are talking about a construction. I doubt seriously, for instance, if the Smithton women would agree with the necessity of understanding the reading of romance fiction in the categorical terms of critique or celebration.

If analyses such as Radway's are to be based on taking other readers seriously then they must also mean taking ourselves seriously as readers – and by "seriously" here, I mean putting our own constructions to the test. Tania Modleski has argued that with the turn to ethnography as a revitalized strategy for the analysis of mass culture, a curious assumption has been made that critics and researchers are not valid readers or viewers of mass culture, but rather detached observers (1989). I think Modleski is correct in assuming that the analysis of spectatorship is an analysis of one's *own* fascination and passion. Unless this is acknowledged, then we are left with a series of fuzzily defined "ideal readers" in whom it is difficult to know how much of their responses are displaced representations of the critic's own.

From another perspective, it could be argued that the "ideal reader" has not been challenged so much as displaced from one realm, that of the textual properties of address, to another, that of the empirically observable woman. One of the most important strategies of Radway's analysis is, as I've indicated, the juxtaposition of the ideal reader assumed by the romance-fiction industry with women who *do* fit that profile, who are therefore the desired audience for romance novels, but who are also at the same time irreducible to structure, formula, or cliché. Unfortunately, however, this challenge to the presumed homogeneity of the ideal reader does not go quite far enough. One of Radway's most important sources is Nancy Chodorow's *The Reproduction of Mothering*, a study of the asymmetrical gender patterns whereby men learn to be mothered and nurtured and women learn to provide mothering and nurturing (1978). Whereas Chodorow argues that women are socialized into mothering precisely through the (often unfulfilled) promise that the pre-oedipal patterns so central to their own development will be recreated, Radway argues that romance fiction provides precisely the kind of nurturance otherwise absent or largely missing from these women's lives.

In the appeal to Chodorow's analysis I sense most strongly the need to specify the particular nature of the needs being fulfilled. To what extent are we talking about white women whose lives are missing the kind of community network and patterns often characteristic of the lives of black women, for instance? What kind of "middle-class" identity is at stake – the kind of precarious middle-class life characteristic of many white-collar workers? Or rather an economic identity defined largely by life style? Is the heterosexual identity of the women as stable as they, and Radway as well, seem to take great pains to stress? I am aware that these questions will strike some readers as the kind of checklist of accountability that characterizes some holier-than-thou political criticism. But my goal here is not some kind of standard of inclusivity. Rather, it is the notion of an "ideal" reader – no matter who defines it as "ideal" – that I think is severely limiting.

Radway's study remains the most influential example of an analysis that attempts to account, simultaneously, for the power of institutions (what she calls an "institutional matrix") and the complex ways in which real women accomplish the "construction of texts" (11–12). The positive critical reception that Radway's book has received suggests at the very least enormous dissatisfaction with just those limitations of exclusive textually based theories of readership. I am wary, however, of some of this positive critical reception, since I am not convinced that the notion of the "ideal reader" has been problematized or undone so much as it has been displaced. What this suggests to me is the need to be careful of the appeals that are made in the name of empirical audiences or ethnography as the truth that will set us free from the overly abstract theorization of the past. I suspect that it may be

85

impossible to do away entirely with the notion of an ideal reader, since we all live this culture's fictions and institutions and participate in them to some extent. I do not say this in order to imply cynically that no alternative positions of spectatorship are possible, but rather to suggest that one of the most persistent myths of spectatorship (and of theory) that has perturbed and in many ways hindered the analysis of spectatorship is the belief that it is not only possible, but necessary, to separate the truly radical spectator from the merely complicitous one. The recognition that we are all complicitous to some extent (and the "some" is clearly what needs to be investigated) does not mean that alternative positions are impossible. Rather, that recognition would make it possible to speak of readership or spectatorship not as the knowledge the elite academic brings to the people, nor as a coded language that can only be deciphered by experts, but as a mode of encounter – between, say, Radway and the women whose responses she collected and studied.

FANTASY

While I share many of the criticisms of psychoanalytic theory that have been made in film studies in the past twenty years, the failure to take seriously psychoanalytic investigation can only lead to spectatorship studies that posit one limited definition of the subject in place of another. It is mistaken to assume, however, that all psychoanalytic film theorists subscribe to all aspects of apparatus theory, or that psychoanalytic investigations have remained unchanged in orientation since the early to mid–1970s. Indeed, one of the most significant rethinkings of psychoanalytic film theory has been in the area of fantasy, which Constance Penley specifically claims as an alternative to the "bachelor machines" characteristic of Metz's and Baudry's approaches to the cinema. "The formulation of fantasy," she writes, "which provides a complex and exhaustive account of *the staging and imaging of the subject and its desire*, is a model that very closely approximates the primary aims of the apparatus theory: to describe not only the subject's desire for the film image and its reproduction, but also the structure of the fantasmatic relation to that image, including the subject's belief in its reality" (1985: 54).

Two essays in particular have been extremely influential in the development of a model of spectatorship which draws upon the psychoanalytic definition of fantasy. Freud's "A Child Is Being Beaten" (1919) has been read as offering a theory of multiple masculine and feminine positions, thereby lending itself to a definition of spectatorship as oscillation rather than "identification" in a univocal sense (Rodowick 1982, 1991; Doane 1984; Hansen 1986). The specific definition of fantasy upon which Penley draws is located in an extremely influential essay by Jean Laplanche and Jean-Bertrand Pontalis, "Fantasy and the Origins of Sexuality" (1964/1986). Elaborating upon their claim that "fantasy is the fundamental object of psychoanalysis" (1967/1973: 317), in this essay the authors explore a variety of components of fantasy which suggest, even more forcefully than the dream analogy so often claimed as the basis for psychoanalytic exploration of the cinema, a situation which is embodied in the cinema.

Laplanche and Pontalis distinguish three "original" fantasies, original in the sense that they are bound up with the individual's history and origins: "Like myths, they claim to provide a representation of, and a solution to, the major enigmas which confront the child. Whatever appears to the subject as something needing an explanation or theory, is dramatized as a moment of emergence, the beginning of a history." Hence, Laplanche and Pontalis define three such fantasies of origins: "the primal scene pictures the origin of the individual; fantasies of seduction, the origin and upsurge of sexuality; fantasies of castration, the origin of the difference between the sexes" (1964/ 1986: 19). These fantasies are "original" not in the sense that they always "produce" or "cause" a given scenario, but that they form the structure of fantasy which is activated in a variety of ways.

Three characteristics of fantasy as read by Laplanche and Pontalis are particularly crucial for an understanding of the cinema as fantasy, and toward a revision of theories of the apparatus whereby the subject of the cinematic fantasy can only always be male. First, the distinction between what is conscious and what is unconscious is less important in fantasy than the distinction between those original fantasies described above, and secondary fantasies. Laplanche and Pontalis stress what they describe as the "profound continuity between the various fantasy scenarios – the stage-setting of desire – ranging from the daydream to the fantasies recovered or reconstructed by the analytic investigation" (1964/1986: 28). As we have seen, one of the problems with much apparatus theory is a mechanistic notion of the unconscious, due largely to the fact that the desire for regression is always postulated as the repetition of the same oedipal scenario. The three original fantasies of which Laplanche and Pontalis speak are not so regimented. And given that fantasy occupies such a distinct place in psychoanalysis insofar as it extends across the boundaries of conscious and unconscious desires, then the analysis of the cinema as a form of fantasy does not require what almost inevitably amounts to a decoding approach, a rigid distinction between manifest and latent content. The area of fantasy is one where the notion of homology operates quite differently than is the case with the cinematic apparatus, since here the homology is between different types of fantasy, of which cinematic spectatorship is one example (21). Put another way, fantasy is more useful for its implications than for its possible status as equivalent to or anticipatory of the cinema.

Second, it is the very nature of fantasy to exist for the subject across many possible positions. Noting that " 'A father seduces a daughter' " is the skeletal version of the seduction fantasy, Laplanche and Pontalis describe this function as follows: "The indication here of the primary process is not the absence of organization, as is sometimes suggested, but the peculiar character of the structure, in that it is a scenario with multiple entries, in which nothing shows whether the subject will be immediately located as *daughter*; it can as well be fixed as *father*, or even in the term *seduces*" (22–3). Despite the claims to anti-essentialism of many apparatus theorists, there is a consistent tendency to conflate literal gender and address; to assume, that is, that if the film addresses its subject as male, then it is the male viewer who is thus addressed. The reading of cinematic fantasy allows no such reduction. Indeed, the notion of fantasy gives psychoanalytic grounding not only to the possibility, but to the inevitability and necessity, of the cinema as a form of fantasy wherein the boundaries of biological sex or cultural gender, as well as sexual preference, are not fixed.

Finally, emphasis is placed throughout Laplanche and Pontalis's discussion on fantasy as the *staging* of desire, fantasy as a form of mise-en-scène. "Fantasy . . . is not the object of desire, but its setting. In fantasy the subject does not pursue the object or its sign: he appears caught up himself in the sequence of images" (26). Elizabeth Cowie has noted that the importance of the emphasis on fantasy as a scene "cannot be overestimated, for it enables the consideration of film as fantasy in the most fundamental sense of this term in psychoanalysis" (1984: 77). While I am somewhat suspicious of any mimetic analogy, the understanding of film as fantasy does open the door to some questions and issues about spectatorship which apparatus theory tended to shut out. In any case, I think the value of fantasy for psychoanalytic readings of the cinema needs to be seen less in terms of a "better" analogy than dreams, the mirror stage, or the imaginary, and more in terms of the series of questions it can engender.

In Cowie's reading of fantasy in film which relies extensively on the Laplanche and Pontalis essay, two such questions are raised: "if fantasy is the *mise-en-scène* of desire, whose desire is figured in the film, who is the subject for and of the scenario? No longer just, if ever, the so-called 'author'. But how does the spectator come into place as desiring subject of the film? Secondly, what is the relation of the contingent, everyday material drawn from real life, i.e. from the *social*, to the primal or original fantasies?" (1984: 87). Cowie notes how, in *Now, Voyager*, there is an oedipal fantasy, "but where the subject positions are not fixed or completed, Charlotte is both mother and daughter, Mrs. Vale and Tina." In partial response to her first question, then, Cowie says that it is not enough to define the fantasy as Charlotte Vale's; rather, it must be defined as the spectator's:

> This is not Charlotte's fantasy, but the "film's" fantasy. It is an effect of its narration (of its *énonciation*). If we identify simply with Charlotte's desires, that series of social and erotic successes, then the final object, the child Tina, will be unsatisfactory. But if our identification is with the playing out of a desiring, in relation to the opposition (phallic) mother/child, the ending is very much more satisfying, I would suggest. A series of "day-dream" fantasies enfold an Oedipal, original fantasy. The subject of this fantasy is then the spectator; inasmuch as we have been captured by the film's narration, its *énonciation*, we are the only place in which all the terms of the fantasy come to rest.
>
> (1984: 91)

Cowie's response to her second question – concerning the relationship between the psychic and the social which the analysis of fantasy can comprehend – focuses on the illicit desires which the subject's pleasure in the fantasy fulfills. In *Now, Voyager*, this concerns the evacuation of the father; in another film discussed by Cowie, *The Reckless Moment*, what she describes as an "unstoppable sliding of positions" results in pairings and oppositions whereby a set of equivalences is set up, and an inference is made "which is an attack on the family as imprisoning" (1984: 101). These claims are reminiscent of the kinds of implications in "reading against the grain" arguments about the classical cinema – i.e., that what appears to be a smooth ideological surface is marred, rather, by rebellion, critique, or even implicit rejection of those norms. What the reading of fantasy brings to such claims, however, is the insistence that investment and pleasure in film watching involve a range of subject positions. Apparatus theory tends to pose a spectator so aligned with one subject position that anything departing from that position would have to seem radical or contestatory by definition. The exploration of the classical cinema in terms of fantasy enlarges considerably what possibilities are contained within the fantasy structures engaged by film viewing, and in so doing inflects differently the notion of a "reading against the grain." For from the vantage point of fantasy, the distinction between "with" and "against" the grain of the film becomes somewhat moot.

Constance Penley assesses the importance of Cowie's approach to fantasy in terms of its assumption that positions of sexual identification are not fixed: "Cowie's model of identification involves a continual construction of looks, ceaselessly varied through the organization of the narrative and the work of narration. The value of such a model is that it leaves open the question of the production of sexual difference in the film rather than assuming in advance the sexuality of the character or the spectator" (1988: 11). However, while it may be a matter of indifference in psychoanalytic terms whether the spectator encouraged or enabled to adopt a variety of positions is male or female, it is a matter of crucial importance within the context of spectatorship, to the extent that spectatorship involves a spectator who always brings with her or him a history, and whose experience of spectatorship is determined in part by the ways in which spectatorship is defined outside of the movie theater.

Cowie emphasizes that whatever shifting of positions occurs in the fantasies of the cinema, they "do so always in terms of sexual difference" (1984: 102). It is one thing to assume "sexual difference" to refer to the way in which any definition of "femininity" is inevitably bound to accompanying definitions of "masculinity," and another thing to assume that the only possible relationship between the two is in some version of heterosexuality. Put another way, the insistence upon sexual difference has had a curious history in film studies, by collapsing the shifting terms of masculinity and femininity into a heterosexual master code. Interestingly, the model of fantasy elaborated by Laplanche and Pontalis has the potential to challenge film theory's own compulsory heterosexuality. In a study of Sheila McLaughlin's film *She Must Be Seeing Things*, for instance, Teresa de Lauretis argues that the film articulates a *lesbian* version of the primal scene, where the positions of onlooker and participant are occupied by women (1989).

Barbara Creed has observed that despite the fact that the castration scenario is but one of three originary fantasies in Laplanche and Pontalis's account, it has been the near-exclusive focus of 1970s film theory (1990: 135). Creed suggests that perhaps "the fantasy of castration *marks* all three primal fantasies to some degree" (135). The same could be said of any of the three fantasies. What might rather be the case is that the classical Hollywood cinema is made to the measure of the fantasy of sexual difference, which is of course what 1970s film theory claimed. It is unclear, in other words, just how much of a critical advantage the fantasy model offers, if it emerges as just another way of affirming the primacy of one particular configuration of desire. Alternatively, it could be argued that this is precisely where fantasy offers an understanding of the tension between the demands for regulation and homogeneity, on the one hand, and the mobility of spectatorial investment, on the other. The positions offered the spectator may be multiple, but the multiplicity finds its most cohesive articulation in the fantasy of sexual difference.

Jacqueline Rose has made a more pointed observation about the

90

current interest in fantasy, particularly insofar as it functions as a "saving device" against the "depressing implications" of the psychoanalytic position that the classical cinema offers the female spectator only an impossible relation to its fictions (1990: 275).

> Unconscious fantasy can . . . be read in terms of a multiplicity of available positions for women (and men), but the way these positions work against and defensively exclude each other gets lost. . . . [W]hile we undoubtedly need to recognize the instability of unconscious fantasy and the range of identifications offered by any one spectator of film, this can easily lead to an idealization of psychic processes and cinema at one and the same time (something for everyone both in the unconscious and on the screen).
>
> (275)

Rose's warning echoes an earlier debate in film studies concerning the monolithic quality of film narrative, with psychoanalysis functioning as a nagging reminder that the "resistance" of the unconscious cannot in any easy or simple way be equated with "resistance" understood in political terms.

Fantasy does offer the possibility of engaging different desires, contradictory effects, and multiple stagings. A certain version of the scenario of sexual difference emerges again and again in film theory as obsessive structure and point of return, and it is not always clear when the obsession and return are an effect of the cinema or of the theorist. In any case, it appears as though the homogeneous effects of the cinematic apparatus are understood in limited terms in the fantasy model – limited to the extent that they have only one point of reference, a notion of sexual difference which assumes the kind of essentialist quality otherwise so disavowed by psychoanalytic critics. I have no intention of reviving the political fantasy of "integrating" Marxism and/or feminism and/or psychoanalysis; rather, it is psychoanalysis on its own terms that requires investigation, not "rescue" by some other discourse. For it is questionable whether fantasy can engage with the complex effects of spectatorship without some understanding of how its own categories – of sexual difference, the couple, and desire – are themselves historically determined and culturally variable.

NEGOTIATION

To put this problem a bit differently, as well as to make the transition to the next tension I want to address, the institutional models of spectatorship have been read as so rigid that there has been a real temptation to see any response that differs slightly from what is assumed to be the norm or the ideal as necessarily radical and contestatory. Such claims to alternatives require that the theory of the institution that gave rise to it be challenged simultaneously. What remains nonetheless peculiar about many theories of the cinematic institution is that they give particular and sometimes exclusive signifying possibilities to the individual film. That is to say, the individual film is taken to be a well-functioning instance of the larger effects of the cinematic institution. When other practices are taken into account, like advertising or consumer tie-ins, they are assumed to create a narrative flow every bit as seamless as that of the classical scenario itself.

Once the cinematic institution is defined and analyzed as consisting of a number of different forms of address, however, it should be possible to unpack and question the excessive monolithic quality of the apparatus. But as I suggest above, I think it is crucial to resist the temptation to see difference or multiplicity as liberatory or contestatory qualities in themselves. This attention to difference (and simultaneous inquiry into the difference that difference makes) can be understood in a variety of ways, both in terms of a single film within which a variety of not necessarily harmonious discourses collide, and in terms of the various components that define film-going in a cultural and psychic sense.

One of the key terms that has emerged in this context is *negotiation*. In an influential essay associated with cultural studies, Stuart Hall's "Encoding/Decoding," three decoding strategies – that is, practices of reading and making sense of cultural texts – are proposed. The dominant reading is one fully of a piece with the ideology of the text, while the negotiated reading is more ambivalent; that is, the ideological stance of a product is adjusted to specific social conditions of the viewers. The oppositional reading is, then, one totally opposed to the ideology in question (Hall 1980).

As influential as this model has been, particularly in the foregrounding of reception contexts, it raises some problems of its own, particularly insofar as the "dominant" and "oppositional" readings are concerned. What is the relationship between activity and passivity in the reader/viewer, whether the reading is dominant or oppositional? If a reader/viewer occupies an oppositional stance, how does this square with the process of interpellation necessary for any response to a text? Dominant and oppositional readings may be more usefully understood, perhaps, as horizons of possibility, as tendencies rather than actual practices of reading. However, in order to foreground the activity of reading, viewing, and consuming mass culture, what Hall's model leaves relatively intact is the notion of a text's dominant ideology. This is peculiar insofar as the activity/passivity of the apparatus model appears to be reversed in favor of an active reader/viewer and a relatively stable, if not completely passive, text.

It may well be more useful to designate all readings as negotiated ones, to the extent that it is highly unlikely that one will find any "pure" instances of dominant or oppositional readings. In other words, a purely dominant reading would presume no active intervention at all on the part of the decoder, while a purely oppositional reading would assume no identification at all with the structures of interpellation of the text. In that case, some notion of textual determination must still be necessary in order for the negotiation model to be useful.

I stress this because there is a tendency to assume that because the model of negotiation posits both the activity of the reader/viewer and the heterogeneity of the different elements of social formations, it conceives of a variety of readings, and that very heterogeneity, that very activity, is then taken to be indicative of a resistance to dominant ideology. Since I do not think that individual texts can be any more easily categorized as purely "dominant" than spectators or readers can, I find it difficult to be quite so enthused about different or unauthorized readings as necessarily contestatory. As I suggested earlier in this chapter, one of the problems in spectatorship studies is the desire to categorize texts *and* readings/responses as either conservative or radical, as celebratory of the dominant order or critical of it. This duality forecloses the far more difficult task of questioning what is served by the continued insistence upon this either/or, and more radically, of examining what it is in conceptions of spectators' responses and film texts that produces this ambiguity in the first place.

One of the severe limitations of much apparatus theory is the assumption that certain textual strategies will necessarily produce desired reassignations of dominant subject/object relationships and subject positions. A textual strategy does not *necessarily* produce anything. But if, consequently, there is no such thing as an inherently radical technique, then there is no such thing either as an inherently conservative one. While I think most contemporary film scholars would agree with the former – would agree, that is, that this particular aspect of 1970s film theory is in need of severe revision – I am not sure that the latter will meet with such agreement, since the notion of a dominant narrative structure still appears with great regularity.

I am alluding to two extreme positions which can be sketched as follows. For many textual theorists of the 1970s, Raymond Bellour and the editors of *Camera Obscura* in particular, the value of textual analysis was to demonstrate that classical narrative produces a variety of ruptures, deviations, and crises only to recuperate them in the name of a hierarchical closure or resolution. From this point of view, any validation of those ruptures is at best naive voluntarism and at worst a refusal to acknowledge what one does not want to know – that the cinematic appratus works with great efficiency to channel all desire into male, oedipal desire. The apparatus works; closure and resolution are achieved. Inspired in many cases by the work of Hall and cultural studies, others, like John Fiske (1987), insist upon the social formations of audiences as the only ultimately determining factors. Both positions ascribe an unqualified power to the text, on the one hand, and socially defined readers/viewers on the other. The problem in each case is that the activity of making meaning is assumed to reside in one single source – either the cinematic apparatus, or the socially contextualized viewer. To be sure, variations are allowed in either case, but they are never significant enough to challenge the basic determinism of the model in question.

While there are advantages to both of these positions, I do not want to suggest that one can take what is most appealing about two different sets of assumptions and put them together in a happy integration. Unfortunately, while the notion of negotiation is potentially quite useful, it can inspire precisely a kind of Pollyanna dialectics – the institution remains monolithic, but never *so* monolithic that readers cannot be actively oppositional. Now I do think that spectatorship studies are most useful when "local," that is, when examined – as I suggest in the critique of Radway's book – insofar as they problematize the ideal reader or viewer. But there still needs to be some recognition of the theoretical questions at stake. There is no necessary discontinuity between theory and local analysis. Indeed, theory becomes much more challenging when contradiction and tension, for instance, exist not as textual abstractions but as complex entities which do not always lend themselves easily to one reading or another. Film theory of the 1970s erred in attempting to account for a cinematic subject in categories that are absolute. (Even when labeled "Western," this usually amounts to the same thing – e.g., some will confess that they speak only of the "Western" [white, male, etc.] subject and then proceed as if "Western" and "universal" were still fully commensurate terms.) But surely the conclusion is not that all theorizing is doomed to such levels of abstraction.

One particularly influential invocation of negotiation is instructive in this context, since it sets out the issues that the concept is meant to address. Indeed, in Angela McRobbie's essay "Dance and Social Fantasy," a study of how teenage girls respond to dance and how those responses read in relationship to the films *Flashdance* and *Fame*, negotiation seems to describe not only the teenage girls but McRobbie herself as a researcher (1984). Noting that the significance of extra-textual codes and knowledge in the reception of mass culture leads to

94

the necessity for the researcher to "limit strictly the range of his or her analysis," McRobbie continues:

> It also means working with a consciously loose rather than tight relation in mind, one where an inter-discursive notion of meaning structures and textual experience leads to a different working practice or methodology. Instead of seeking direct causal links or chains, the emphasis is placed on establishing loose sets of relations, capillary actions and movement, spilling out among and between different fields: work and leisure, fact and fiction, fantasy and reality, individual and social experience.
>
> (142)

Several negotiations form the core of McRobbie's analysis, not least of which is the juxtaposition of the responses of teenage girls to dancing as both a social and an individual activity, and the textual forms that seem to encourage such fantasies in two dance films, *Flashdance* and *Fame*. Within the two films, there are several processes of negotiation at work. In *Flashdance*, McRobbie notes that while the dance scenes are very much directed at that ubiquitous entity, the male spectator within the film, other narrative elements of the film are drawn so clearly from the woman's film that it is impossible to say with certainty that the address of the film is directed toward the woman defined unambiguously as the object of the male gaze (138). The process of negotiation here concerns, then, two different genres – the musical and the woman's film – the conventions of which may rub against each other rather than function compatibly. McRobbie also notes that in both films, there is a sometimes peculiar juxtaposition of old and new elements; the films "place together images and moments of over-whelming conformity with those which seem to indicate a break with Hollywood's usual treatment of women" (150). In other words, the classical formulae of both films could be said to acknowledge and retreat from their own limitations insofar as representations of women are concerned.

McRobbie also insists upon the importance of understanding films like these in an intertextual network, and in the case of these two films, the expectations of dance culture can inflect the readings of the films, and vice versa. Thus the process of "negotiation" refers to how the films are structured as cinematic texts, as well as to how the meanings of these films are "negotiated" in relationship to one's knowledge of the dance scene outside of the movie theater. Noting that the dancehall or disco shares some similarities with the movie theater (a "darkened space" where the spectator/dancer "can retain some degree of anonymity or absorption"), McRobbie notes as well a significant difference: "Where the cinema offers a one-way fantasy

95

which is directed solely through the gaze of the spectator toward the screen, the fantasy of dancing is more social, more reciprocated" (144). Such a mapping of one context onto the other may account for a reception of these films that departs sharply from the pronouncements of film theory about the inevitability of the colonization of the female body.

Two particular points of reference recur in McRobbie's essay, and they echo some of the questions I raised in relation to Radway's *Reading the Romance*. Richard Dyer has suggested that one of the basic appeals of the movie musical is the utopian dimension, a way of providing pleasures and satisfactions that are otherwise unavailable in the culture at hand, and yet which are defined in such a way as to suggest that they can only be satisfied within capitalism (1977). Radway suggests that this utopianism – defined within the context of Nancy Chodorow's reading of women's desires for re-creation of their pre-oedipal bond – is a function of the reading of romance novels, and McRobbie's reading of dance and dance films is equally suggestive of a utopian impulse.

I do not wish to evoke a traditional and moralistic Marxism, whereby art provides us with a glimpse of the truly integrated human beings we will all become in the communist future. But I find that sometimes the utopian dimension becomes clouded by the understanding of desire as always in conflict with the dominant culture. McRobbie notes, for instance, that *Fame* presents a desire for community and family as necessarily intertwined (158), and certainly an interesting area of research is the way in which films articulate definitions which both reflect dominant ideology (the family is the basis for all community) and challenge them (communities provide what families do not, or cannot, in our culture). What makes me somewhat suspicious is the way that the discussion of utopianism seems to fall into exactly the kind of large abstractions – having to do with the "human subject under capitalism and/or patriarchy" – that McRobbie sets out (specifically in the passage cited earlier) to challenge. In case I sound as if I am contradicting myself as far as the necessity of combining "local" analyses with theoretical reflection is concerned, let me say that I do not think that theory means falling back into large clichés about the human subject – or the female subject.

The second recurring point of reference in McRobbie's essay is an illustration of the first. Noting that dance "carries a range of often contradictory strands within it," she affirms the conformity of dance with conventional definitions of femininity, but says that at the same time the pleasures of dance "seem to suggest a displaced, shared and nebulous eroticism rather than a straightforwardly romantic, heavily heterosexual 'goal-oriented' drive" (134). In another context, McRobbie

96

describes the dance scene and suggests that as it offers a "suspension of categories, there is not such a rigid demarcation along age, class, ethnic terms. Gender is blurred and sexual preference less homogenously heterosexual" (146). Curiously, this "suspension of categories" is itself suspended when McRobbie reports that her sources on the pleasures of dance are "predominantly heterosexual;" hence "these fantasy scenarios make no claim to represent gay or lesbian experience" (145). While gay and lesbian experiences of dance may well be different, this disclaimer erects the categories of sexual preference just when the analysis of dance seems to put them into question.

I suspect that since the question of sexual preference is far more controversial than, say, the desire for a community (whether based on the family or not), and is perhaps threatening to those very viewers/participants whose desires one is attempting to take seriously, then the temptation is to shelve a consideration of it for some future analysis, or to open the question about the permeability of sexual boundaries without really pursuing it in any depth. But the deployment of gay and lesbian identities in popular culture, and the complicated responses the viewers bring to homosexuality as a moral, sexual, and political issue, seem to me just the kind of *specific* area of inquiry for investigation into the utopian impulse that desires for community avoid.

Film theory has been so bound by the heterosexual symmetry that supposedly governs Hollywood cinema that it has ignored the possibility, for instance, that one of the distinct pleasures of the cinema may well be a "safe zone" in which homosexual as well as heterosexual desires can be fantasized and acted out. I am not speaking here of an innate capacity to "read against the grain," but rather of the way in which desire and pleasure in the cinema may well function to problematize the categories of heterosexual versus homosexual. To be sure, this "safety zone" can also be read as a displacement, insurance that the happy ending is a distinctly heterosexual one. But as has been noted many times, the buddy film, if it affirms any kind of sexual identity aside from a narcissistic one, is as drawn to a homosexual connection as it is repelled by it.

Taking into account the complexity of the range of responses to the stability of sexual identities and sexual categories would require an approach to negotiation that specifies the psychic stakes in such a process, rather than just stating that the psychic remains significant or important. I am not referring here to the kind of psychoanalytic theorizing typical of much 1970s film theory, where the "unconscious" usually meant a master plot repeated again and again, an inevitable source of meaning and comprehensibility. What has been surprisingly absent from much psychoanalytic film theory is an investigation of the ways in which the unconscious refuses the stability of any categorization. The example of heterosexuality and its various "others" seems to me a particularly crucial one to take into account, since so much of the ideology of the cinematic institution is built simultaneously on the heterosexual couple as the common denominator, on the promise of romantic fulfillment, at the same time that that couple seems constantly in crisis, constantly in need of reassurance. One would have thought this an area where the concept of negotiation would provide a useful corrective.

To take this in a somewhat different direction: The notion of negotiation is only useful if one is attentive to the problematic as well as "utopian" uses to which negotiation can be put by both the subjects one is investigating and the researchers themselves. While I have not seen this spelled out in any detail, negotiation seems to be a variation of the Marxist notion of mediation – the notion, that is, of a variety of instances that complicate or "mediate" in various ways the relationship between individuals and the economic structure of capitalism. Raymond Williams has noted that while the concept of mediation has the advantage of complicating significantly the cause-and-effect notion of "reflection" so typical of a traditional Marxism, and of indicating an active process, it remains limited in its own way. Williams notes that "it is virtually impossible to sustain the metaphor of 'mediation' . . . without some sense of separate and pre-existent areas or orders of reality. . . . Within the inheritance of idealist philosophy the process is usually, in practice, seen as a mediation between categories, which have been assumed to be distinct" (1977: 99).

Negotiation can replicate the problems that inhere in the notion of mediation by replacing the language of "subjection" and "imposition" with that of "agency" and "contradiction" but without significantly exploring how the notion of an active subject can be just as open to projections and subjections as a passive subject can. While the field of cultural studies, with its emphasis on "negotiation" as the way readers/viewers shape mass culture to their own needs, has had an enormous impact on film studies, another direction in literary studies also makes persistent use of "negotiation" in a rather different way. The so-called "new historicism" has had only a limited relationship with film studies, yet some of the ways in which the concept of negotiation has emerged in new historicist studies offer a useful counterpoint to the inflection offered by cultural studies.

New historicism is most immediately associated with English Renaissance studies. But the problems new-historicist work addresses are not so different than those central to film studies, particularly insofar as a reckoning with both the advances and the limitations of 1970s film theory are concerned. Louis A. Montrose, for instance, has said that "the terms in which the problem of ideology has been posed and is now circulating in Renaissance literary studies – namely as an opposition between 'containment' and 'subversion' – are so reductive, polarized, and undynamic as to be of little or no conceptual value" (1989: 22). That this assessment "applies" to film studies, particularly in relation to spectatorship, may have less to do with a striking coincidence between film studies and the new historicism, and more to do with questions central to virtually all forms of cultural analysis in the 1980s and 1990s which attempt to develop new forms of criticism and theory at the same time that they engage with their own historical legacies, particularly insofar as the 1960s and 1970s are concerned in their status as simultaneous political turning points and mythological burden.

While it is not my purpose either to align myself with a new-historicist project or to provide an extended introduction to this field, it is noteworthy that the term *negotiation* in its new historicist usage tends more toward questioning those very possibilities of radical agency that the cultural-studies approach finds in its negotiations. Stephen Greenblatt notes that capitalism "has characteristically generated neither regimes in which all discourses seem coordinated, nor regimes in which they seem radically isolated or discontinuous, but regimes in which the drive toward differentiation and the drive toward monological organization operate simultaneously, or at least oscillate so rapidly as to create the impression of simultaneity" (1989: 6). From the vantage point of this simultaneity, then, the immediate assumption that all unauthorized uses of films, and therefore spectatorial positions that depart from the presumed ideal of capitalist ideology, are virtually or potentially radical is a reading of the nature of discourse and power in our culture as more dualistic than it is.

A large part of the problem here is that the analysis of spectatorship in film studies has as a significant part of its legacy a commitment to the creation of alternative cultures and political identities which refuse to comply with dominant ideology. Phrases like "alternative cultures" and "refusal to comply" can of course mean a variety of things, including contradictory things. The reactions of black male spectators to the filmed popularization of Alice Walker's novel *The Color Purple* cannot be squared in any easy or even complex way with the feminist critique of the "woman as object of the male look," yet both constitute claims to validation by marginalized groups (see Bobo 1988). Part of the 1960s/1970s legacy of film studies is a romanticized vision of the politicized past, based on the assumption (erroneous and inaccurate) that the common denominator "socialist" could account for any and all kind of radical and progressive social change – a utopian definition of socialism which was quickly enough put to rest by feminism and gay and lesbian liberation movements. Curiously, what seems to have persisted is a vague discourse of "subversion" and "alternative scenarios," amidst conceptual confusion about just what is being subverted and for what.

Catherine Gallagher says – in what could easily function as a critique of the tendencies present in much writing about spectatorship – that new historicists have attempted to show "that under certain historical circumstances, the display of ideological contradictions is completely consonant with the maintenance of oppressive social relations" (1989: 44). It has been crucial to spectatorship studies to understand that visions of the cinema as the inflexible apparatus of the ideological subject are as much projections of theorists' own desires as they are hypothetically interesting and useful and also historically conditioned postulates about going to the cinema. But it is equally important for such an inquiry to take place in what amounts to a new "stage" of spectatorship studies, where the model is no longer the passive, manipulated (and inevitably white and heterosexual) spectator, but rather the contradictory, divided and fragmented subject.

The new-historicist reminder that "negotiation" is a marketplace term tempers too quick an enthusiasm about what may ultimately be strategies of consumerism. But it is too easy to assume the cynical route (which is, after all, only the reverse of romanticism), that is, to assume in a kind of more-Foucauldian-than-thou posture that there are no alternative positions, only fictions of them. What remains vital, in the critical examination of spectatorship, is the recognition that no "negotiation" is inherently or purely oppositional, but that the desire for anything "inherent" or "pure" is itself a fiction that must be contested.

What I am suggesting, in this extremely schematic encounter between new historicism and cultural studies, is that a desire for unproblematized agency – whether that of the critic or of the imaginary or real spectator(s) under investigation – persists. Even though McRobbie does question the notion of the "ideal viewer" which, as I suggest above, is one of the limitations of Radway's analysis, there remain some echoes of an idealized female subject in her account. In an extremely provocative essay on the status of negotiation as a critical concept in studies on female spectatorship, Christine Gledhill sees negotiation as providing a possible way out of the limitations of the implications of feminist/psychoanalytic film theory and the attendant split between text and reception, particularly insofar as texts were seen as capable of situating alternative subjective positions. "The value of 'negotiation' . . . as an analytical concept is that it allows space to the subjectivities, identities and pleasures of audiences," writes Gledhill (1988: 72). But "subjectivity," "identity," and "pleasure" are here defined in a way that acknowledges the critique of the fictions of bourgeois identity that has been central to Lacanian-inspired film theory. At the same time, those critiques are fictions, too, in supposing that any notion of identity may supposedly be "done away with."

In a move somewhat reminiscent of Jane Gallop's claim that "identity must be continually assumed and immediately put into question" (1982: xii), Gledhill says that

> the concept of negotiation stops short at the dissolution of identity suggested by avant-garde aesthetics. For if arguments about the non-identity of self and language, words and meaning, desire and its objects challenge bourgeois notions of the centrality and stability of the ego and the transparency of language, the political consequence is not to abandon the search for identity. . . . The object of attack should not be identity as such but its dominant construction as total, non-contradictory and unchanging.
>
> (72)

I am suggesting, as is perhaps obvious by now, that this "dominant construction" enters into the ways in which researchers themselves construct their audiences. This should not, of course, come as startling news to anyone familiar with the dynamics of transference and counter-transference. But in order for studies of spectatorship to engage fully with the complex dynamics that define the process of negotiation, such constructions need to be accounted for.

As Gledhill's comments suggest, one of the key issues at stake here is the competing claims of "identity," which have been associated with some of the most fervent debates in film studies and related fields in the past two decades. Studies of reception and negotiation are often meant to challenge the ways in which post-structuralist theorists are seen to critique any notion of the self as an agent as an inevitable fiction of bourgeois/patriarchal/idealist culture. What becomes quite difficult in that process of challenge is acknowledging the necessity of the critique of the fictions of the self without resurrecting them yourself. Somewhat curiously, the challenges to apparatus theory described in this chapter return to the problem of identification, as if to suggest that however mobile and multiple subject positions may be, spectatorship still engages some notion of identity. But then theorists of the cinematic apparatus never banished identification from film theory, but rather redefined its terms beyond those of character or a one-to-one correspondence between viewer and screen. In any case, the current visibility of identity as a problem in film studies – whether as spectre, curse, or positive value – speaks to the continued friction between subjects and viewers.

A colleague of mine once commented that much of what passes for film theory is a finger-wagging list of everything that is "wrong" with a given position or argument. I recognize that I have indulged in some of that syndrome in this chapter, since I have focussed critically on address/reception, fantasy, and negotiation as important concepts for spectatorship studies; that is, I have attempted to examine the concepts closely, in a symptomatic way, without simply assigning them positive or negative marks. Two criticisms have consistently emerged in my discussion of these concepts. First, I have suggested that there is a considerable reluctance on the part of theorists to acknowledge their own investment in the process of spectatorship analysis. I do not mean by this that all critics should write in a confessional mode, or impose a first-person account in every discussion of spectatorship. I see theoretical self-consciousness, rather, as an attention to how and why certain modes of theoretical discourse, certain tropes, certain preoccupations, are foregrounded in specific critical and cultural contexts.

Second, I return frequently in this chapter to the need for more specific, local studies, where the focus would be less on large theories that can account for everything, and more on the play and variation that exist at particular junctures between the competing claims of film spectatorship – as the function of an apparatus, as a means of ideological control, on the one hand, and as a series of discontinuous, heterogeneous, and sometimes empowering responses, on the other. In the remaining chapters of the book, I turn to four such specific instances, each of which focuses on particular areas of spectatorship inquiry that have been important in film studies – textual analysis, stars, reception, and "subcultural" audiences. My aim is to approach these topics with the same attention to the tension between homogeneity and heterogeneity, between domination and resistance, that has structured this chapter, but to do so in a way more attentive to the stakes of specific, local studies. The point is not to construct yet another theory or concept of "the" cinematic spectator, but to suggest areas of inquiry which reveal both the importance of conceptualizing spectators, and some directions these conceptualizations can now take.

Part II

READINGS OF SPECTATORSHIP

5

TEXTUAL ANALYSIS AND PORTRAITS OF SPECTATORSHIP

Textual analysis is one of the most important theoretical and practical legacies of 1970s film theory. Yet when 1970s film theory is assessed, whether sympathetically or critically (or both), textual analysis is frequently one of the first targets. It is argued that textual analysis relies too exclusively on the formal and technical aspects of the cinema, and therefore gives exclusive signifying authority to a single film and ignores the complex nature of the cinematic institution. Or, by exploring in exhaustive detail the signifying structures of the individual film, textual analysis creates a film text that has only the most remote connection with the ways in which films are actually received (an issue which has not been ignored by practitioners of textual analysis; see Bellour 1975a). Textual analysis is criticized for resurrecting the old dichotomy of text and context, privileging the former and ignoring the latter; for generalizing from very specific examples, and for assuming that if any classical Hollywood film operates in a certain way, then it has to possess a certain degree of typicality, or that a model of classical Hollywood cinema will be demonstrated in any single example one might choose.

Such criticisms of textual analysis have emerged from a range of responses to 1970s film theory, from the sympathetic to the highly critical. David Rodowick suggests that "contemporary film theory has often totalized complex questions of sexual difference and identification within a singular unity which merges the 'forms' of spectatorship with the 'forms' of the text" (1991: 136). Rodowick does not in any way reject psychoanalytic film theory and attendant questions of textual analysis, but rather argues for more rigorous and pointed examination of their range of inquiry. Whereas Rodowick sees the legacy of psychoanalytic film theory as crucial to considerations of film, ideology, and social change, Jackie Byars is less optimistic about that legacy. Speaking specifically of feminist film theory in its "psychological" versus its "sociological" forms, she says that the "duality of the 'social' and the 'psychic' may be tired, but its presence lingers, influentially" (1991: 29). Specifically, Byars focuses on how feminist film theory's preoccupation with spectatorship has ignored how the "social subject and the discursive subject" are "overlapping but not entirely congruent phenomena" (35). Rodowick and Byars occupy very different positions vis-à-vis the issue of the continuing value of psycho-analytic models of textual analysis, but the limitations to which they point – the tendency to generalize too much from the analysis of textual systems – are strikingly similar.

The textual analyses that have become "classics" of film theory are virtually all performed on classical Hollywood films: Stephen Heath's detailed reading of *Touch of Evil* (1975), Raymond Bellour's analyses of a number of films by Hitchcock, but especially *North by Northwest* (1975b), Thierry Kuntzel's analysis of *The Most Dangerous Game* (1972/ 1978). While these analyses are different in scope, they share an emphasis on understanding classical film narrative as a pattern of interweaving oppositions, a system that is threatened and restored, corresponding to the overall movement of plot, narrative, and mise-en-scène. Virtually without exception, the "threat" has something to do with Woman. The system thus excavated in classical Hollywood cinema is located at the intersection of structuralism – concerned with the various codes that make exchange possible, a privileged mode of which is the exchange of women; and psychoanalysis – concerned with the various ways in which sexual difference is displaced, denied, or otherwise negotiated.

At the same time, textual analysis in film studies is marked by the transition from structuralist studies of narrative, concerned with the overall modes of coherence and stability in the text, to post-structuralist studies, concerned more with what exceeds or puts into question those very modes of coherence and stability. While this shift has influenced virtually all areas of contemporary theoretical endeavor, the changing status of textual analysis in film studies nonetheless represents a particularly important area of inquiry. For the classical Hollywood film, the preferred object for textual analysis, is the kind of dominant, transparently realist text which in a classical structuralist narratology would lend itself quite easily to a series of predictable patterns. But through the lens of post-structuralism, classical film would put into question the totalizing dominance of such transparency. As I suggest in chapter 1, the influence of Roland Barthes's detailed analysis of "Sarrasine," the novella by Balzac, in *S/Z*, cannot be overestimated in this context (1970/1974). Just as the classical narra-tive cinema would appear to be, in structuralist terms, perfectly "read-erly," so it would acquire, in post-structuralist terms, a "writerly" status informed at the very least by a notion of "limited plurality."

When described in the structuralist terms of opposition and resolution, one could assume mistakenly that textual analysis is concerned with form and structure in a purely aesthetic or thematic sense. While it is true that some of what is called "textual analysis" is indistinguishable from formalist analysis, it is important to specify that as textual analysis developed in film studies, it was linked with psychoanalysis, particularly insofar as theories of the subject were concerned; to anthropology and cultural analysis, particularly through the work of Claude Lévi-Strauss; and to a lesser extent with Marxism, particularly insofar as the Althusserian notions of symptomatic reading and interpellation are concerned. As I have indicated in previous chapters, despite the efforts of many theorists to separate absolutely the "subject" from the "viewer," some slippage occurs. Hence, one of the legacies of textual analysis is a notion of the film viewer as held, contained, or otherwise manipulated by the mechanisms of a cinematic institution which finds its most succinct expression in the various textual strategies of delay, resolution, and containment that engage the spectator. The psychoanalytic and ideological ramifications here are both connected to a concept of regulation.

Despite the significance of Marxism, anthropology, and psychoanalysis in the development of textual analysis in film studies, descriptions of textual analysis often proceed as if it were just another kind of formalism. As stated in previous chapters, the psychoanalytic inquiry that characterized apparatus theory emphasized an "unconscious" that is tamed and turned into yet one more crisis of male subjectivity. A far more pervasive psychoanalytic influence is the assumption that whenever a structure is created or imposed, something is repressed. The process of textual analysis therefore is the attempt to retrace the evolution of structure and attendant process of repression. The assumption is that the film text functions for the spectator in much the same way that Freud saw works of art, as particularly condensed instances of unconscious processes, desires, and fantasies. At the same time, this particular psychoanalytic influence was reinforced by Althusserian Marxism, specifically insofar as "symptomatic readings" were concerned – e.g., the assumption that within any structure there remains a symptom of what has been repressed or marginalized.

In this chapter I address the relationship between textual analysis and spectatorship by focussing on a particular case study, the trope of portraiture and its narrative function in a 1945 film directed by Albert Lewin, *The Picture of Dorian Gray*. Like many of the films that have been immortalized (at least within film studies) through textual analysis, this film demonstrates a visible and foregrounded preoccupation with spectatorship. To some extent, of course, *all* films do; the advantage, however, of analysis of a film so visibly preoccupied with spectatorship is obvious, since it is an opportunity to observe how the classical cinema creates a narrative about itself, engages in self-reflexive myth-making. *The Picture of Dorian Gray* is interesting as well in that in order to designate a space of viewing, it must engage with potentially controversial material, the most obvious being the gay persona of Oscar Wilde and the gay implications of the novella upon which the film is based. It is not my purpose here to enter into the question of censorship and the impact of the production code on this film, although it is worth noting that one of the most interesting developments in textual analysis of recent years is the exploration of the interaction between film texts and industry texts. Indeed, critics like Mary Beth Haralovich, Lea Jacobs, and Annette Kuhn have suggested that censorship was a dynamic, complex relationship, and not one of simple negativity (Haralovich 1990; Kuhn 1988; Jacobs 1987, 1988, 1991).

Albert Lewin, the director of *The Picture of Dorian Gray*, directed only six films, and all of them demonstrate a peculiar blend of the Hollywood commonplace and the excessive (particularly true of *Pandora and the Flying Dutchman* [1951]). In his *Biographical Dictionary of Film*, David Thomson says of Lewin's films that "arty aspiration showed like a teenage slip" (1981: 347). *The Picture of Dorian Gray* is both exceptional and typical; exceptional in that it has obvious pretensions to show artistic sensibility and upper-class mores, and typical in that it reflects a core structure evident across a wide range of classical Hollywood films. The question of typicality is a nagging one for textual analysis, although the question may be more one of excessive claims for the analysis than for the film under scrutiny. The use of textual analysis to find "a" subject position that typifies "the" classical cinema is both futile and pretentious. Rather, individual films – which are always a blend of the typical and the exceptional – offer, through the lens of textual analysis, a series of hypotheses about the varieties of spectatorship. *The Picture of Dorian Gray* may lean a bit more toward the exceptional than the typical, but the figures of spectatorship drawn in the film find parallels in other films of the period, particularly in the combination of, first, a painting and responses to it, and second, a foregrounding of different modes of spectatorship, from naive investment in the image to ironic detachment (*Laura* [1944], *The Woman in the Window* [1944], *Scarlet Street* [1945]).

It is not my intention, within the limits of a necessarily short chapter, to engage in a detailed textual analysis of the film. In any case, textual analysis is less a matter of exhaustiveness than of strategy – the recognition, say, that a detail which might initially appear insignificant provides a perspective from which other seemingly insignificant details suddenly emerge in another kind of coherence, or that within the large oppositions that form the overall structure of the film, there is nonetheless a pressure, a sense of something always at the horizon or on the edge of the opposition. It would of course be ludicrous to assume that what I, in the name of film theory and academic film studies, see in my reading of an individual film is necessarily what any and all spectators will see. While the notion of a textual unconscious is crucial to the development of film studies, the necessarily metaphoric implications of that assumption are frequently lost. For texts may inspire unconscious responses, but they don't "have" an unconscious – only people do.

In Oscar Wilde's 1891 novella, a triangle connects three men – Dorian Gray, a handsome aristocratic young man; Basil Hallward, a painter; and Lord Henry Wotton, an idle aristocrat who assumes a tutorial role of sorts in relationship to Dorian. The novella opens as Basil puts the final touches to his portrait of Dorian. In the presence of both Basil and Lord Henry, Dorian makes his fatal wish: "If it were I who was to be always young, and the picture that was to grow old! For that – for that – I would give everything!" (1962: 42). Influenced by Lord Henry's philosophy, Dorian pursues pleasure for its own sake. During an outing to a London slum, he happens across a theater where Shakespeare is being performed. The star of the show is a young actress, Sibyl Vane. She possesses an uncanny gift for performance which is highlighted even more by the incompetence of her colleagues. Dorian immediately falls in love. When he brings his two male friends to observe Sibyl's talents, however, she is wooden and dull.

Sibyl later explains that since she found love with Dorian, she is no longer capable of performing well. That is, having found "art" in the realm of everyday life, she can no longer produce it. Dorian promptly abandons Sibyl. She commits suicide, after which Dorian begins to degenerate – in several senses of the word. But the changes in Dorian's life are manifested, not in his own body, but in Basil's portrait of him. Dorian eventually shows Basil the transformed portrait, and then murders him. While attempting to destroy the painting, Dorian himself dies. His body finally records the changes previously visible only in the painting, while the painting is restored to its original state.

Even though Wilde's *The Picture of Dorian Gray* is superficially about heterosexual love, it is widely recognized as gay in inspiration and in its none too subterranean subtext. As Richard Ellmann writes, "More than any other writer of his time in England, Wilde recognized that homosexuality was the great undercover subject. . . . To express his point of view as directly as he could, Wilde wrote *The Picture of Dorian Gray*. . . . Wilde was attacked for immorality, but he had cagily left Dorian's sin unspecified, while clearly implying involvements with both sexes" (1977: 6). It comes as no great surprise that the most significant changes made in the adaptation of Wilde's novella to the screen are the foregrounding of heterosexual desire as the motor force of the film. True, the relationship between Dorian and Sibyl (with Sibyl now a singer in a music hall) functions in the film as in the novella to render somewhat ambiguous the simultaneous identification and desire between Dorian and the two principal men in his life. But another female character is added to the film, Gladys, the niece of painter Basil Hallward. Lewin's film begins, as does the novella, with the completion of the portrait of Dorian, but with the difference that a female signature is added to the painting – Gladys is portrayed as a small child who puts the letter "G" under her uncle's signature. After Sibyl's suicide (provoked, as in the novella, by Dorian's rejection of her, but now as a result of her failure to act unpredictably when Dorian invites her to spend the night with him), the passage of time allows Gladys to mature into a young woman whose childish devotion becomes adult love for Dorian, with somewhat incestuous overtones since Dorian is so closely affiliated with Glady's uncle. In the film, Dorian asks Gladys to marry him in an attempt to reform and to atone for his guilt over Sibyl's suicide. The same desire for salvation motivates his destruction of the painting, and – as in the novella – he dies while the painting is restored to its original state.

While the character of Gladys lends a more obvious heterosexual component to the film, there is a link between her and the Wilde novella. Two minor female characters in the novella – one actually named Gladys – have some connection with the film character; one is a hostess at a gathering attended by Dorian and Lord Henry, and the other is Hetty, a briefly mentioned "village girl" abandoned by Dorian to protect her from inevitable corruption through his influence. Most important, however, is the familial connection established with Basil Hallward, since the character of Gladys is largely created by dividing the character of Basil in two. Thus Gladys, present at the portrait sitting and co-signer of the portrait, becomes a figure upon whom is displaced any possible sexual attraction between Basil and Dorian.

The addition of Gladys to the film occasions its division into two distinct parts, the first dominated by Dorian's relationship with Sibyl, the second by his relationship with Gladys. As objects of Dorian's affections, the two women are not typed according to the virgin/whore dichotomy, but rather according to a class dichotomy as well as one of performance – Sibyl the performer, Gladys a perpetual onlooker. There is a symmetry as well in the representation of the two women, particularly insofar as their male protectors are concerned – Sibyl's brother James, who dies when he attempts to kill Dorian in revenge for his sister's suicide, and Gladys's sometime suitor David, who discovers the secret of Dorian's painting in an effort to obstruct their marriage by whatever possible means.

In what has become known as typical of the classical cinema, then, *The Picture of Dorian Gray* is structured by a series of rhyming oppositions. The restoration of order in the film occurs when the painting is restored to its original status, and Gladys and David are united in a relationship that is free of the quasi-incestuous overtones of a possible relationship between Dorian and Gladys. The most obvious and foregrounded oppositions in the film center on the representation of the portrait. While Dorian's portrait is described in Wilde's novella, it is not a description that is – to use Roland Barthes's term – "operable;" that is, much of the force of the portrait in the novella is a result of its status as a function of discourse. Not only is the portrait shown in Lewin's film, but its appearance introduces a striking opposition between black-and-white and color, for the display of the portrait at three crucial moments in the film occasions the use of technicolor. The use of color gives the painting(s) a certain autonomy, and also makes the difference between the early and late versions of the painting all the more striking.

In one of the most influential essays in the theorization of film narrative in the late 1970s, "Narrative Space," Stephen Heath begins with an analysis of a scene in Hitchcock's *Suspicion*. Two policemen arrive at Lina's home. A play is established in the scene between two paintings, one the realistic portrait of Lina's father which functions as a constant reminder of his law and his authority, the other a somewhat abstract, "modernist" painting hanging on the wall in the entry hall to the house, and toward which the puzzled attention of one of the policemen is drawn as he enters and again as he leaves. The scene in question serves as a demonstration of the construction of narrative space, as a "perfectly symmetrical patterning [that] builds up and pieces together the space in which the action can take place, the space which is itself part of that action in its economy, its intelligibility, its own legality" (1976/rpt. 1981: 20). The tension between the two paintings, one traditional, one modernist, and the function of the modernist painting as "useless," serve "to demonstrate the rectitude of the portrait, the true painting at the centre of the scene, utterly in frame in the film's action" (23). The implication in Heath's analysis is both that the classical cinema constructs a narrative space controlled by the order represented by the father's portrait, but that always at the edges of this construction are the possibilities, so forcefully demonstrated in the Hitchcock scene, of "missing spectacle: problem of point of view, different framing, disturbance of the law and its inspectoring eye, interruption of the homogeneity of the narrative economy, it is somewhere else again, another scene, another story, another space" (24).

111

A common assumption about textual analysis, and about Heath's contributions to it, is that whatever ruptures, disturbances, or differences emerge are smoothed over and contained by the homogenizing force of classical film narrative. While this is true of some textual analysis, I do not think it is an accurate assessment of Heath's work. The analysis of the scene in *Suspicion* may demonstrate how the articulation of space in classical film narrative marginalizes and relegates to "uselessness" figurations that threaten to upset its order. But the analysis suggests just as forcefully the way in which classical narrative engages a constant process of flirtation with its own margins. To be sure, no film directed by Hitchcock can be taken as representative of classical Hollywood as a whole – despite claims to the contrary by those who have analyzed the mechanisms of male desire in his films – and the whole painting episode could perhaps be described as a typical "Hitchcock joke," as Heath suggests. But the scene analyzed by Heath finds echoes in other classical Hollywood films. The portrait of Dorian Gray does not function in the same way as the father's portrait in *Suspicion*; in Hitchcock's film, the portrait is a metaphoric condensation of the authority that dominates Lina and the film, whereas in Lewin's film, the portrait is much more literally the focus of the film. Yet I find echoes of Heath's analysis in *The Picture of Dorian Gray*, specifically insofar as the articulation of narrative space is concerned.

For in the film, spectatorship is represented with clear and sharp divisions between innocence and corruption, yet those very divisions are more permeable than what first appears. Spectatorship as it is defined in the film operates on two levels. The first has to do with the portrait itself and responses to it, with the narcissism of Dorian Gray, and the nurturance it finds in Lord Henry, defined as the excesses which the film must put right – all variations on the common theme of male specular identity, of men as mirrors for other men. This process of mirroring establishes the painting as a means of representing spectatorship. The second level has to do with how the film constructs a scenography evocative of certain codes and conventions of painting, but in more diffuse ways than actual and literal portraits within the film. Here, the objects of such painting-inspired mise-en-scène are usually women. Put another way, portraiture in *The Picture of Dorian Gray* occurs on two levels, only one of which has to do with the actual portrait itself; rather the implications of framing and mise-en-scène unite the two different levels. Yet the levels are separated by the difference between men and women.

The Picture of Dorian Gray begins with Lord Henry in a carriage on his way to Basil's. While Lord Henry reads, a male narrator speaks in voice-over: "Lord Henry Wotton had set himself early in life to the

112

serious and great aristocratic art of doing absolutely nothing. He lived only for pleasure, but his greatest pleasure was to observe the emotions of his friends while experiencing none of his own. He diverted himself by exercising a subtle influence on the lives of others." The form of spectatorship sketched out here is situated immediately within the realm of an aristocratic aesthete's ideal pleasures. Once he has arrived at Basil's studio, to which he has come out of curiosity about the secrecy of his current painting project, the three men who form the core of Wilde's novella are introduced. Each man performs the activity that will define his spectatorial role throughout the film: Basil creates an image that he will assess, Dorian poses and eventually contemplates his own image, and Lord Henry chases and captures a butterfly – presumably yet another metaphoric activity for observing the emotions of others and influencing (not so subtly in this case) their lives. An equivalence is established between the levels as well, since Lord Henry pursues his butterfly at the same time that Basil puts the finishing touches on his portrait and Dorian poses. A dissolve from the live creature, to the dead mounted butterfly, to the portrait makes a clear connection between killing a creature and immortalizing it through art.

While Lord Henry functions in the film, as in the novella, to present a philosophy of pleasure to Dorian, he also – and far more obviously – functions in the film as a spectator within the film, to the extent that the portrait is initially as shrouded in secrecy to him as it is to the viewer. Rarely, if ever, do such spectators within the film function unequivocally in the literal "positions" of address that spectators adopt (see Browne 1975–6). In Lord Henry's case, the fact that a voice-over narrator, never associated with any single character in the film, introduces and contextualizes him makes it even more difficult to identify him as an authoritative presence in any simple sense. Rather, the central terms of spectatorship in the film are defined by the two polarities which Dorian and Lord Henry represent; mesmerized absorption in his own image, in the case of Dorian; somewhat distanced detachment, in the case of Lord Henry. Basil's role as an artist combines both forms of spectatorship without succumbing to either extreme – he is absorbed and obsessed by his painting, but with the image of another.

While the display of the painting occurs early in the film, in Basil's studio, its appearance is accompanied by enough delay and foregrounding to make the painting the central enigmatic object of the film. Our first sight of it coincides with Dorian's first look at the finished product. The portrait is thoroughly realist, an example of classical portraiture. The portrait also is a straightforward representation of what has been seen of Dorian, with two important exceptions

– the painting is presented in technicolor, and whereas Dorian has posed for the final moments of his sitting before another painting depicting a group of women bathers, the painting is not shown in the background to his portrait (Figures 1 and 2). The other objects surrounding him – a highbacked chair, a statue of a cat, and a clock – remain in the painting, so that the only erasure is that of the painting. The finished portrait is, of course, entirely in keeping with conventional portraiture, but what remains a matter of some curiosity is the placement of the painting of the women bathers behind Dorian as he poses. This painting is not insignificant in the initial mise-en-scène of the studio, since it creates a rhyming structure, against which the still unseen portrait of Dorian is measured.

The next view afforded of the painting occurs within the context of Dorian and Sibyl's relationship. Knowing that Dorian intends to marry Sibyl, Lord Henry has suggested that Dorian test her by asking her to spend the night with him. If she refuses, then she is truly the superior creature that Dorian believes her to be; if not, then Dorian will know not to marry her. But when Dorian asks her to spend the night, she agrees, and Dorian promptly rejects her. The rejection leads to her suicide, after which the portrait of Dorian is shown (again in technicolor) with a subtle change: the appearance of what the narrator, in voice-over, describes as a "cruel look about the mouth" (Figure 3).

The painting is not seen again until it has been completely transformed, with Dorian portrayed as a grotesque old man whose image records the kind of life he leads. The style of the painting has also changed. It is now in an expressionist mode, with excessive strokes, bold colors, and a myriad of indistiguishable objects within the frame (Figure 4). The revelation occurs after Basil has seen the changes that have occured in his painting, and Dorian murders him. Whereas Sibyl's death caused the "cruel look about the mouth" in the earlier painting, Dorian's murder of Basil causes blood to form on the hands of the deformed and deranged Dorian represented in the later version. Curiously, there is a change as well in the sexual quality of the transformed painting. While the evocation of aristocratic wealth in the film allows gay sexuality to be summoned and repressed simultaneously in the name of the effete taste and effeminate behavior presumed to be characteristic of the wealthy, there is nonetheless a delicate androgyny in the figure of Dorian represented in the first version of the painting. If the women bathers have disappeared in the portrait, it would be easy to see them as having been absorbed into it. But in the final painting, Dorian has become a parody of deranged masculinity.

The most striking changes in the painting, then, are the transformation of a young, somewhat androgynous gentleman into a decrepit old man, and the shift in style from realism to "expressionism."

114

Figure 1 The Picture of Dorian Gray. Dorian poses for the portrait before the painting of women bathers

Figure 2 The portrait without the painting in its background

Figure 3 The portrait develops a "cruel look about the mouth"

Figure 4 The portrait finally represents a horribly deformed Dorian

The painting changes location, as well. The first part of *The Picture of Dorian Gray*, concerned with the relationship between Dorian and Sibyl, and with the painting as an accurate projection of what we see, contrasts two radically different spaces, the aristocratic home (whether Dorian's or Basil's) and the music hall where Sibyl Vane performs, and where Dorian is treated in awe as a gentleman. The second part of the film, taken up with Dorian's relationship with the grown-up Gladys, contrasts two spaces within the house. When Dorian first notices what the narrator has called the "cruel look about the mouth" in the painting, he decides to hide it away in a room at the top of the stairs. The narrator describes Dorian's decision: "It would be mayhem to allow the thing to remain, even for an hour. Even in a room to which only his friends had access. Henceforth he must always be on his guard. Against everyone. At the top of the house was his old schoolroom, which had not been used for years. No one ever entered it." The painting thus acquires an aura of secrecy that rhymes with the opening of the film, but transforms secrecy into a threat.

Whereas Dorian negotiated comfortably the spatial opposition characteristic of the first part of the film, between two radically different class environments, the tension generated between the two areas of the house initiates conflict heretofore absent, with the added component of temporal opposition – the schoolroom is virtually the only reference in the film to Dorian's childhood. While the room is not often shown, it acquires narrative importance. The narrator says, for instance, that "He could not endure to be long out of England or to be separated from the picture. It was such a part of his life." The self-absorption present in the first part of the film is here quite literal. The risk of homosexual implications is managed by drawing an imaginary line across the threshold to the room, a line crossed only by men and never by women, thus identifying bonds between men in the past of childhood.

If the problem generated by the play of the two paintings in *Suspicion* concerns the authority of the father under siege, in this film there is no such equivalence between the classical, realist portraiture of the painting and an authoritative order. Rather, the two versions of the painting are both threats to an implied order, one which can only be set right by the realignment of reality and representation, and the emergence of that legendary resolution principle for which the classical Hollywood cinema is so famous and so derided – the happy heterosexual couple. For once the death of Dorian brackets the incestuous overtones of his relationship with Gladys, and once the restoration of the portrait to its original state and Dorian's accompanying death erases implicit homosexuality, the male-female couple, Gladys and her patient suitor David, can be united.

117

What remains a matter of some curiosity in this relationship between male/female, homosexual/heterosexual, incestuous/nonincestuous pairs, however, are the different ways in which painting is evoked in the course of the film to articulate narrative space. For while the portrait of Dorian in its changing status is the key image of the film, other devices of mise-en-scène partake of the conventions of painting. Particularly striking in this context is an opposition established early in the film between the portraiture of men and the framing of women. Basil's studio is defined as belonging to a community of men, with women framed in a literal and ostensible way. Before Dorian's arrival at the studio at the beginning of the film, Basil and Lord Henry are seated in the garden. In the background we see a woman sewing, framed in a doorway (Figure 5). The pose and the framing are familiar representations of women in Western oil painting, with the woman depicted as if she is observed, unawares, while engaged in a solitary activity, and of which Jean-Honoré Fragonard's *A Young Girl Reading* (1776) is one representative example (Figure 6). Men are defined in terms of how they "look," in both senses of the word, while women are defined in terms of how they look in only one sense of the word. That the only living, breathing female in this scene is the child Gladys emphasizes the rigid sexual hierarchy at work. And Gladys herself enters the scene of the studio through a doorway, and the construction of the shot echoes the scene outdoors.

So far, this sounds like the standard "man looks, woman is looked at" argument – e.g., that painting establishes only an apparent equivalence between the male or female object of the look, one betrayed by the status of woman as only the object of the look. The matter of curiosity to which I referred above, however, is that the mostly anonymous women who are framed in the film are done so in relationship to the position of the spectator *of* (not within) the film, i.e., not in relationship to the three male figures whose spectatorial activities function so centrally. Laura Mulvey's analysis of the classical Hollywood cinema assumes that the masculine film viewer is aligned in fairly unproblematic terms with the "ego ideal" represented by the male protagonist, but in the case of *The Picture of Dorian Gray*, no such alignment exists. The woman framed in the doorway is an object of spectacle in spite of the looks of the male characters, not because of them.

The composition of the woman in the doorway engaged in a solitary activity is repeated when the three men go to the "Two Turtles" to see Sybil Vane perform. We see Sibyl before them, singing in front of a *trompe-l'oeil* store front. Behind the three men, at the opposite end of the theater, there is an office, where a woman is seen through the open door at work at a desk (Figure 7). At one point during the

Figure 5 Basil and Lord Henry in the garden with a woman sewing framed in the doorway

Figure 6 Woman observed unawares: Jean-Honoré Fragonard's *A Young Girl Reading*

Figure 7 Basil, Dorian and Lord Henry at the "Two Turtles" with a woman at a desk framed in the doorway

Figure 8 Women framed on three levels off and on stage

performance, we see the stage at such an angle that images of women, framed identically, are seen on three levels: Sibyl on stage, her mother backstage sewing, and a woman dressing before a mirror (Figure 8). While these women so obsessively framed within doorways or stages are stereotypical objects of the presumably male gaze, there is a curious contradiction. For the male "spectators" – Dorian, Basil, Lord Henry – seem to be less interested in the spectacle before their eyes, and more interested in each other. And while each of the women, on her own terms, is a fairly straightforward "frame" of representation, the juxtaposition of the three levels creates an odd, asymmetrical effect. Between the first image of the woman framed in the doorway and the image of the three women, there is a relationship not unlike that between the original and transformed portrait of Dorian.

Another matter of some curiosity is that while the element of framing has been written about extensively in relationship to gender in film, in this case social class is as much of a determination as gender is; at the very least, the device of framing results from the intersection of class and gender determinations. For the woman framed in the doorway at the beginning of the film is a servant, and the women seen at the "Two Turtles" are defined not just by their sexual status but by their class status as well. While it is much more common for women to be represented as "framed," there are some instances where men – either working-class men at the music hall, or servants – are framed in ways similar to the woman sewing. At several moments in the film, servants are portrayed standing stiffly to attention while the wealthy people they serve eat or converse, and the effect here is quite similar to the woman-in-the-doorway motif.

I am suggesting, then, that the trope of portraiture is a figure of spectatorship to the extent that in each case, a mode of observation – from narcissistic self-absorption to detached mockery – is foregrounded. There is no single position authorized by each individual instance of portraiture, from Dorian's portrait to the framing of women and servants; rather, spectatorship takes shape as the possible relationships between these different views and the corresponding sites of observation. What seems to me most crucial about this particular example, however, is that it puts into question the automatic equivalence some have assumed between spectatorship in the classical cinema and men possessing women. Not that men don't possess women in this film, but rather, even within the textual system, "possession" is a complex process involving the evocation and denial of male homoerotic bonds. In addition, the intersection between gender and class in the film does not reduce in any obvious way to a "pure" example of sexual difference, because the notion of property is so excessively defined in class terms as well as gendered ones.

121

As an instance of that ubiquitous entity, the classical Hollywood cinema, *The Picture of Dorian Gray* is both typical and atypical, as is undoubtedly the case with any Hollywood film. Like many literary adaptations of the 1940s, there is a self-aggrandizing quality about the film, and the numerous references to high art and aristocratic privilege serve simultaneously as windows to a fantasy land and as a self-promoting strategy. Unlike other films of the 1940s which deploy opposing definitions of "realist" versus "modern" art in order to elevate the status of the former at the expense of the latter (Waldman 1982), Lewin's film does not condemn any particular version of the aesthetic as inherently corrupt; rather, any and all forms of representation are susceptible to excess. Within the specularity of portraiture in the film, there is the suggestion that spectatorship involves the simultaneous erection of boundaries and their dissolution. Does this therefore mean that *The Picture of Dorian Gray* is "subversive," or the exception to the rule of classical cinema? I think not. That a film like *The Picture of Dorian Gray* sits so comfortably within the classical cinema, while engaging with an undeniable homoerotic component for spectatorship (at least as far as men are concerned), suggests that textual analysis will perhaps always uncover forms of spectatorship that both conform to and exceed what is assumed to be typical.

6

STAR-GAZING

The analysis of stars has become one of the most significant areas of inquiry in recent film studies, largely in response to the limitations of apparatus theory. The study of stardom has obvious importance for the understanding of spectatorship in mainstream cinema. No matter how significant the textual details of individual films or the scope of a director's vision, for instance, the role of the star is the most visible and popular reference point for the pleasures of the cinema. It has taken some time for the study of stars to re-emerge in film studies of the past ten years, and this is due in part to the changing definition of the field. One tradition of film criticism to which 1970s film studies reacted and situated itself negatively was characterized by a focus on the star, but in uncritical terms. In other words, so-called traditional film critics did not problematize or analyze the actor's signifying role – i.e., the place of the star within the larger system of the classical cinema. If the study of stars and stardom has, then, re-emerged in film studies as an important area of concern, this is due both to the influence of theories of the apparatus, and to challenges to those theories.

For in apparatus theory, the star is just one more element of the signifying system of the classical cinema, an instance like many others of Metz's "secondary cinematic identification" (Metz 1975: 47). And in textual analysis, the star is a function of the narrative and visual system at work within the film, perhaps *inflected* by the aura of the star constructed outside the film, but nonetheless contained by that system. It is interesting in this respect to compare Raymond Bellour's textual analysis of the crop-duster sequence in Hitchcock's *North by Northwest* (1959) with James Naremore's analysis of Cary Grant's role in the film, which foregrounds attributes of performance largely absent from most textual analyses (Bellour 1975b; Naremore 1988: 213–35). Contemporary studies of stars have challenged the assumptions of apparatus theory and textual analysis, primarily by focussing on the intertextual system at work in the creation of the personae of stars. If

123

the cinematic institution consists of a wide range of texts, from individual films to fan magazines to televised entertainment programs to advertising, then unifying models of the apparatus or textuality may well be in need of serious revision, at the very least in order to accommodate the fact that different signifying systems function in not necessarily harmonious ways. So too does cinematic spectatorship take on a different cast when perceived through the phenomenon of stardom understood intertextually, since the power of Metz's primary cinematic identification or Baudry's transcendental subject is less easily reduced to the camera or the projection situation itself.

The work of Richard Dyer has provided many of the fundamental assumptions for the study of stars upon which later work has been based. In *Stars* (1979), Dyer explores stars and responses to them in terms of the issues of contradiction they raise, thus challenging the notion of a seamless flow of meaning. Since "contradiction" is a widely used term throughout contemporary critical theory, it is worth examining the different ways in which the term is used in Dyer's analysis. In relation to what Dyer calls "structured polysemy" (quite similar to Barthes's "limited plurality"), the star image consists of a variety of complex interwoven elements, the complexity ("polysemy") held in check by some kind of institutional force ("structured"). While these elements may not necessarily be in contradiction with each other, the very presence of multiple determinations makes it possible to conceptualize tensions among them.

Star images may conceal or hide tensions, and a concept of "negotiation" (similar to that discussed in chapter 4) thus emerges as a way of understanding how the relationships between different determinations function successfully, or not. One example Dyer cites is Jane Fonda. The "sex star" and the "actor" parts of her persona were considered, early in her film career, as "separate and perhaps contradictory." Dyer also notes that "[h]er adoption of radical politics raised much sharper contradictions" (1979: 89). According to this line of reasoning, her more recent incarnation as exercise-video superstar is yet another level of negotiation of those contradictions, but one which is much more successful. For through the celebration of exercise and fitness, apparent feminist ideals of autonomy and self-determination are made compatible with a stereotyped view of the female body. One could argue, of course, that the two stereotypes – the sex kitten and the healthy, fit female – are not interchangeable, thus allowing the potential contradiction of which Dyer speaks. But a close look at numerous segments of Fonda's exercise tapes (the "buttock tucks" are particularly good examples) demonstrates that the conventional codes for representing the objectified female body are not so far removed from those of the exercise videos.

Dyer's larger point is that these contradictions made visible through stars speak to fissures within dominant ideology. In this sense his work is representative of a major movement in film studies, toward affirming contradiction as the site where radical contestation begins. In a discussion of Orrin E. Klapp's categories of "reinforcement," "seduction," and "transcendance" as the three possible relationships people may have to dominant norms, Dyer questions the ease with which one can distinguish between "seduction" and "transcendance" (1962; cited in Dyer 1979: 27–8). Dyer asks: "Can one not see both, and especially transcendence, as simply providing a 'safety-valve' for discontent, and by providing expression of it siphoning it off as a substantial subversive force?" The specific example to which Dyer responds is Klapp's suggestion that a teenage girl who enjoyed and identified with Sandra Dee as Gidget because of her own love for surfing was offered "a springboard by which . . . [she] can vicariously leap from femininity into a role usually reserved for boys" (1962: 234; cited in Dyer 1979: 28). In response to his own question, Dyer goes on to suggest, as have many others, especially those influenced by cultural studies, that "the system is a good deal more 'leaky' than many people would currently maintain. In my view, to assert the total closure of the system is essentially to deny the validity of class/sex/ race struggle and their reproduction at all levels of society and in all human practices." Furthermore, the Sandra Dee example cited by Klapp stresses "both the possibility of a leak at a very unprestigious, ordinary, exploitative part of the system, and the role of the spectator in making the image subversive for *her*" (28).

The "role of the spectator" alluded to is, of course, indicative of the force behind much of the interest currently paid to stars. Dyer himself is careful to specify that not all contradictions speak to radical possibilities, and the question about "safety valves" raised above emerges again, for instance, in considering the tension between anomie and alienation ("You feel anomic because you are outside society in general; you feel alienated because you are outside the ruling groups in society" [59]). For how, Dyer asks, does one distinguish between what are "real challenges to the status quo and the dominant ideology" from what are simply "holidays from it" (59). As I've suggested elsewhere in this book, the persistence of this duality between "real" and "ungenuine" alternatives has made it difficult to find a "real" alternative to the limitations of the apparatus model. For in criticizing the notion of dominant ideology as monolithic, an unfortunate reluctance to see *any* ideology as dominant has occurred. In the Gidget example cited above, for instance, it seems to me that far more crucial than conventional femininity versus activity reserved for boys, and even more crucial than the implicit distinction between the passive female consumer of the ideal femininity embodied by Sandra Dee and the active teenager who "subverts" that image, is the fact that – perhaps like a Jane Fonda exercise tape – images such as Gidget offer *simultaneously* the embodiment of stereotypical femininity and releases from it. Certainly it has been crucial to contest readings that would posit a wholly successful system of control and manipulation as the essence of mass culture, but all too frequently what is left out of the "leaks" is the complex way in which subversion and the status quo are not necessarily neatly opposed, but rather constantly enmeshed with each other.

In this context, it is useful to look back at a book originally published in 1957 by Edgar Morin, a figure whose work has far more relevance to the agendas of contemporary film studies than is generally recognized. In *Les Stars* (1972), Morin argues, as he does in other works, like *Le Cinéma, ou l'Homme imaginaire* (1956), that distinct to the experience of film viewing is the capacity of the medium to maintain a connection between two apparently contradictory entities, whether ancient mythology and technology or human agency and robotized motion. Morin's argument in *Les Stars*, that film actors are the equivalent of twentieth-century gods, and that the cinema therefore is a medium which satisfies ancient desires, is not particularly provocative or original in itself. But the argument calls upon a notion of contradiction that provides a useful perspective on the concept of contradiction in contemporary theory. For Morin, the cinema embodies contradictory desires, and the star is perhaps the most stunning and condensed version of this embodiment. Hence, Morin speaks of the actor as the "unique synthesis" of physical beauty and mask, as simultaneously a unique personality and an automaton (43, 105). He describes the star system itself as a curious mixture of accessibility and inaccessibility: "A prodigious technique of encouragement/discouragement. The access to stardom depends on chance" (49). The god-like quality of the star is simultaneous with the commodity quality of the star; indeed, Morin stresses that the two sides of the star's status as both god and commodity are "two aspects of the same reality: the needs of man in twentieth century capitalist society" (102). Such invocations of an entire century are not particularly useful in specifying how stars function differently than any other component of twentieth-century capitalism, yet Morin does suggest that specific to stars is, precisely, that contradictory quality.

Morin describes, then, a contradictory quality which is fully part of the institution of the cinema, while for Dyer this contradictory quality is more crucially defined as a path of resistance to dominant ideology. The difference is more than one of degree, since the contradictory quality of stardom in Morin's analysis is not necessarily linked to any subversion of ideology. This isn't to say that Dyer's account presup-

126

poses all contradiction to have a radical inspiration. But since Dyer's point of departure is the opposition common in 1970s theory between an ideological monolith and contradiction, then virtually any example of the latter acquires, by definition, a potentially oppositional function. Many theorists accepted this opposition too quickly, assuming that the nature of classical narrative is such that all tensions, disruptions, and contradictions are regulated and contained by the hierarchical patterns of dominant ideology. But I find the opposite extreme equally problematic – the assumption, that is, that "contradiction" and "subversion" are indistinguishable.

I would like to consider this issue of contradiction and star personae in relation to a specific example – the star image of Bette Davis. Like virtually all actresses of the golden age of Hollywood, Davis's image circulated in a variety of contexts, including fan magazines, women's magazines, and advertising. Davis's appeal was obvious from the kinds of letters – genuine or not – on display in fan magazines. One fan writes to *Photoplay* in 1933, for instance, that unlike Constance Bennett, "Bette Davis has glamour – gorgeous glamour. Maybe I owe Constance Bennett an apology, but I have written the way I feel" ("With Brickbats and Bouquets" 1933a). Another fan encourages "all true Southerners" to see *Cabin in the Cotton*, in which Davis was "never more exquisite" ("With Brickbats and Bouquets" 1933b). During World War II, she was visible as a promoter of worthy causes, like the USO. Davis's signature appears on inspirational essays in the fan magazines encouraging women to behave responsibly and patriotically during the war, like "Code for American Girls" and "Don't be a Draft Bride" (Davis 1940; 1941a).

Davis's star persona is typical to the extent that like other stars – female stars in particular – her image circulated in a wide variety of forms. Nonetheless, the sheer visibility of Davis is exceptional, particularly since that visibility lasted for such a long time, from the early 1930s until her death in 1989. In the popular fan magazine *Photoplay*, for instance, no single actress appears in as many contexts as Davis does – advertisements for her films as well as for consumer products, letters to the editor, gossip columns, advice columns (Davis authored the advice column "What Shall I Do?" in *Photoplay* in 1943), and feature stories. Davis was also a popular focus for women's magazines like *Ladies' Home Journal* (Davis 1941b; 1952), *McCall's* (Cameron 1974), and *Good Housekeeping* (Baskette 1963), and the range of dates of this sampling of articles is indicative of Davis's staying power. Although Davis may have been particularly appealing to women fans, features in other magazines and revues without a specific gender focus are evidence of her wide and diverse appeal.

Richard De Cordova has noted that the emergence of the star system is the result of a series of stages, beginning with the foregrounding of the cinematic apparatus itself rather than the human figures it depicted, and moving later to attention to the "picture player," that is, the actor as purely the embodiment of a cinematic role. The film "star" was the result of a fascination with the actor's life outside the movie theater (1985, 1990). The possibility for overlap is obvious, whether in real-life relationships that mirror the movies (Marlene Dietrich and Josef Von Sternberg, Katharine Hepburn and Spencer Tracy) or in real-life stories that seem to imitate the films in which an actor is featured. But the possibility for dissonance is there as well. Morin claims, for instance, that the attention to the private lives of the stars makes for more intimacy between spectator and actor, but this is only the case if one assumes that "private life" always signifies intimacy. In chapter 3 I mentioned the example of Marlene Dietrich; the constant attention in fan magazines to her role as devoted mother and *hausfrau* at heart was a means of managing her provocative image (in several senses – as sexually powerful and sexually ambivalent, as masculine and feminine, heterosexual and lesbian simultaneously) projected on screen, and not exclusively of bringing actor and fan in a closer relationship. In the case of Bette Davis, too, the constant attention to her belief that a woman should be a devoted wife (during her first and second marriages, at least) functioned as much as a way of regulating her on-screen image as of drawing fans closer to her.

One of the difficulties and challenges of analyzing "a" star image is that the sheer wealth and diversity of material resists any easy categorization. This is particularly true in the case of someone like Davis whose image was constructed across so many different forms. Indeed, inconsistency, change and fluctuation are characteristic of star images, as if the "real" person constituted by star publicity is as open to a change of definition as the actor's roles themselves. Maria LaPlace has noted that the fan magazines tended to portray Davis as a woman for whom domestic considerations were secondary, and who was totally devoted to her career. I have found contradictory evidence in this regard, including fan magazine articles which take great pains to stress that Davis was a traditionally minded wife *at the same time* that she was devoted to her career. In addition, Davis's own description of her failed marriages in her autobiographies suggests the supposed incompatibility (for women) of career and family in a cynical rather than an emancipatory sense (Davis 1962; Davis with Herskowitz 1987). Thus I think it is important to stress that, much more than the narratives that unfold on screen, the "text" of an actor's image is full of discrepancies and incoherencies. The complexity of this "text" might well serve as a useful counter-example for analysts of the textual system of the classical cinema. The very nature of the texts one has to analyze in the case of stars makes it impossible to come to any homogenizing conclusions. In other words, the analysis of stars may serve to dispel many of the illusions about the very possibility of non-contradictory theoretical absolutes, which still seem to characterize much work in cinema studies, especially insofar as classical narrative is concerned.

In an analysis of how the persona of Bette Davis functions in the 1942 film *Now, Voyager*, LaPlace offers a series of speculations concerning the relationship between the female star and female spectators. LaPlace notes that the film very definitely presents an itinerary of consumerist perfection – the dumpy, neurotic spinster Charlotte Vale is transformed into a healthy, glamorous independent woman, and the primary yardstick of that change is her appearance – weight loss, cosmetics, elegant coiffure, and glamourous clothing. LaPlace argues, however, that this discourse of consumerism is not totalizing or monolithic, mainly because of two factors. First, to whatever extent consumerism may rely on the definition of woman as an object to be made desirable to men, nonetheless consumerist discourse situates woman as subject, and therefore opens many unintentional possibilities for the articulation of female desire. Noting, for instance, that cigarette advertising directed at women relied on notions of choice and freedom and implicit feminism, LaPlace says: "Choice and freedom for women in the ads became synonymous with the mass-produced goods of the market, robbing them of their connotation of structural social change. Nevertheless, the effects of the idea that freedom and choice were legitimately desirable for women could not be entirely contained by Big Business" (1987: 140).

Second, Laplace says that the discourse of consumerism in *Now, Voyager* intersects with two other discourses, those of female fiction and of the star image of Davis, both of which mediate the objectification of woman with her autonomy and self-determination. Davis does function in the film as a mistress of consumerism; LaPlace notes that the film was promoted as "a how-to-be-beautiful guide with Davis as chief instructor" (141). Yet, given how consumerism engages with both the image of Davis as an unconventional woman devoted to career and the dynamics of woman's fiction, the film does not function exclusively as a socializing tool for conventional female desirability. Describing the conclusion of the film, in which Charlotte Vale commits herself to raising her former lover's child rather than to a romantic relationship with him, LaPlace says that "spectators with the knowledge of the Bette Davis discourse can interpret the ending such that it can be made to speak for women: knowing that Davis values work, mastery, and creativity, Charlotte's 'motherhood', as much as her new activities with Cascade [the psychiatric hospital where she began her recovery], takes on the connotations of the Davis image" (165).

Discussions of female spectatorship in mainstream film have been so influenced by Laura Mulvey's model of the woman as object and the man as subject that readings like LaPlace's, in which women are defined as subjects as well as objects, challenge the always–already dichotomous model of the classical cinema. Indeed, much of the current interest in stars needs to be understood within the specific context of film studies, particularly insofar as challenges to theories of the cinematic apparatus are concerned. Yet what has proven difficult to the challenge to the apparatus model in question is precisely *how* to theorize the simultaneity of opposing positions and points of view. LaPlace makes limited claims for the Bette Davis image, but they are feminist claims in that textual analysis here provides the possibility of contestatory subject positions. In LaPlace's analysis, the Bette Davis image offers, if not a feminist ideal, then at the very least a progressive grid through which the debilitating effects of consumerism are mediated.

The polarity of sexual difference, of the active male and the passive female, has been read in recent film theory as totally synonomous with the subject/object relationship. As a result, any relations that either do not conform to the active male/passive female model, or are not male/female in the literal sense, have been the object of two completely divergent responses. Consider, for instance, the relationship between two females, Davis and the child she chooses to raise, in *Now, Voyager*. According to the institutional model, this relationship should be merely a substitute for the classic male/female dichotomy; Charlotte's relationship to Tina is totally mediated by the absent father. Alternatively, those who challenge the apparatus model (like LaPlace) see in the foregrounding of the female–female relation a displacement of the male subject. As Lea Jacobs puts it in her reading of the film, "Tina, the stars, they all serve as replacements for the man, yet the fact remains that Charlotte refuses the man" (1981: 103.)

LaPlace's discussion does not rely exclusively on the terms of the film, and the analysis of stars has offered, precisely, a way to move beyond textual analysis, particularly its tendency to repeat the same structure again and again (although Jacobs' analysis of *Now, Voyager* demonstrates that textual analysis need not be so invested in the repetition of oedipal narrative). As convincing as LaPlace's argument about Davis's autonomy is, that sense of autonomy is defined strictly in terms of a notion of "independence" synonomous with career. Yet Davis's much publicized (and self-confessed) "failures" at marriage serve to emphasize the continued duality of the private and the public for women. I noted above the sheer diversity of material about stars, and I do not want to suggest that underlying that diversity is a master narrative holding all the different threads together. But particularly striking in Davis's case is a notion of self-promotion that seems to me more complicated than concepts of a "progressive" discourse would suggest. Self-promotion is contradiction personified. Self-promotion allows – indeed, encourages – one to see Bette Davis as a product of and contained by the power of the marketplace, and at the same time as an autonomous subject making choices.

I am not so convinced that the apparent control exercised by Bette Davis over her own image constitutes a feminist alternative. Certainly, autonomy and self-determination are important ideals of feminism, but in Davis's case those ideals are so channeled into readily available myths of female power – i.e., patriarchal myths of women's power – that one has to question their contestatory value. And while feminist film theory has so insisted upon the polarity of the male as subject and female as object, and woman's identification with the ideal of "to-be-looked-atness" (to cite Laura Mulvey's phrase), this does not necessarily mean that attending to other possibilities (like female-to-female relationships) will liberate radical potential.

LaPlace notes in her discussion of each of the discourses informing *Now, Voyager* that relationships between women are central. When consumerism, for women, is defined in terms of "to-be-looked-atness," then the ubiquity of the male gaze is affirmed. The importance of relations between women thus becomes obscured. Yet advertising specifically, and the appeals of consumerism in general, often take competition and rivalry among women as a distinct theme. This means that we can isolate two threads – the relationship between Bette Davis as a self-promoter and the institutions of the cinema, on the one hand, and the ideal of consumerism (whether in advertising or films) as it relates to competition between women, on the other. Both of these threads foreground the problematic dualism between the active, dynamic, and potentially progressive spectator and the passive, controlled, and manipulated spectator. As has undoubtedly become obvious by now, I think it is impossible to separate them with any certainty. Any such separation risks affirming, in the name of radical alternatives, a very limited view of the complexities of spectatorship.

In the construction of Davis's star persona, relationships between women take several forms. Her "advice column" in *Photoplay* was aimed specifically at women; and Davis was a familiar presence in the advertising of various products aimed toward female consumers. In these advertisements, Davis's image wavers between accessibility and inaccessibility. An advertisement for jewelry shows Davis, seated alone, in an image from *Juarez*, and a title announces "This Glamour can be Yours" (*Photoplay* 1939). The jewelry is a tie-in with the film;

the text reads: "With heirloom jewelry definitely in, what more thrill-ing costume accessories imaginable than these divine adaptations from the Empress' priceless court jewels in Warner Bros.' two-million-dollar production *Juarez*." Davis's pose is virtually identical in an advertise-ment for Westmore make-up, although she is now dressed in a bath-robe, seated at a vanity table (*Photoplay* 1940). If the jewelry advertise-ment draws the inaccessible into the realm of the accessible ("Now at your favorite shop!"), the make-up advertisement plays more strongly on the theme of accessibility. An anonymous young woman is pictured in miniature next to Davis, her pose quite similar to that of the star. "Playing the lead on a big date?" reads the caption underneath her photograph. "You'll be a standout in the crowd, center of all eyes, with Westmore make-up, as used by Hollywood stars."

Now many female stars have advertised and (fictitiously or not) authored advice columns; indeed, the very nature of the star system requires such activity. In Davis's case, what is unique is not only her visibility, but also the way her on-screen persona plays so consistently across the register of female-to-female relationships. In other words, there is an ideal fit between the address to female consumers in advertising and the film roles themselves. Female rivalry is central to the construction of Davis's star image. Virtually all of her film roles play upon competition between women in one form or another. Her self-promotion through advertising draws simultaneously on her simil-arity to other women and her nonetheless unique status as a star. Numerous myths about female rivalries, whether with important women in her own life or other actresses, inflect the narrative of her career. These intertwining motifs of female rivalry in its different forms and Davis's star image exemplify the shifting values and inflections that film spectatorship acquires.

If one of the most persistent motifs in Davis's screen roles is female rivalry, the motif is all the more striking for the match it makes with the construction of Davis's off-screen persona. In her films, the theme of female rivalry takes two particular forms: struggle between the mother and the daughter over autonomy, or competition between two women for the affections of a man. Sometimes the two forms overlap, as in *Mr. Skeffington* (1944), in which Davis is threatened by her daugh-ter's youth as her own beauty wanes, a threat which culminates in the daughter's marriage to her mother's former suitor. Sometimes the two forms inflect each other, as in *Now, Voyager*, in which the rivalry with the unseen wife of Jerry (Paul Henreid) develops at the same time as Charlotte Vale's battle with her own mother for autonomy, and Charlotte's "adoption" of Jerry's child Tina becomes a way of negotiating both forms of female rivalry. Frequently, when the rivalry between two women takes place over a man's affections, the relation-

Figure 9 Miriam Hopkins and Bette Davis in *Old Acquaintance*

ship between the two women is far more foregrounded than either of the women's relations to the man in question. In *Old Acquaintance* (1943) a requisite love triangle operates, but the intense and complicated friendship between Davis and Miriam Hopkins provides far more dramatic fodder than the attraction to the man (Figure 9). And at the same time, the two female stars are contrasted, with Hopkins's ruffled blonde femininity in opposition to Davis's far more androgynous, and often almost butch seriousness. Such visual and behavioral contrast is a typical feature of the rivalries. In *The Old Maid* (1939), Davis and Hopkins play cousins (Figure 10), both of them are typically feminine

133

Figure 10 Miriam Hopkins and Bette Davis in *The Old Maid*

at the film's beginning; but the aftereffects of Hopkins's bitter jealousy turn Davis into a stereotypical spinster, in sharp contrast to her cousin.

Again, there is a "real life" echo. One of the most consistent elements in stories of Davis's life and career is the influence of her mother Ruthie. In various narratives of Davis's life, the strength of the connection between the mother and the daughter wavers between obsession and simple devotion. Whereas in some cases Ruthie can be read as a model of the devoted mother determined to give her daughter the chances she herself didn't have, in others Ruthie comes across as a stereotypical stage mother. One often repeated anecdote supposedly relates an episode early in Davis's stage career. As Davis tells the story in one of her autobiographies, *The Lonely Life*, she had won a bit part in a summer stock company in Rochester, New York. Her mother was unable to accompany Davis, but told her daughter as her train left the station to "[l]earn the part of Pearl. The actress playing the part is going to have an accident." While Davis describes her skepticism, she also claims to "have learned by then that Ruthie's hunches were not to be sneezed at." Sure enough, the actress playing the part of Pearl suffered a fall, and Davis's advance preparation earned her the part (1962/1990: 55–6).

There is the proverbial chicken-and-egg enigma about Davis's "real life" versus her "screen life," and which imitates which. The "life imitates art" (and vice versa) syndrome is a crucial component of the construction of star personae. The anecdote about Ruthie's premonition is worthy of many scenes in Davis's own films. In fact, the episode echoes uncannily a scene in Davis's most famous female-rivalry picture, *All About Eve* (1950). Karen (Celeste Holm), wanting to teach Margo Channing (Davis) a lesson, fakes car trouble and forces the actress to miss her performance, so that understudy Eve (Anne Baxter) – who apparently adores Margo but wants her success – can take over. Of course, one presumes that Ruthie did not deliberately arrange for the actress to fall (as Karen arranged for car trouble in *All About Eve*); but the anecdotal quality of the episode with Ruthie gives the mother–daughter relationship a variety of possible contours, including the relationship later enacted in *All About Eve* by Celeste Holm and Bette Davis. Many years later, Davis's own maternal role in the mother–daughter bond was villainized in the story told by her own daughter B. D. Hyman, who wrote a *Mommie Dearest*-style memoir of her years with Davis. Hyman offers her own interpretation of Davis's relationship with Ruthie. As Davis's daughter tells it, Ruthie "had seen in her older daughter the chance to grab for the gold ring" and the rivalry thus described once again echoes Davis's on-screen rivalries (1985: 47).

Part of Davis's image has been built on her supposed actual rivalries with other women, particularly Miriam Hopkins and Joan Crawford (Stine 1974/1984; Considine 1989; Quirk 1990). That lesbian rumors circulated about both of these women – Hopkins in particular – evokes the homoerotic component of female rivalry, and in any case lesbianism was not far removed from Davis's own star image (Quirk 1990: 23, 425–6). Indeed, some of Davis's films have been re-read by lesbian viewers, including a hilarious send up in *Dry Kisses Only* (1990), a video by Kaucyila Brooke and Jane Cottis. While Brooke and Cottis's tape challenges the presumed exclusive heterosexuality of Hollywood, the lesbian rumors about Davis do not, on their own terms, provide a radical or otherwise contestatory edge to Davis's career. For such rumors create the possibility for endless denial, speculation, and – most important – narrative. While the rivalries with other women often emphasized *their* presumably lesbian attraction to Davis, Davis herself offered enough comments about other actresses simultaneously to confirm the rumors some of the time and deny them at others. Such radically opposing interpretations are integral to the persona.

The difference between Davis's reputed relationships with Miriam Hopkins and Mary Astor is illuminating in this respect. For in the two films featuring Davis and Hopkins (*The Old Maid* and *Old Acquaintance*), as well as in *The Great Lie* (1941), which features Davis and Astor, the dynamics of female rivalry are quite similar. In all three films, two women compete over a man, but far more importance is given to the relationship between the women. The relationship between Davis and Hopkins emphasizes the hostile aspects of female rivalry. Hopkins was known as a difficult actress in any case, and various stories have circulated in Davis biographies to explain Hopkins's particular hostility to Davis, from romantic rivalry over a man, to lesbian rivalry, to Hopkins' jealousy over her loss of plum roles (especially *Jezebel*, in which she had played the role of Julie on stage) (see Considine 1989: 148–51). Davis herself claimed late in her career that Hopkins and Faye Dunaway (with whom she worked on *The Disappearance of Aimee*) were the only two actresses who were impossible to work with ("Any race for witchery featuring Miss Hopkins and Miss Dunaway would most definitely end up in a tie" [Davis 1962/1990: 258]). Famous physical confrontational scenes in *The Old Maid* and *Old Acquaintance* have served, then, in accounts of Davis's life and career, as legendary culminations of life-meets-art (Quirk 1990: 196–9, 256–60).

Davis's relationship with Mary Astor in the filming of *The Great Lie*, however, emphasizes the more positive and mutually supportive elements of female rivalry (Figure 11). As Mary Astor described the production of the film, Davis was unhappy with the triteness of the original script, and persuaded Astor that it was up to them to spice it up. The script held promise, precisely in terms of the dynamics of female rivalry. *The Great Lie* tells the story of a man caught between two women, Julie, a sweet, honest creature (Davis), and Sandra, a self-centered bitch (Astor). Briefly and illegally married to the latter, he comes to his senses and marries the former. But the husband disappears in Latin America, and the first wife discovers she is pregnant. Davis convinces Astor to give the child to her. When the husband miraculously returns, Astor decides she wants to renege on the bargain, but once the "great lie" is revealed, the man chooses to remain with Davis.

136

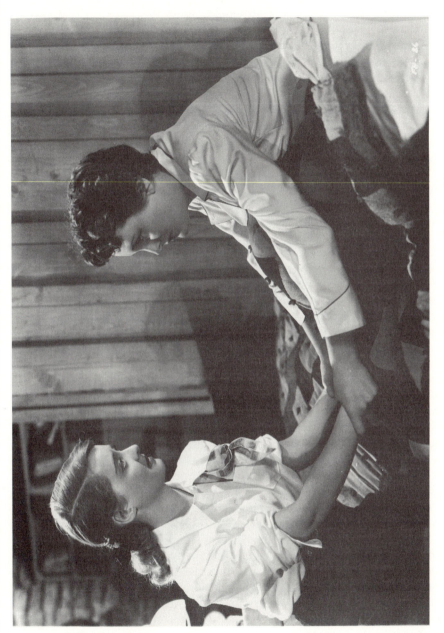

Figure 11 Bette Davis and Mary Astor in *The Great Lie*

Astor describes the "interesting part, the fun part" of the rewritten script (with the emphasis on the two women more than the couple) as "the relationship between the two women – the savage bargaining – their strange life together . . . while awaiting the child. These are the scenes that Bette and I rewrote, and they were real 'female' scenes. A couple of cats who had to shield their claws for expediency, with the continual threat that one or the other would blow the whole setup" (1967: 153–4). Yet the rivalry was only possible, as Astor tells it, by virtue of the collaboration between the two women, who became "as simpatico as a pair of dancers as we worked out the story, constantly by building up the importance and impact of the character of Sandra" (Astor 1959: 203). The Astor–Davis collaboration stands, then, as a corrective of sorts to the Hopkins–Davis hostility; according to Astor, "Bette has always had the wisdom, rare in this business, to know that a star cannot stand alone; she appears to much better advantage if the supporting actors are good" (Astor 1959: 204). Like the advertisements in which she is featured, with their competing and often simultaneous themes of accessibility and inaccessibility, the motif of female rivalry in Davis's star persona encourages opposing interpretations.

I have emphasized in this chapter that the dynamics of stardom and spectatorship in the case of Bette Davis encourage the opposing terms of love and hate, devotion and obsession, life and the movies, butch and femme, to inflect each other constantly. I am suggesting that the appeal of stardom is that of constant reinvention, the dissolution of contraries, the embrace of wildly opposing terms. It has been important to some feminist critics to recognize actors as artists who contribute actively and passionately to the cinema, particularly when those actors are women whose creative roles are so often denigrated or subjugated to the authority of the male director or producer (see Clarke and Simmonds 1980), and I think this represents a crucial revision of 1970s film theory. Yet at the same time, the appeal to agency, creativity, and autonomy needs to recognize the historical and cultural limitations of these notions. The homilies of resistant-versus-complicit readings that have been so central to film studies in general, and spectatorship studies in particular, are bound by such limitations, particularly insofar as they project an either/or alternative echoing 1970s theory. The persistent duality of being inside dominant ideology and complicit, versus being outside it and therefore resistant, reduces politics to a question of reading, and the complexities of spectatorship to facile and static opposition.

The dynamics of female rivalry as I have described them in Bette Davis's career play on a variety of oppositions. But one more dimension not so often played out in the intertextual commentary that constructs a star persona is race. Davis is known for anti-racist stances, and a black magazine writer once described her as far more appealing to black audiences than other white female stars, in part because of her "underdog" status in her films: "she came from behind and, win or lose, always played the game. Blacks wanted this kind of rebellion and this chance of winning in the 1930s and 1940s; we didn't have it, but we could root for those who did" (C. Davis 1978: 30). This enthusiasm is reiterated by James Baldwin, who described Davis's performance in the 1942 film *In This, Our Life* (in which she plays a rich, spoiled woman who commits a hit-and-run accident and puts the blame on a black chauffeur) as "ruthlessly accurate." Davis became, in Baldwin's words, "the toast of Harlem" (1976/1990: 70).

In the construction of female rivalry in *The Great Lie*, a significant contrast between Julie and Sandra concerns their relationships with their servants. A sour white maid tends to Sandra's apartment with disdain and sarcasm, while Davis's household is presided over by a black maid Violet, played by Hattie McDaniel (Figure 12). Violet is a maternal surrogate to Davis, and the supposed warmth and devotion of their relationship is contrasted with Astor's haughty, detached attitude toward her servant. The celebration of the wedding of Davis and George Brent is even marked by festivities among the black servants. Hattie McDaniel's role may be racist, but her performance is as distinctive as Davis's or Astor's. I have no idea whether her role was in any way influenced by the reported changes that Mary Astor and Bette Davis made to the script of the film; since McDaniel was on loan to Warner Brothers after the success of her Oscar-winning performance in *Gone With the Wind*, it seems likely that her role was intended from the start to be important. Yet according to McDaniel's biographer, Davis feared that McDaniel would be a scene-stealer, and campaigned to have some of her scenes cut (Jackson 1990: 74). This anecdote contradicts other stories about Davis's career; in 1962, for instance, she was one of the first women to receive the Opportunity Pioneer Award, and she was cited for being "the first to encourage the casting of Negroes in other than stereotype movie roles" (*Jet* 1962).

If *The Great Lie* dramatizes the ever shifting dynamics of Bette Davis's rivalries with women, then, those dynamics cannot be easily fitted into a model of "progressive" spectatorship. The female rivalry between Astor and Davis needs to be specified as having to do with *white* women. But if it is easy, in purely textual terms, to see McDaniel's role as serving primarily to supplement the opposition between Davis and Astor, the perspective of spectatorship – in this case, of examining how spectators view black and white and how spectators view in and through black and white – problematizes an easy division between a text and its reception. At the same time, while the gendered contours of spectatorship have received extensive attention in film studies, rarely is spectatorship examined in terms of

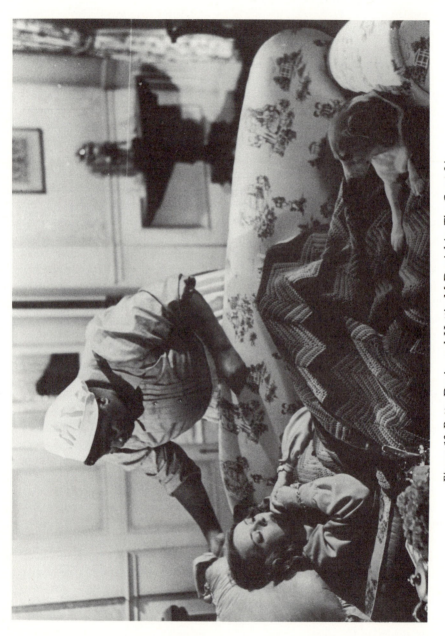

Figure 12 Bette Davis and Hattie McDaniel in *The Great Lie*

race – in the case of Bette Davis, for instance, rarely is it acknowledged that feminist readings of her appeal may project specifically white ideals of feminism onto the female spectator. In the next chapter, I turn in more detail to a consideration of the components of white spectatorship.

7

WHITE SPECTATORSHIP AND GENRE-MIXING

Prior to the televised broadcast of the Academy Awards in 1991, Barbara Walters' traditional pre-Oscar interview show included a segment with Whoopi Goldberg, who was highly favored to win the supporting-actress Oscar for her role in *Ghost*. Goldberg noted that were she to win (which she did), it would be the first such award in fifty years – referring, of course, to Hattie McDaniel's supporting-actress Oscar in 1939 for *Gone with the Wind*, in the stereotypical maid/mammy role that she re-created shortly after in *The Great Lie*. Intentionally or not, Goldberg's remark suggested that as far as black actresses and the roles they enact in Hollywood cinema are concerned, little has changed in the years separating Hattie McDaniel and Whoopi Goldberg.

To be sure, Goldberg has demonstrated versatility far beyond the mammy stereotype that defined McDaniel's career. Yet there is something odd about the fact that Goldberg's Oscar-winning performance should have come for a role in which she serves as handmaiden to the interrupted romance of two white yuppies. Indeed, the similarity between Goldberg's role in *Ghost* and McDaniel's portrayal of the mammy has been noted by Donald Bogle. The character Goldberg portrays in *Ghost*, says Bogle, is "decades old – the matronly black woman who deals with spirits and whose eyes pop open wide at the appropriate moments. . . . The role is a nurturer for a white couple, and Goldberg has this feistiness that mammies in the past often had" (Jones 1991: 69, 88). Versatility notwithstanding, Bogle describes Goldberg as a "talented woman, but she's no stranger to mammy roles" (88).

The recycling of the mammy role in *Ghost* is facilitated by the various recyclings characteristic of the film. The retroactive quality of Goldberg's role may also have something to do with a new genre of ever increasing importance in contemporary commercial cinema, of which *Ghost* is a prime example – the "surprise hit." *Ghost* was a "surprise hit" in some of the same ways as 1989's *Field of Dreams*

142

which, while not nearly as successful at the box office, was nonetheless afforded some of the same reception as *Ghost* – the surprise that such an improbable, blatantly sentimental film should garner such popular success. *Ghost* and *Field of Dreams* also share, in their status as "surprise hits," another quality insofar as their critical reception was concerned – they evoked passionate, extreme, either/or responses. Critics found them either ludicrous and stupid or innovative and charming. There was little middle ground for either film. That each was nominated for an Oscar for best picture was read as "surprising" as well, if not a nod to their unexpected success then at the very least the sign of some kind of disturbance in the category of "best picture."

Among the common "surprising" aspects of *Ghost* and *Field of Dreams* are that both films foreground the mixing of genres character- istic of many of the most interesting contemporary commercial films (romantic drama and screwball comedy in the case of *Ghost*; sports picture and save-the-farm film in the case of *Field of Dreams*). Addition- ally, both films were seen as throwbacks to the golden age of Holly- wood filmmaking, and both are blatant fantasy films in the most literal sense, featuring the dead returning to make amends. In both films, the fantasy was read as a unique (and somewhat peculiar) combination of New Age spirituality and classical Hollywood filmmaking; reviews of both films were accompanied by capsule histories of the films that preceded them, from baseball films (*Pride of the Yankees*) to return- from-the-dead films (*Here Comes Mr. Jordan*).

Ghost and *Field of Dreams* share another coincidence. In both cases, a black character functions centrally and crucially to enable the fantasy of the white participants. The fantasies in question are the two classical scenarios of oedipal desire theorized by white psychoanalytic criticism, the troubled identification of father and son (*Field of Dreams*) and the heterosexual romance as measure of identity and loss (*Ghost*). The settings of these films are most emphatically and distinctly white, from the gentrified Tribeca of *Ghost* to the Iowa cornfields of *Field of Dreams*.

My purpose in this chapter is to examine how the stretching of genre in these two "surprise hits" may be read in relationship to the fantasies of color and race in which both films engage. The connection here, between mixing genres and race, is not as coincidental as might first appear. Manthia Diawara notes in a discussion of black spectator- ship and the film *Forty-Eight Hours* that "Hollywood requires that the black character [portrayed by Eddie Murphy] must be punished after he has behaved like a hero (albeit a comic one) and humiliated the white people in the bar" (1988: 71). Diawara says that the film "mixes genres (the police story and the comedy, the serious and the fake authority figures) and achieves a 'balance' whereby the black character is only good at subverting order, while the white character restores

143

narrative order" (71–2). Although he doesn't pursue the effect of genre-mixing further, Diawara suggests, I think, that the simultaneous play with and confirmation of racial stereotypes in the film has an immediate relationship with the play on genre.

One only has to think of a film like *Alien Nation* (1988) to see a bold example of this connection. The film combines at least two genres – the alien-invader science-fiction film and the cop-buddy film, particularly in its black/white form. By pairing an earthling and an alien as the cop buddies, the film displaces onto the alien white stereotypes about blacks, particularly insofar as sexual prowess and drug use are concerned. Robyn Wiegman has analyzed a similar dynamic in *Enemy Mine* (1984), where "the mythology of the interracial male bond is woven through the space world of the twenty-first century; the human is a white man, and the alien, though clothed in reptilian fashion, is played by black actor Louis Gossett, Jr., the 'dark brother' in the interracial paradigm" (Wiegman 1989: 93–4).

In chapters 5 and 6, I examined spectatorship in areas that have been of central importance to contemporary film studies – textual analysis and stars. In this chapter I examine the racial dynamics of spectatorship, and it has been noted more than once that contemporary film theorists have had little regard for questions of race. While the works of historians like Donald Bogle, Thomas Cripps, and Dan Leab have traced both the development of black film and the history of blacks in film, they are rarely cited in film theory (Bogle 1973/1989; Cripps 1977; Leab 1976). Even feminist film theory, which would appear to have a large stake in understanding and accounting for the complexities of race in film, has been notoriously slow to undertake analysis of the interlocking paradigms of gender and race (Gaines 1986; Wiegman 1989, 1991). Recent developments suggest, however, a challenge to the lily-white complexion of film studies. These developments take a number of forms, from a consideration of black spectatorship, particularly as it challenges many of the assumptions of 1970s film theory (Diawara 1988; Bobo 1988), to an examination of the particular structures of black cinema (Yearwood 1982; Gaines 1986; Reid 1991; Diawara 1991), to a consideration of film insofar as race and ethnic differences are concerned (Friedman 1991). I am most concerned in this chapter with white spectatorship, and with the underlying question of whether and how the model of spectatorship which has been established and revised in film studies has been a specifically *white* model. I am assuming, then, that attention to race and spectatorship means not only questioning the difference that being black makes, but also the difference that being white makes. The risk in such an undertaking is obvious, since this can be yet another way of establishing white concerns as primary, albeit in a self-conscious way. Nonetheless, I think the consideration of race and spectatorship needs to account for what it means to be a white spectator; otherwise, spectatorship only acquires the contours of race through the classic dichotomy of dominance and marginality.

The case of gender is instructive in this context. Feminist film critics and theorists insisted upon forgrounding questions of the *female* spectator in order to challenge film theory. But this challenge polarized and in some cases essentialized positions, giving the female spectator the qualities of mobility and subject multiplicity that were denied to any subject in models that took male subjectivity as the norm (see Waldman 1988). I think spectatorship is better defined as always involving the intersection of different and differing gendered modes, rather than ascribing to the female spectator those very qualities that have been seen as characteristic of the woman's role in classical Hollywood cinema. I fear that attempts to define spectatorship in racial terms will encounter the same kinds of problems, with an always resistant and critical (black) spectator posed in opposition to the always complicit (white) one. This tendency is not limited to race, but is rather a function of any "marginality" model (a similar tendency occurs with gay and lesbian audiences – which will be examined in the next chapter). In other words, the marginalization model is limited, particularly when (as has been the case in many studies of the female spectator) the "marginalized" spectator is largely a projection of the presumably "dominant" one.

The myths of male subjectivity and patriarchal identity have been studied and probed and foregrounded exhaustively in contemporary film theory, but the same cannot be said for the category of whiteness. Marilyn Frye has observed that "sexuality" only becomes "heterosexuality" when a lesbian or a gay man walks in the room. As a starting point, the same could be said for race – that, in a predominantly white culture, race is an issue only where "other" races – i.e., "other" than white – are concerned, as if (paralleling early feminist criticism) to be white is unmarked, unspecified, neutral (1990). As Richard Dyer puts it, in one of the few examinations of "whiteness" in film studies, "black is always marked as a colour . . . and is always particularising; whereas white is not anything really, not an identity, not a particularising quality, because it is everything – white is no colour because it is all colours" (1988: 45). I want to foreground the ways in which the black characters in *Ghost* and *Field of Dreams* function to articulate fantasies of race in North America, specifically in terms of white spectatorship. While I am concerned with structural and textual details of the films, my concern is not so much to demonstrate that the films are racist, but rather to show the dynamics of white spectatorship. I am thus following Dyer's suggestion that "[t]he representation of white qua white begins to come into focus – in mainstream cinema, for a white spectator – in films in which non-white characters play a significant role" (1988: 47).

My point of departure is the reception apparatus for spectatorship, specifically the differing ways that the racial dynamics of spectatorship are marked in film reviews. Reception study is one of the directions which I described in chapter 3 under the rubric of historical approaches to spectatorship meant to challenge theoretical models which posit the cinematic apparatus as monolithic. Given the institutionalized network of film reviewing, the possibilities for reception study based on how film reviews create horizons of expectation (to use Jauss's phrase) and, more crudely, box-office returns, are rich indeed. At the same time, this "evidence" is still textual material, and while it can offer a series of hypotheses about spectatorship, it cannot be seen as any definitive or foolproof gauge of response. Indeed, responses to film involve an entire range of processes, unconscious and conscious, immediate and long-term, individual and social. As I have already mentioned, *Ghost* and *Field of Dreams* inspired diametrically opposing opinions, the function of which seemed primarily to add to their cachet as "surprise hits." What interests me in the context of the present discussion is the extent to which, in the white mainstream press, race is mentioned at all.

Field of Dreams tells the tale of a thirtysomething struggling Iowa corn farmer, Ray Kinsella (Kevin Costner), who hears a voice tell him: "If you build it he will come." Through a series of myths having to do with North America (specifically Berkeley) in the 1960s, the writer as exile, the disaffection between father and son, and most of all, baseball as the symbolic structure uniting all of these myths, Ray understands that he must build a baseball field. The ghost of Shoeless Joe Jackson (one of the 1919 Chicago White Sox players associated with the fixing of the World Series) soon appears, followed by other players of the past. Ray Kinsella's quest leads him to author Terrence Mann (James Earl Jones), the spirit of the 1960s now living in seclusion in Boston, and then to the ghost of small-town doctor and one-time (literally) baseball player Moonlight Graham, and eventually back to Iowa. Ray's devoted wife Annie and child Karin are supportive background figures; they, like Ray, can see the ghosts; nonbelievers cannot. The fantasy connecting Ray, Shoeless Joe, Mann, and Graham is resolved when the ghost of Ray's father appears on the field, younger than Ray himself. Ray and his father play the game of catch that Ray refused as an adolescent and has regretted as an adult.

The ludicrous plot and bald fantasy of *Field of Dreams* inspired wondrous praise as well as sarcastic mockery. Sharp criticisms of the film were often accompanied by pointed commentary concerning the irony of "integrating" a black author into the fantasy of baseball, since the era evoked by the film was one in which blacks were not permitted to play in the major leagues (see Jacobson 1989; Gretton 1990). Describing the film as "the male weepie at its wussiest," Richard Corliss in *Time* called Terrence Mann "a crusty black author . . . who doesn't mind that all the old major-leaguers were white" (Corliss 1989). In his syndicated column, Charles Krauthammer called *Field of Dreams* the "limit of baseball cliche," particularly insofar as the fact that baseball was "most cruelly segregated for over half a century" is actively elided in the film (Krauthammer 1989).

Any considerations of race conveniently disappear from the glowing accounts of the film, most of which tend to embrace its fantasy with wholehearted enthusiasm. The one exception I found in the positive reviews was, perhaps not coincidentally, Philip French's review in the London *Observer* – i.e., a view from outside North America. Noting that the role of James Earl Jones represents a change from the novel *Shoeless Joe* upon which the film is based, in which Ray pursues J.D. Salinger, French suggests that "[t]he change enhances this aspect [the 1960s memory] of the film by making Mann a fan of the Brooklyn Dodgers infielder Jackie Robinson, the first black American to become a baseball star. The 1957 transfer of the Dodgers from Long Island to Los Angeles and the destruction of their ballpark, Ebbets Field, is evoked as a turning point in American social history" (French 1989).

The role of Terrence Mann is the most obvious revision in the transposition of W. P. Kinsella's novel *Shoeless Joe* to the screen. Reportedly because of potential legal problems, the role of J.D. Salinger was changed, and as James Earl Jones put it in an interview, the change was as radical as possible, from a "white Jewish novelist" to a black one. "I guess I was a damn good choice – I could certainly throw them off when it comes to confusion with Salinger," said Jones (Maychick 1989: 31). Curiously, the transition situates Mann in a Jewish neighborhood in Boston, and by all appearances he is virtually the only black person there. I have no idea how this peculiar mise-en-scène occurred in the production of the film, but its effect is to make the "addition" and "contrast" of a black novelist all the more obvious and awkward.

Less commented upon in the reception of the film is another significant shift that occurred in the transposition of novel to film. The nostalgia for the 1960s evoked through Ray and Annie is absent from the novel. While this nostalgia has been commented upon by many reviewers, it is hardly ever noted that it represents a significant shift from Kinsella's novel. The film begins with a montage of Ray Kinsella's past with Costner's voice-over, and stock images of Berkeley in the 1960s illustrate how he and Annie met. The novelist Terrence Mann is introduced first as a connection to the 1960s, supposedly as the author who coined the phrase "make love not war." Annie refers to Mann at a public meeting about book banning, while Ray is attempting to figure out the meaning of the latest phrase from The Voice, "ease his pain." The mention of Mann inspires Ray to travel to Boston to find the author, assuming that it is Mann's pain he is destined to ease.

Hence, Mann is first evoked in the film as a bridge connecting the 1960s to present-day Iowa. Just as the version of the 1960s presented in the film is curiously devoid of any reference to blacks or the civil-rights struggle, so the evocation of Mann is first and foremost as a 1960s author representing supposedly "universal" values of "love" and "peace." Indeed, one reviewer described the novelist – seemingly unironically – in the film as a "cross between J.D. Salinger and Bob Dylan" (Denby 1989), and another described him as a "former political activist along Abbie Hoffmann lines" (Stack 1989).

One of the most efficient ways to evoke and deny race simultaneously is to make a black character a projection of white anxieties about race. This occurs in seemingly opposite ways in the two films under consideration here, but through an identical device. In case anyone should notice the irony of a baseball heaven harking back to the years when blacks could not play professional baseball, Terrence Mann is revealed to be an avid fan of the Brooklyn Dodgers – the team on which Jackie Robinson broke the color barrier in 1947. Jackie Robinson's name is mentioned only briefly in the film, however, and Mann recites the speech that waxes the most poetic about the mythic quality of baseball, thus emphasizing that baseball ostensibly transcends racial division. Even James Earl Jones, in the interview mentioned above, speaks of his own love of baseball in tones that match and echo those of his character. Jones told the interviewer that "several interviewers have wondered about the credibility factor. 'They've all asked me if I felt my character . . . would be accepted by a team of white men, albeit ghosts, from 70 years ago.' " Jones replied that "it's like Jackie Robinson. Except for the times he was spiked on the field, regardless of what real prejudice existed, once you're on the field, baseball is pure" (Maychick 1989: 31–2).

In other words, race is both evoked and denied in the film, and vanishes into the mythology of baseball just as surely as Terrence Mann vanishes into the cornfield. Everything is set up in *Field of Dreams* to suggest that race is incidental, and that if it has to be an issue, then it can be integrated into the mythology of baseball as part of the simple, good times of the past. Indeed, as the reviews of this film suggest, race only becomes an issue when the critic is a cranky soul who cannot or will not buy into the fantasy world of the film.

In other words, to be conscious of race and the curious racial politics of the film is to refuse to be a good sport (in several senses of the term).

This marginalization of race could be read as an attempt to bring 1960s "activism" and 1980s "conservativism" together as seamlessly intertwined eras, thus requiring the repression of any factors that might problematize the fit. But then the question of race is more perturbing, for why mention or evoke race at all? Why bother to introduce an element that "integrates" so facilely yet so superficially? One of the most important insights of 1970s film theory is the emphasis on the signifying importance of seemingly insignificant details. For in its simultaneous evocation and denial of race as a signifying factor, *Field of Dreams* offers a particular vision of white spectatorship which *requires* and depends upon the presence of blacks. The presence of James Earl Jones in this film (and Whoopi Goldberg in *Ghost*) is, in part, a strategy that is meant to appeal to black viewers, but I think white spectatorship is let off the hook too easily if one assumes that these roles are only designed to provide the proverbial "something to appeal to everyone." Terrence Mann may function in *Field of Dreams* to attract a black audience, but he also functions to reassure a white one. For as "not-Jewish," as a baseball fan, as the depoliticized spirit of the 1960s, Mann becomes a narrative facilitator, a reassuring measure that some myths really are universal.

Ghost is every bit as much of a fantasy film as *Field of Dreams* is, but its mythic range is less of a temporal one – baseball as the unifying force for America, a son's reconciliation with a father brought back as a young man – and more of a spatial one, having to do with the boundaries, imaginary and real, that divide a city and its activities into "white" and "black." Most obviously, of course, the fantasy of *Ghost* is less mythic, in that the fantasies of love and coupledom, life and death, and urban space present in the film do not have quite the range that baseball does. *Ghost* has more racial specificity than does *Field of Dreams*; its major black character, Oda Mae Brown, actually lives in a black and hispanic neighborhood, has a context, and is recognizable as more than a seemingly accidental transposition from a novel to a film. Yet the dynamics of the two films are quite similar insofar as Oda Mae Brown, like Terrence Mann, speaks the anxieties of white spectatorship.

Ghost tells the tale of a young couple, Sam and Molly, and the seemingly random mugging that kills Sam. As a spirit visible to the spectators but invisible to the rest of the characters in the film, Sam discovers that his best friend and co-worker Carl was responsible for his death, and he tries to warn Molly that her life may be in danger. When Sam discovers his murderer, Willie Lopez, who was hired by his co-worker, he follows him to the Brooklyn neighborhood where he lives and by chance encounters Oda Mae Brown, a phony psychic who turns out to be genuine, since she is the only human being able to hear (although not see) Sam and communicate with him. He convinces her to visit Molly, and after a series of complications involving embezzlement, fraud, and disbelief, Molly not only believes that Oda Mae is in touch with Sam, she engages, through her, in one last embrace with him. At the conclusion of the film, the evil friend is dead and so is Sam, but each has gone his separate way, while Molly and Oda Mae are left in the land of the living.

I have noted that negative reviews of *Field of Dreams* in particular take note of the race factor. In the case of *Ghost*, race is rarely called attention to. Kathi Maio's review of the film in *Sojourner: The Women's Forum* criticizes its racist implications; the fact that her review appears in the alternative feminist press makes it the exception that proves the rule (1991: 26). The only other specific mention of race that I have seen in reviews of *Ghost* occurred not in a review of the film, but of its video release. Ty Burr notes that Goldberg's role has an

> ironic subtext: While Goldberg's own movies have flopped noisily, she wins respect playing supporting loon to white actors. Indeed, a tinge of stereotype casting becomes clearer with repeat video viewings. At its core, *Ghost* is about an upscale pair of generic white lovebirds who are threatened by a slavering, rape-minded Hispanic . . . and helped by a loudmouth con artist who makes her living scamming superstitious, eye-rolling black folk.
>
> (Burr 1991: 78)

Burr's review has as much to do with how well the film stands up "with repeat viewings" as with how well it works in a movie theater, and it is interesting that the racist stereotypes should only become evident when the film is seen more than once.

Aside from a cursory mention of Jackie Robinson and the Brooklyn Dodgers, *Field of Dreams* quickly puts explicit acknowledgement of race aside in the pursuit of a white fantasy of a mythic world where blacks articulate the myths that exclude them. In *Ghost*, however, not only are familiar racial divisions apparent from the outset, but the only character in the film who actually mentions race is Oda Mae Brown. Sam and Molly inhabit a downtown New York of Wall Street and gentrified Tribeca lofts, and Sam's discovery of Willie Lopez leads to the neighborhood where he eventually encounters Oda Mae. The Brooklyn neighborhood stands in obvious contrast to Tribeca, a contrast marked by the sharp difference between the trendy yuppie loft and the shabby apartment of Willie Lopez as well as the cramped, decidedly non-trendy home of Oda Mae and her two sisters. In addition, a subway ride is required to move between the two worlds of white and black/hispanic, a ride marked as a most significant passage in that it eventually becomes the means for Sam to learn how to function more actively in the world of the living. It does not require too much imagination to see that if the white dust and angel statues of Sam and Molly's loft suggest heaven, the Brooklyn neighborhood of dark corridors and cramped surroundings suggests hell.

Like *Field of Dreams*, *Ghost* provoked widely disparate responses but tended to be ridiculed more consistently, largely for two reasons – a combination of genres even more excessive than in *Field of Dreams*, and a "mystery" (i.e., who was responsible for Sam's death?) so obvious that a child could figure it out. Richard Corliss described *Ghost* as a "bad movie that a lot of people will like. It's got suspense, comedy, a big chase and a little sex" and said of Sam's death that it is a "plot twist that anyone can unravel in an eyewink" (Corliss 1990). Similarly, Georgia Brown criticized the way in which "[t]oo many genres are contending for ascendancy here," one symptom of which is precisely the "telegraphing" of the murder of Sam; "anyone half-attuned to mystery plots will be way ahead of this one" (Brown 1990). *Variety*'s reviewer did not comment specifically on the obvious murder plot, but noted in general of the film that "demanding filmgoers won't buy it," largely because of its "unlikely grab bag of styles" and "far-fetched effort" (Daws 1990). And while Janet Maslin in the *New York Times* is less critical than others of the film's mixture of genres, she does note its "odd inconsistencies" and its "uncertain" attitude about ghosthood, and once again a symptom of this confusion is the fact that "the audience is already miles ahead" of Sam when he discovers Carl's guilt (Maslin 1990).

There is no necessary connection, of course, between the mixture of genres, the obviousness of the mystery, and the racial dimensions of the life-and-death themes in *Ghost*. Yet the easy-to-solve mystery is like the prologue to a dream or a fantasy, an accessible entrée that makes the much more implausible events to follow palatable and acceptable – including the mixture of genres and the presence of spirits from the world of the dead. Whoopi Goldberg's role as Oda Mae is significant in this context, since she has, as Caryn James put it in a thought piece on the "ghost" film (such articles were common after *Ghost* became a hit, as if figuring out why this film had become so successful had become part of its reception), "the most crucial role. . . . In her move from skeptic to believer, she reflects the audience's own cynical stance" (James 1990). Goldberg's role as mediator – between the audience and the improbability of the film, between the widely different stylistic reference points of the film – is not unlike James Earl Jones's role in *Field of Dreams*. Why, then, should the race factor be worthy of explicit mention with respect to *Field of Dreams*, even if sporadically, yet be virtually unmentioned in reviews of *Ghost*?

If *Field of Dreams* obscures its own potentially racist implications by having Terrence Mann function as a voice of truth, which speaks the transcendental quality of baseball more enthusiastically than any white character in the film, *Ghost* works in reverse terms. The only commentary on race in the film comes from Goldberg's Oda Mae. When she sees a picture of Sam in the loft, she says he is "cute. White, but cute." When she translates Sam's information about his killer to Molly, she editorializes at one point, telling Molly that Willie Lopez is Puerto Rican, a fact that Sam does not mention. The difference in neighborhoods is remarked upon only by Oda Mae, who at one point complains about going downtown; the white yuppies never utter a racist remark about Brooklyn. And in a most peculiar case of preventive medicine, Oda Mae refers to the "spooks" that surround her – all of them black or Hispanic – once her genuine psychic powers have been revealed, thus translating the title of the film into racial slang.

Meanwhile, in a move somewhat reminiscent of another spirit-returns-from-the-dead film which appeared at the same time as *Ghost*, Bill Cosby's *Ghost Dad*, race is something to which whites are oblivious. In *Ghost Dad*, Cosby plays Elliot Hopper, the lone black executive in the company of white men, and early in the film we see him with a group of white businessmen in an elevator. One of the men introduces Hopper as the man responsible for an important merger who will therefore be the youngest man to sit on the board of their firm. Whatever characterization of Hopper viewers might imagine for the white men in the elevator, "youth" would surely be far down on the list. Similarly, when Oda Mae conspires with Sam's revenge fantasy against Carl and enters the bank, never once does a white player react to her in racial terms; rather, it is understood that her wild costuming provokes the response. With Oda Mae virtually the only character in the film who speaks of race, a central tenet of racial ideology is confirmed, i.e., that white people only have a race when a black person walks in the room, and that (in *Ghost*) it is blacks who have a race, and who are conscious of race, not whites.

By designating Oda Mae as the only character in the film who is aware of race, the film handily deals with another potential problem: it is free to engage in the symbolic imagery of black and white in a near-infantile way, mobilizing the black, menacing figures who carry the evil dead (Willie Lopez and Carl) off to hell, as opposed to the shimmering white spectres who await Sam in heaven at the film's conclusion (Maio 1991: 26). Curiously, *Field of Dreams* also alludes to the black/white dichotomy and its symbolism of evil versus good in its centering of the fantasy of baseball and father and son, for after

152

the fixing of the 1919 World Series the Chicago White Sox became known as the Black Sox. I am not trying to argue that any reference to "black" or "dark" as synonomous with evil or foreboding is necessarily racist; rather, in two films so preoccupied with the racial dynamics of fantasy, it is no small coincidence that so many allusions to "color" emerge.

Both James Earl Jones and Whoopi Goldberg are actors who have achieved large appeal to black and white audiences, and in the case of Goldberg, *Ghost* was widely perceived as a film that delivered on the promise of her acting abilities demonstrated earlier in *The Color Purple*. I have said that the roles they enact play upon the anxieties of white spectatorship, and their reputations as gifted actors with large followings outside of these individual films are important in this context. Indeed, Jones's reputation as a quality actor with an authoritative presence gives a certain cachet to the role of Terrence Mann, and Goldberg's turn as Oda Mae Brown played on the snappy wit and comic gifts that have constituted her star persona. If Goldberg and Jones are actors with large followings among black and white spectators alike, consideration of reception suggests that a significant difference between black and white spectatorship emerges in the arena of *performance*.

I have referred to the reviews of *Field of Dreams* and *Ghost* I've cited as examples of the white, mainstream institution of film reviewing. But characterizing these newspapers and magazines as "white" can easily give the impression that the dominant ideology of an institution is the same as its readership. This, of course, returns me to the problem of white as unmarked, neutral, without distinctive features. The reviews of these films in daily newspapers or national-circulation magazines do not always seem particularly white until they are compared with examples in a magazine like *Jet*, for instance, aimed at a black readership, or at newspapers like *The Chicago Crusader* or *The Amsterdam News* aimed at black communities. And the difference has less to do with how much attention is called to the fact of race (white reviewers critical of *Field of Dreams* are quite attentive to its racism), than with how that attention is focussed. For emphasized in the film reviews of black publications are the performances of black actors and their achievements, no matter whether the roles are small or large. *Jet*'s story on *Ghost* focuses on its importance in Whoopi Goldberg's career (Collier 1990), and the review of *Field of Dreams* in the *Chicago Crusader* emphasizes Jones's role as the cynic in need of transformation (the review concludes: "If you are one who has trouble believing in miracles, dip yourself in magic waters before you go into the theater; and transform yourself like the character in the film, Terrence Mann played by James Earl Jones, and be prepared to believe in life again" [Blair 1989]).

According to standard accounts of audiences for commercial films, blacks constitute 12 per cent of the US population and 25 per cent of the audience for motion pictures (Bates 1991: 18). Black publications attest to this enthusiasm of black audiences for motion pictures, but the enthusiasm is often misunderstood by whites. *Field of Dreams* provides an example of this. Ray Kinsella confronts Terrence Mann with what he assumes to be definitive evidence of Mann's love for baseball – an article Mann wrote for *Jet* magazine in April, 1962. In fact, the April 26, 1962 issue of *Jet does* have a major story on black baseball players, with the cover announcing "Black Gold on Green Diamonds" (Barbee 1962). In the film, the simple fact of Mann's story is presented as evidence of his great love of baseball; yet the story by *Jet* writer Bobbie E. Barbee has much more to do with a celebration of black players than with any mythic investment in the game itself as a metaphor for life. Were a film like *Field of Dreams* to take black spectatorship seriously, Jackie Robinson would be much more than a passing reference to justify the presence of James Earl Jones.

For white audiences, one of the most stereotypical and therefore comfortable relationships between black and white is that of performer and onlooker, and it has been noted many times that one of the ironies of race in the US is that many whites see no contradiction between, say, enjoying black music or watching black athletes or observing black actors, and retaining decidedly racist views outside the arena of performance. The two films under consideration in this chapter seem to offer strategies for the representation of race and fantasy, and fantasies about race, that avoid blatant racism and racial stereotyping. For in both *Field of Dreams* and *Ghost*, the appeal to spirituality is not only about white male fantasies of father and son or white heterosexual fantasies of the couple; it is also about the appropriation of the spiritual life of black people as whites imagine it, but with so many displacements that the characters in question are barely recognizable as black. How do white people imagine the spiritual life of black people? In *Field of Dreams*, Mann represents the spirit of the 1960s as a wimpy "love" that denies difference, and in *Ghost* Oda Mae is a charlatan with an authentic soul who only recognizes her true gifts once a white man has enabled her to.

An element of self-justification emerges quite frequently when whites write about race, a desire for racism to involve only them, the "dominant ideologues," and never me, the critic. I have in this chapter discussed white spectatorship from the vantage point of a white spectator. What I, as a white critic writing about race and whiteness might say, is different from what a black critic writing about race and black spectatorship might say. However painfully obvious this might seem, the discussion of race in film theory follows too often from the assumption that black spectatorship will follow the model that white film theory has constructed to account for various and sundry forms of "resistant," "marginal," or otherwise "oppositional" spectatorship.

This isn't to say that notions of resistance and opposition should not be central to theories of black spectatorship as they have been developed by black theorists. But a white film theorist looking at film reviews and comments in the black press is not likely to find the same notion of "resistance" that has dominated film theory. Rather, the notion of resistance elaborated by some black authors has far more to do with performance, that is, with how black actors perform in several senses of the term – how well they act, certainly, but also and especially how they bring both passion and distance to their roles. Black spectatorship is thus inflected by performance and becomes a re-enactment of what W.E.B. Dubois called the "double consciousness" of black people (1903/1961) (see in particular Bogle 1973/1989). This is a notion of contradiction that seems to me quite different from the textual processes central to 1970s film theory. According to that model, the contestatory value of a film is revealed through narrative structure and mise-en-scène, not through the actual performance of the film, which I mean in both senses of the term – the actors' performance in the film, and the reception of the film by specific kinds of viewers (there are no specific viewers in 1970s film theory; there is only the subject).

In *The Devil Finds Work*, James Baldwin describes eloquently the process of resistance central to black spectatorship. Baldwin describes Sidney Poitier's role in *The Defiant Ones* (1958) as a performance "which lends the film its only real distinction [and] also, paradoxically, smashes it to pieces. There is no way to believe both Noah Cullen *and* the story" (Baldwin 1976/1990: 74). *The Defiant Ones* tells the tale of two escaped prisoners, one white (Tony Curtis) and one black (Poitier). During most of the film they are handcuffed to each other and through their relationship a parable of race relations in North America is told. Like *Field of Dreams* and *Ghost*, however, *The Defiant Ones* tells a white myth of black and white relations, and as a result the film contains numerous "blind spots" (to use the language of 1970s film theory) wherein Poitier's character acts, not as a black man, but as a white image of what a black man is. According to Baldwin, Poitier's performance makes the incomprehensible logic of the film visible; the "unmistakable truth of his performance was being placed at the mercy of a lie" (75).

The Devil Finds Work, which contains numerous analyses of other films, was published in 1976. Baldwin's discussions of films echo some of the preoccupations of 1970s film theory – the contradictions within films that reveal the "gaps" in dominant ideology, in particular. Aside from the obvious fact that Baldwin is a far more eloquent writer than most film theorists, the most striking difference to accompany this echo of 1970s film theory is the discussion of audiences, specifically of how black audiences see films. The abstracted "subject" of 1970s film theory takes on concrete shape. But the facile opposition which 1970s film theory has used to define its theoretical sophistication – the subject versus real people – has no place in Baldwin's account. For "the subject" is present in *The Devil Finds Work*, as both an ideological entity (informed by white fantasies of race relations) and a psychic one (the simultaneous attraction to and repulsion by male homosocial bonds, the function of the woman as projection of threats and fears, both evident in *The Defiant Ones*). But so are film audiences, from liberal white viewers who cheered as Sidney Poitier jumped off the train at the conclusion of the film, sacrificing his own chance to escape to remain with his white buddy; to the black Harlem audience who "was outraged, and yelled, *'Get back on the train, you fool!'* " (Baldwin 1976/1990: 76). The examination of white and black spectatorship may well offer a unique opportunity to move beyond the facile oppositions of "subjects" and "real people," of "ideology" and "resistance," that have characterized film theory.

8

THE CRITICAL AUDIENCE

Throughout this book I have stressed that the distinction between "viewers" and "subjects" is the foundation for contemporary theories of spectatorship in film studies. At the same time, this distinction too often hardens into a rigid abstraction. It seems altogether fitting, then, that in this last chapter I turn to the subject of film audiences. The distinction between subject positions and real film viewers (for whom the activity of watching the movies can mean many different things) has acquired different inflections in the course of the past two decades of film theory. During the heady years of apparatus theory, the film viewer was bracketed altogether, while in more recent years pronouncements about those viewers have been more visible, in direct proportion, it seems, to the waning influence of apparatus theory.

In the rush to criticize apparatus theory, however, and the attendant reclaiming of spectatorship as the domain of audiences and not just subject positions, some disturbing assumptions about the study of real people have entered the discussion. Many methods and devices have been embraced as more closely approximating how movies are actually watched and enjoyed, like reception theory, ethnography, or audience surveys. But I do not see how examinations of film reviews or surveys, designed largely by academics, bring us any closer to the actual experiences of film audiences than psychoanalysis or textual analysis. In the previous chapter, I used film reviews in relationship to race and mixed-genre films, but I do not think that this attention to reception provides any more direct access to spectatorship than textual analysis does.

Yet the study of documents like film reviews, as well as the study of audiences, is part of a general tendency toward discrediting, or at least problematizing, the excessive emphasis on cinematic textuality in film studies. To be sure, film reviews are "texts," and as such they cannot be defined as more immediately reflective of the real conditions of spectatorship. Such an assumption is in part a reaction to the knee-jerk emphasis on textuality of much film theory, and particularly to one of its attendant problems. For too often the naive assumption is made of homologies between textual patterns and responses to them, i.e., a classical narrative produces its own ideal spectator, a decentered text produces an equally decentered spectator. But to discredit the analysis of textuality altogether is a classic case of throwing the baby out with the bathwater. Between the notion that the textual system of the individual film is all, and the argument that exclusive attention to textuality is at best an academic view of the real, complicated, heterogeneous business of viewing, there must be other alternatives. In order to avoid the simple duality of abstract versus real spectatorship, it is important to acknowledge, from the outset, that any analytic conception of *the audience* involves a considerable amount of projection, myth-making, and fabrication.

Part of my focus in this chapter will be on the difficulties of identifying the film audience, and I have purposefully chosen an audience which is politically charged – gays and lesbians. To be sure, the components of white spectatorship examined in the previous chapter are politically charged as well, although in that case I was more concerned with how spectatorship is constructed within specific films. Yet my point of departure in both chapters is similar to the extent that I am asking what it means to define spectatorship in terms of identity, in both cases identities that I share. I assume, from the outset, that all so-called members of so-called communities live that membership in complex, contradictory, and radically different ways. One of my frustrations in reading much film theory is the tendency to identify a limit or a horizon and then shirk from exploring its ramifications, and so in choosing to focus in this chapter on the question of a gay/lesbian audience, I am attempting to further observations I have made in previous chapters about the homosexual components of film spectatorship. I will approach the question of this audience critically, but I do not intend to indulge in what has become an unfortunate exercise, reciting all of the fictions of identity that make "knowledge" impossible.

I am, as has undoubtedly been evident throughout this book, ambivalent about both the claims of contemporary spectatorship studies and criticisms of that work. But when ambivalence leads only to finger-pointing about everyone else's errors, then the important work leading to more understanding – and knowledge – about the ways in which spectatorship is lived by real film viewers is obscured. If this strikes some readers as wanting to have it both ways – wanting to criticize the fictions of identity while affirming nonetheless the importance of research that inquires into how individuals partaking of identities (fictively constructed or not) understand the movies – I would argue that this is, rather, the necessary paradox involved in examining spectatorship productively *and* critically at the same time.

Curiously, the "subject" of apparatus theory is assumed to possess the attributes of "dominance" – white, male, heterosexual, middle-class, etc. – while the "audience" consists of all that is left out of the subject. For example, if one is to believe the pronouncements of film exhibitors, women have constituted, from the 1930s through the 1950s, the most significant *audience* for the movies. This assumption was interpreted in various ways; for instance, a 1942 poll published in *Variety* indicated that as many men as women attended the movies. The following week a writer nonetheless affirmed that women were the ones who *chose* the films to be seen ("It is not the percentage of men as against women that counts. It's *how* did *most* of them get there?") (*Variety* 1942a, 1942b). But in relationship to apparatus theory, for which the ideal spectator of the classical cinema was implicitly male, the female *spectator* became "marginal" in the sense that she was the "other" against whom the illusions of the self could be critiqued. As I suggested in previous chapters, many of the theories that have circulated about female spectatorship have less to do with how women watch films, and much less to do (to use the terms of the discourse) with how women are "positioned" by the apparatus, than with an excavation of what is repressed in the apparatus model. This return of the repressed, projected upon a "marginal" audience, occurs across a variety of contexts – working-class and black spectators, for instance, "resist" (whereas "dominant" spectators melt symbiotically into the screen). Attention paid to specific audiences tends often to focus on the so-called "marginal" or "subcultural" audience (Hebdige 1979; McRobbie 1980; Marchetti 1986; Staiger 1992, chapter 8).

If the model of the cinematic subject assumes homogeneity, then projecting heterogeneous "activity" onto so-called marginal audiences may be more attractive, but "activity" can be just as vapid and indistinct a term as "passivity." While it may be preferable to speak of black spectators as always resisting the fictions of mainstream cinema (preferable, that is, to ignoring race altogether), I fear that the continuing dualism of "dominant" spectators versus "marginal" (and therefore resisting ones) perpetuates the false dichotomy of us and them. Defining the other as the vanguard of spectatorship only reverses the dichotomy.

The increasing interest in audience research in film studies is often conflated with the interest in defining spectatorship in critical terms, that is, understanding spectatorship as empowering, as contestatory, as part of an overall political agenda. At the time I am writing this chapter, few audiences in the US could be more politically charged than gay men and lesbians, given the current crisis about AIDS and the National Endowment for the Arts controversy in particular (Carr 1990; Hughes and Elovich 1990). The visibility of gays and lesbians is frequently defined in terms of spectatorship, and the success of advo-cacy by 1970s gay organizations in relationship to television, for instance, has been documented by Kathryn C. Montgomery (1989: 75–100). That the constitution of gays and lesbians as an audience presents a threat is suggested by the obsessive assumption made by right-wing groups that audiences are all heterosexual, with the attend-ant fear that anything other than blanket condemnation of homo-sexuality will upset the subject/object dichotomy, that is, will make homosexuality something other than the object of heterosexual scorn.

A recent example of striking coincidences foregrounds questions of definition of gay and lesbian audiences. Greta Garbo (Figure 13), who like many Hollywood stars has a devoted following across genders and sexualities, died in March 1990. There had always been, especially among lesbians and gay men, speculations about Garbo's sexuality, but another event which occurred shortly after Garbo's death put those speculations in a specific context. In March 1990, *Outweek*, a New York-based gay and lesbian weekly, published an essay about the "secret gay life" of recently deceased Malcolm Forbes (Signorile 1990). A variety of national publications announced that Malcolm Forbes had been "outed." Ever since, the practice of so-called "outing" (a term now used in gay and lesbian publications) has inspired heated controversy, and numerous celebrities and public figures whose supposed gay and lesbian identities had been well-known among gays and lesbians were highlighted as potential "victims" of the outing craze.

While "outing" is a feature of the news media, it depends for its existence and its controversy on spectatorship of many kinds, and film spectatorship has a particular function to the extent that wondering about the sexual identities of film stars perpetuates their visibility and vulnerability. Many in film studies believe that the cinema acquires its institutional quality, its ability to permeate dreams and fantasies, through a wide-ranging web of texts and contexts. Film researchers have made use of a wide variety of these texts and contexts, many of which (like fan magazines, tabloids, television news) challenge any notion of sanctity of the autonomous film. Gay and lesbian spectator-ship, however, highlights a channel of information which may stretch even these larger and more expansive definitions of context and inter-textuality. For much of gay and lesbian spectatorship depends upon gossip, on sources of information which certainly vary as to their reliability, but which provide common assumptions and myths about film. As Andrea Weiss puts it, "rumour and gossip constitute the unrecorded history of the gay subculture" (1991: 283).

When Rock Hudson died of AIDS, the revelation of his gay sexuality

Figure 13 Greta Garbo

161

was supposedly a shock, yet Hudson's gay identity had been common knowledge in gay and lesbian circles for years. The "outing" controversy has taken gossip and gay/lesbian information and gone public with it – or rather, has taken one very specific alternative public sphere, that of gay and lesbian cultural life, and projected it onto the public sphere in the largest and most general sense, that is the more dominant and presumably anonymous public sphere of print and broadcast journalism. The criticism of "outing" as an invasion of privacy seems to me to miss the far more extensive implications of "privacy," for what "outing" threatens (in cinematic terms) is the relationship between the public, relatively anonymous sphere of film-going and the private knowledge of gays and lesbians. In chapter 3, I described attention to the cinema as a unique public sphere as one of the attempts to historicize spectatorship. Gay and lesbian spectatorship suggests the importance of the cinematic public sphere in the shaping of marginal communities.

That Greta Garbo's death should coincide so closely with the advent of "outing" gave a particular and sometimes peculiar inflection to her obituaries and to the numerous articles and tributes and evaluations of her career published after her death. Three such pieces, published in gay/lesbian journals with a national readership, foreground significant and often contradictory definitions of gay/lesbian spectatorship. All of these pieces draw upon the kind of gossip and rumor that are part of all marginal communities. My point here is not reception analysis, but rather a use of a sample of this discourse as an entry into questions of spectatorship and audience in relationship to the desires of lesbians and gay men.

Even though *Outweek* was best known for its "outings" of various public figures, the obituary for Garbo written by Otis Stuart only alludes briefly and cautiously to rumors about her sexual preference (Stuart 1990). Rather, Stuart focuses on Garbo as a contradictory entity about whom any sure and secure knowledge was an impossibility: "the mistress of self-determination was also contradiction incarnate" (60). Stuart refers to some anecdotes about Garbo's life, but he is more concerned to concentrate on the rich sexual ambiguity and sexual power that she projected on screen. "Whatever its offscreen reality," Stuart writes, "Garbo's sexual potency was a moveable feast onscreen. In fact, it was rich enough never to have made the question an issue, however unorthodox *Queen Christina*'s behavior might have been on the street" (61).

In sharp contrast to Stuart's essay is Michael Bronski's piece in *Gay Community News*, which proposes that contradiction and mystery notwithstanding, Garbo's life is easily read and interpreted in terms of a lesbian identity protected and nurtured by the star's famous defection from Hollywood. Bronski writes: "Unlimited reasons have been offered to explain her passion for secrecy, as well as the retirement, but the obvious reason – her lesbianism – is never mentioned. The ordeal of remaining in the closet, of divorcing the personal life from the public image, is a terrible hardship. Rather than live a lie, Garbo decided to live for herself" (Bronski 1990: 20). Bronski goes on to note that while there is plenty of evidence of gay and lesbian Hollywood stars, Garbo's case is nonetheless unique, for she "understood the severe limits placed upon her and made her choice" (20). Whereas Stuart emphasizes the sexual ambiguity that made Garbo an object of fascination for gay and lesbian audiences, Bronski offers the life as well as the screen image as a gay and lesbian icon, and stresses what is only implied in Stuart's obituary, that "[i]f the straight world had inklings of Garbo's lesbianism, the gay world certainly had no doubts" (20).

The certainty of Garbo's lesbianism is even more emphatically stated in Margie Adam's brief elegy to the actress in *Outlook* magazine. Adam describes her identification with Garbo as the knowledge of shared identity. From the first moment she saw Garbo in *Grand Hotel*, shortly after her own coming out, Adam says "I knew, right down to my molecular structure, that the shimmering beauty with such a jawline up there on the screen was a dyke, just like me" (Adam 1990: 25). Her knowledge is due to "a sixth sense that all lesbians have which I would liken to the heightened sensibility possessed by animals that live in the dark" (25). Like Bronski, Adam assesses Garbo's infamous need for privacy as a result of her lesbianism, but Adam goes considerably further than Bronski. One of the frequently cited justifications for "outing" is the need for lesbians and gay men to have public role models, and Adam alludes to this argument when she regrets that Garbo "never came out" and will therefore "always be lost to us" (25).

Those familiar with debates about "identity politics" will recognize, in the different shadings of these tributes to Garbo after her death, conflicts among gays and lesbians about the very nature of gay/lesbian identity and its relationship to other kinds of identity. Adam's certitude about Garbo's lesbianism is an obvious example of projection, and I find it disturbing that such projections are not recognized as part of the complexity of the spectator experience rather than as certainties about the actress in question. I know many lesbians for whom the discovery of strong attractions to other women was accompanied by various fixations on movie stars, from Natalie Wood to Doris Day; to assume that these women therefore must be lesbians is at best disingenuous. A confusion is made between spectatorship and identification, in that pleasures taken in watching are assumed to be fully of a piece with projected ideals.

Yet the case of Garbo *is* different, to the extent that her "private life" (which is always a part of star personae) was shrouded in the kind of mystery that has been central to coming-out narratives. Put another way, Bronski's reading of Garbo's career offers, at the very least, a coherent narrative within which the mystery is somewhat dispelled. The difference between gay/lesbian readings of Garbo and a controversial biographical exposé published shortly after her death is one of perspective and degree. Antoni Gronowicz, in *Garbo: Her Story*, offers a series of anecdotes (most often transposed into a most peculiar first-person account) which confirm Garbo's love affairs with women (1990). While Gronowicz presents himself as a dear friend and confidant of Garbo, there is no more interest in the lesbian Garbo than in the heterosexual (or bisexual) one; this is the perspective of a somewhat detached gossip writer. Nor are the lesbian encounters privileged, as they obviously are in gay/lesbian accounts of Garbo's career, as offering a distinct connection between the life and the work.

At the same time that claims about Garbo's lesbianism may appear to challenge the heterosexual presumption about Hollywood actors, there is something too oddly familiar about those claims, for they rely on the mechanisms of curiosity, mystery, and fascination about the private lives of stars that have always been central to the star system (De Cordova 1990). Put another way, the gay/lesbian interest in Garbo's sexual identity only challenges Hollywood myths up to a point, for in perhaps more profound ways that interest guarantees spectatorship. Generating speculation on whether Garbo was or wasn't does not necessarily function as critical spectatorship; it is an extension of the institutions of stars and films, not critiques of them. And yet, given the extent to which the various institutions of stardom rely on compulsory heterosexuality, the revelation of Hollywood stars as gay, lesbian, or bisexual demonstrates how presumably innate heterosexuality is a myth.

Gay and lesbian adoration of Garbo and subsequent claims to her after her death are only one, isolated example of gay/lesbian spectatorship. There are far more obvious examples of critical spectatorship among gays and lesbians, particularly the actions that have been taken to challenge homophobic representations in films ranging from *Cruising* (Wilson 1981) to the recent *Basic Instinct* (Signorile 1991b). Yet I am not certain that spectatorship is the appropriate word to describe these political actions, which have far less to do with how films are seen and consumed and far more to do with how they are produced. Organized actions against *Cruising* and *Basic Instinct* were based initially on scripts, not on finished films.

A better example, perhaps, is the divided reaction to *The Silence of the Lambs* (1990), the adaptation of Thomas Harris's 1989 novel (Dorenkamp 1991; Kennedy et al. 1991; Taubin 1991). In Harris' novel, the fact that the serial killer is not gay is established clearly; the film, however, presents Buffalo Bill as a peculiar combination of stereotypes, most of which evoke his status as a gay man. Despite the fact that the film inspired extensive debate among gays and lesbians and in the gay/lesbian press, I am not sure how much this debate had to do with gay and lesbian spectatorship, since most criticism of the film focussed on how "middle America" would perceive the gay stereotypes, not on how gays and lesbians themselves responded to the film. Michelangelo Signorile, for instance, who was one of the most vociferous critics of the film, wrote: "The movie is a success because it's smart enough for the sophisticated set and manipulative enough for the sensation-loving masses. While the smaller, more educated audiences perhaps understand the nuances . . . the ignorant majority of film-goers – the millions growing up in gay-hating America – are getting yet another lesson in Homophobia 101" (1991a: 45). Spectatorship in this debate had far more to do with how others watched the film, and in a peculiar way evoked studies that have been done in the past of Hollywood's "moral" effect on viewers.

If gay/lesbian spectatorship in the case of Garbo is not radically different from classical spectatorship, and if militant actions against films that engage in homophobic portrayals have less to do with spectatorship than with controlling the kinds of images seen, then it may begin to seem as though the very notion of critical spectatorship is, if not oxymoronic, then at the very least in need of some qualification. In some obvious ways, of course, the very purpose of academic spectatorship studies was to encourage the development of critical spectatorship, certainly to the extent that the large majority of those who write film scholarship also teach. Endless debates have taken place over whether a given film is contestatory or complicit. More recently these debates have moved to the realm of audience response. In this sense, then, gay/lesbian audiences function as a limit-case, as an ideal testing ground for the notion of critical spectatorship, not in the sense of "informed" viewing but in the sense of the possibility of "contestatory" and "radical" viewing.

But critical spectatorship is not the same as a politicized audience, even though it may be a necessary condition for it. The politicized audience has in fact been the specter haunting spectatorship studies over the past two decades, and one of recent film theory's most persistent fantasies is the fusion of critical spectatorship with political engagement. Aside from the obvious problems in assuming that gay men and lesbians necessarily have anything in common, the very

165

notion of a gay and/or lesbian film audience contains several potentially confusing threads which foreground the problematic relationship between "critical" and "politicized" spectatorship. In the most obvious, simplistic, and essentialist sense, to speak of a gay/lesbian audience may suggest that all gay men and lesbians share some specific identification patterns, such as cross-gender identification with film characters, or some kind of inherent capacity to read against the grain. In a larger, more diffuse, yet more culturally specific sense, film has become a component of the various narratives that constitute the very notion of a gay/lesbian identity, from coming-out stories to shared pleasures in camp to speculations about the real lives of performers. From this perspective (which seems to me much more enlightening than any monolithic notion of a gay/lesbian audience), the question is not what characterizes gay/lesbian spectatorship as common responses to film texts, but rather what place film spectatorship has had in the cultivation of gay/lesbian identity.

In other words, rather than attempt to essentialize some kind of distinct gay/lesbian spectatorship as a set of responses to film, it is more productive to ask what the place of film spectatorship is in gay and lesbian life. Given the particular function of the cinema as a mediation between individual fantasy and public ritual, what is significant in this instance is how going to the movies situates gay/lesbian desire in specific ways. Finally, one could argue that the only viable reason to speak of a gay/lesbian audience is in political terms, whether to argue for consumer pressure (i.e., gays and lesbians attend films and should therefore put pressure on film producers to create more complex roles for gay/lesbian characters) or to stress alternative distribution outlets which would be defined by political notions of spectatorship.

Thus we have three entries into defining gay/lesbian film audiences – first, an essentialist notion of how lesbians and gay men see the cinema; second, an examination of the place of cinema in the development of gay and lesbian identities and the consolidation of lesbian and gay communities; third, a conception of lesbian and gay audiences as constituting a political force, whether to pressure existing film productions or to create new ones. These three entries are not mutually exclusive, but neither are they the same. While defining the importance of film in the creation of one's gay identity is potentially contestatory and threatening, both to unexamined notions of heterosexual Hollywood and to compulsory heterosexuality, it is not political in the same way as conscious organizing as a consumer group is. This may sound obvious, but the recent uproar over "outing" and the peculiar connections forged between the gay press and the tabloids suggest that different notions of what it means to speak of a gay/lesbian

166

audience have become confused. The death of Garbo and its coincidence with the "outing" phenomenon offered, in bold relief, a demonstration of this confusion.

I have suggested in previous chapters that there are strong homosexual currents in spectatorship, and one could begin to wonder about
film theory's enthusiastic embrace of the metaphor of sexual difference
as a massive defense rather than as mere description of the prescribed
forms of sexual and spectatorial behavior (see Mayne 1990: chapter 3).
To put this another way, then, the composition of gay and lesbian
audiences foregrounds the very nature of film spectatorship as an
activity wherein distinctions between center and margin dissolve. This
may well suggest that there is a paradox in talking at all about gay
and lesbian audiences.

I am suspicious, though, of those who cry "paradox" or "contradiction" at the moment that any kind of specific gay and/or lesbian
spectatorship is proposed. Rather, I would insist that the paradox
can be acknowledged without invalidating the spectators in question;
indeed, it is only in acknowledging the paradox of definition that the
spectator can be defined in useful terms. Certainly, I think it is just
as – and no more – impossible to identify a common experience of gay
male or lesbian viewing (not to mention, therefore, gay *and* lesbian) as
it is to identify a single mode of spectatorship for any group consisting
of complex people with variables and differences. Unfortunately, those
critical of the so-called "identity politics" of gay and lesbian groups
and organizations assume too quickly that an essential homosexual
identity is what is affirmed and desired.

So the very notion of a critical audience, and specifically the critical
audience of gays and lesbians, *does* involve a paradox, but an inevitable
one, not the product of some lack of theoretical sophistication. Spectatorship and advocacy are not the same; however much they may
inflect each other – as they should – they are never reducible one to
the other. I would like to consider as a final example a film where
radically different notions of what the phrase "critical spectatorship"
might mean confront each other. One of the first articles I published
(in 1977) was a study of Rainer Fassbinder's film *Ali: Fear Eats the Soul*,
entitled "Fassbinder and Spectatorship" (Mayne 1977). I read the film
in terms of Fassbinder's attempt to appropriate Hollywood melodrama
to political ends. *Ali* is the story of a German cleaning woman in her
60s who meets and falls in love with Ali, an Moroccan immigrant
worker much younger than her (Figure 14). Fassbinder's famous
admiration for the film melodramas of Douglas Sirk is evident in the
film, particularly since it is a rewriting of Sirk's *All That Heaven Allows*.

At the time that I wrote the article, I was aware of Fassbinder's gay
sexuality, but unlike other of his films where authorial display and

Figure 14 Brigitte Mira and El Hedi Ben Salem in *Angst essen Seele auf* (*Ali: Fear Eats the Soul*)

gay desire are central, *Ali* seemed to occupy a completely different terrain. Only after Fassbinder's death in 1982 did I discover the fact that has since been repeated in numerous sources – that El Hedi Ben Salem, the man who plays Ali, was Fassbinder's lover. The details of Fassbinder's relationship with Salem are worthy of the melodramatic formula he adapted in *Ali* and other films. The two met in Paris, and Salem quickly became part of Fassbinder's entourage. Salem had a wife and five children in Morocco, and he and Fassbinder brought two of the sons to live with them in Germany, a brief experiment which ended with the children farmed out to other homes. Salem had small roles in several of Fassbinder's films; his starring role in *Ali* marked the demise of his relationship with Fassbinder. Salem had a history of violence when under the influence of alcohol, and he once attacked several people. Friends got him out of Germany before an arrest could be made. In 1977, Salem hanged himself in a jail cell (Hayman 1984; Katz 1987; Raab 1983).

My own take on *Ali* was that Fassbinder's appropriation of Hollywood melodrama offered an experience in critical spectatorship. Narratively, the devices of melodrama were used critically to explore the political realities of immigrant labor, racism, and class hypocrisy in Germany. Fassbinder's use of melodrama focuses on spectatorship, from the disapproving gazes of friends, family, and co-workers to the framing within the frame which foregrounds conditions of visibility. But two dimensions were entirely missing from my account of critical spectatorship. The first is camp, which is less evident here than in other Fassbinder films, but which nonetheless emerges in the stylized portrayal of the couple, particularly in the "incongruous contrast" of youth and old age, and the overall theatricality of the film's mise-en-scène ("to appreciate camp in things or persons is to perceive the notion of life-as-theater, being versus role-playing, reality and appearance") (Babuscio 1977: 41, 44). The second is what I'm tempted to call referential spectatorship, that is, a reading of a film in terms of the purported real-life events surrounding it. Given Fassbinder's propensity for authorial display in his films, and the notoriety of his life, the films and the anecdotes of the filmmaker's life tend to blend together in the writings about Fassbinder's career which influence, directly or indirectly, the reception of his films.

Fassbinder makes a brief appearance in *Ali* as Emmi's son-in-law, who is the last to leave the room when Emmi presents her new husband. This is the only face-to-face encounter of Salem and Fassbinder in the film, but there is nothing in the encounter to suggest the off-screen relationship. Indeed, even though I've just described two types of spectatorship that I totally ignored in my analysis of the film, it is nonetheless true that little in *Ali* would seem to demand an accounting for either camp or biography. In retrospect, however, it seems to me that what is challenging about Fassbinder's films is, precisely, the collision of different modes of spectatorship. The collision is only superficially described as Hollywood escapism versus political analysis. For two radically different notions of what constitutes spectatorship collide in *Ali*, one playing on distinctly gay styles like camp, and the other playing on Hollywood melodrama. The collision is exemplified in a striking detail of the film, the fact that twice Salem's naked body is displayed, both times in the context of a heterosexual relationship, and both instances striking for the objectification of the male, rather than the female body. Yet *that* challenge to conventional (heterosexual) spectatorship does not mesh easily, if at all, with the more conventional categories of class exploitation.

Indeed, the collision of two different modes of spectatorship is

169

complicated further by the fact that spectatorship is marked by race. The male body may be objectified, but its status as object goes beyond its maleness, for it is a body that is marked as racially other; in other words, the status of Salem's body can be read, simultaneously, in terms of gay male desire and in terms of racism. To be sure, the display of the male body in other Fassbinder films (such as *Germany in Autumn* and *Fox and His Friends*) is not necessarily defined by the intersection of race and sexuality that one sees in *Ali*, but nonetheless the collisions among race, sexuality, and class in this film stand as an appropriate emblem for the complex questions that gay/lesbian spectatorship raises. Kobena Mercer has observed that

> today we are adept at the all too familiar concatenation of identity politics, as if by merely rehearsing the mantra of "race, class, gender" (and all other intervening variables) we have somehow acknowledged the diversified and pluralized differences at work in contemporary culture, politics, and society. Yet the complexity of what actually happens "between" the contingent spaces where each variable intersects with the others is something only now coming into view theoretically.

(1991: 193)

Mercer's observation occurs within the context of an extensive analysis of Robert Mapplethorpe's photographs of black men and their complicated appeals to desires in which race, gender, and sexuality are not easily separated. The constitution of gay and lesbian audiences may well provide the most extended challenge to the study of spectatorship in terms, in Mercer's words, of "what actually happens 'between' . . ."

In the previous chapter, I noted how *Ghost* presents a classic pattern of white heterosexual coupledom threatened and restored through the intervention of Whoopi Goldberg's psychic. Even though that film takes heterosexual desire as its starting point and its conclusion, there is a striking scene that suggests cross-racial and same-sex love simultaneously, only quickly to shut down the possibility. One of the gifts Oda Mae Brown (whose name – as was frequently remarked informally among lesbian and gay viewers – is evocative of that of lesbian novelist Rita Mae Brown) discovers through her encounter with Sam is the ability to be possessed by a spirit so completely that she momentarily embodies that person literally. The first demonstration of this gift occurs when the spirit of a black man occupies her body and speaks to his former wife, but it is Goldberg's body we see. Oda Mae offers her body for such possession by Sam, so that he and Molly can share a final passionate embrace. But this time, Sam's body substitutes for Oda Mae's. The possibility of physical and intimate contact between the two women is broached, then shut down.

170

Reports of uncomfortable audience reaction to the beginning of this particular scene were common among lesbian and gay viewers, as if such scenes inspire gay and lesbian viewers to become, in Ruby Rich's words, "ultimate dialecticians," watching the screen (hopefully) out of one eye, members of the audience (suspiciously) out of the other (Citron et al. 1978: 87). A scene that for many (presumably heterosexual) viewers might well be only of marginal significance, at least consciously, became a major point of discussion for lesbian and gay viewers. This point of entry is complicated and provoked by Goldberg's off-screen commentary on the scene; she is reported to have told an interviewer that she was "relieved" not to have to kiss Demi Moore in the scene; " 'I have just managed to live down the lesbianism of *The Color Purple*' " (Musto 1990: 48). That Goldberg has been a popular performer among lesbians and gay men complicates the significance of the scene further; as Michael Musto put it in an open letter to Goldberg, "Remember when you were considered a daring counterculture performer with a big lesbian following? Now you've sold your soul so cheaply you breathe a sigh of relief when you're not asked to kiss an actress" (1990: 48).

One could point here, as Linda Nochlin has, to a long-standing iconographic tradition in Western art whereby the representation of a black and a white woman together signifies lesbianism (1983). While it is crucial to examine how the flirtation with lesbianism operates in relationship to the politics of race in *Ghost*, it is equally crucial to explore how that relationship functions across several boundaries, between the contingent spaces of which Mercer speaks. Ruby Rich has said, for instance: "I think that racial difference operates for lesbians in the same way as, let's say, butch-femme, or s&m roles do, that is, as a form of differentiation between two people of the same gender." With "issues of power and representation," Rich continues, "nothing can be taken for granted" (Bad Object-Choices 1991: 275).

While I think that Fassbinder's work is exemplary in its engagement with questions of spectatorship, my point is that gay spectatorship in his films collides not only with heterosexual presumptions but also with other definitions of politicized spectatorship having to do with class and race. This encounter seems to me quite similar to what has occurred in the current attention drawn to supposedly "resistant" audiences; resistance is a complicated process like any other, involving, as Rich says, "issues of power and representation." There is no simple, pure site of resistance, and the complicated forms that spectatorship takes make this clear. However much movements of feminists, gays and lesbians, and people of color have challenged a notion of "political" activity that would think only in terms of a master narrative of socialist revolution and attendant socio-economic change, the notion of

171

the personal-as-political cannot be equated with any idea that watching television or going to the movies are in themselves political acts. But theoretical writing about the "politics" of "critical" spectatorship usually remains locked into an either/or situation – a micropolitics where everything is a contestatory act, or a macropolitics where nothing is contestatory unless part of a globally defined political agenda. Despite the regular dismissal of master narratives and notions of the political whereby some clear-cut organizational strategy is required, the possibility of spectatorship as a potential vanguard activity still haunts film studies. Instead, spectatorship needs to be treated as one of those ordinary activities, and theorizing this activity can open up spaces between seemingly opposing terms, thus leading us to attend more closely to how stubbornly our pleasures in the movies refuse any rigid dichotomies.

WORKS CITED

Adam, Margie (1990) "Greta Garbo's 'Mysterious' Private Life," *Outlook* 10 (Fall): 25.

Allen, Jeanne Thomas (1980) "The Film Viewer as Consumer," *Quarterly Review of Film Studies* 5, 4: 481–99.

Allen, Robert (1979) "Motion Picture Exhibition in Manhattan, 1906–1912," *Cinema Journal* 18, 2: 2–15.

—— (1980) *Vaudeville and Film, 1895–1915: A Study in Media Interaction*. New York: Arno Press.

—— and Gomery, Douglas (1985) *Film History: Theory and Practice*. New York: Alfred A. Knopf.

Althusser, Louis (1968) *Lire le capital*, tome I. Paris: François Maspéro.

—— (1971) "Ideology and Ideological State Apparatuses (Notes toward an investigation)," in *Lenin and Philosophy and Other Essays*, trans. Ben Brewster. New York: Monthly Review Press, 127–86.

Appleton, Victor (1913) *The Motion Picture Chums at Seaside Park*. New York: Grosset and Dunlap.

Astor, Mary (1959) *My Story: An Autobiography*. Garden City, New York: Doubleday.

—— (1967) *A Life on Film*. New York: Delacorte Press.

Augst, Bertrand (1980) "The Lure of Psychoanalysis in Film Theory," in Theresa Hak Kyung Cha, ed., *Apparatus*, New York: Tanam, 415–37.

Austin, Bruce A. (1989) *Immediate Seating: A Look at Movie Audiences*. Belmont, California: Wadsworth.

Babuscio, Jack (1977) "Camp and the Gay Sensibility," in Richard Dyer, ed., *Gays and Film*. London: British Film Institute, 40–57.

Bad Object-Choices (1991) *How Do I Look? Queer Film and Video*. Seattle: Bay Press.

Baldwin, James (1976; rpt. 1990) *The Devil Finds Work*. New York: Dell.

Barbee, Bobbie E. (1962) "Players Keep Proving Worth with Opening Week Heroics," *Jet*, April 26: 54–7.

Barthes, Roland (1970; English translation 1974) *S/Z*. Paris: Seuil; New York: Hill and Wang, trans. Richard Miller.

—— (1975) *The Pleasure of the Text*, trans. Richard Miller. New York: Hill and Wang.

—— (1977a) "Writers, Intellectuals, Teachers," in Stephen Heath, ed. and trans., *Image-Music-Text*. London: Fontana, 190–215.

—— (1977b) "The Death of the Author," in Stephen Heath, ed. and trans., *Image-Music-Text*. London: Fontana, 142–8.

Baskette, Kirtley (1963) "Bette Davis' Biggest Victory," *Good Housekeeping*, vol. 157 (August): 30, 32, 34, 38.

Bates, Karen Grigsby (1991) " 'They've Gotta Have Us': Hollywood's Black Directors," *The New York Times Magazine*, July 14: 14–19, 38, 40, 44.

Baudry, Jean-Louis (1970; rpt. 1986) "Ideological Effects of the Basic Cinematographic Apparatus," in Philip Rosen, ed., *Narrative, Apparatus, Ideology*. New York: Columbia University Press, 286–98.

—— (1975; rpt. 1986) "The Apparatus: Metapsychological Approaches to the Impression of Reality in Cinema," in Philip Rosen, ed., *Narrative, Apparatus, Ideology*. New York: Columbia University Press, 299–318.

Bellour, Raymond (1975a) "The Unattainable Text," *Screen* 16, 3: 19–27.

—— (1975b) "Le Blocage symbolique," *Communications* (special issue on Cinema and Psychoanalysis) 23: 235–350.

Bergstrom, Janet (1979) "Alternation, Segmentation, Hypnosis: Interview with Raymond Bellour," *Camera Obscura* 3–4: 71–103.

—— and Doane, Mary Ann, eds. (1989) *Camera Obscura* 20–1: special issue on The Spectatrix.

Blair, Anne (1989) Review of *Field of Dreams*, *The Chicago Crusader*, May 6: 10.

Bobo, Jacqueline (1988) "*The Color Purple*: Black Women as Cultural Readers," in Deidre Pribram, ed., *Female Spectators*. London and New York: Verso, 90–109.

Bogle, Donald (1973; rpt. and updated edition, 1989) *Toms, Coons, Mulattoes, Mammies, and Bucks: An Interpretive History of Blacks in American Film*. New York: Continuum.

Bordwell, David (1985) *Narration in the Fiction Film*. Madison: University of Wisconsin Press.

—— (1989) "A Case for Cognitivism," *Iris*, 9: 11–40.

Bordwell, D. Staiger, J., and Thompson, K. (1985) *The Classical Hollywood Cinema: Film Style and Mode of Production to 1960*. New York: Columbia University Press.

Branigan, Edward R. (1984) *Point of View in the Cinema: A Theory of Narration and Subjectivity in Classical Film*. Berlin, New York, and Amsterdam: Mouton.

—— (1986) " 'Here is a Picture of No Revolver': The Negation of Images, and Methods for Analyzing the Structure of Pictorial Statements," *Wide Angle* 8, 3–4: 8–17.

Britton, Andrew (1984) *Katharine Hepburn: The Thirties and After*. Newcastle-upon-Tyne: Tyneside Cinema.

Bronski, Michael (1990) "She really did 'want to be alone,' " *Gay Community News* 17, 41: 20, 15.

Brown, Georgia (1990) "Blithe Spirit," *The Village Voice*, July 17: 63.

Browne, Nick (1975–6) "The Spectator-in-the-Text: The Rhetoric of *Stagecoach*," *Film Quarterly* 29, 2: 26–38.

Budd, Mike, Entman, Robert M., and Steinman, Clay (1990) "The Affirmative Character of U.S. Cultural Studies," *Critical Studies in Mass Communication* 7, 2 (June): 169–84.

Burch, Noël (1979) *To the Distant Observer: Form and Meaning in the Japanese Cinema*. London: Scolar Press.

Burr, Ty (1991) "Soul Man" (review of *Ghost* on video), *Entertainment Weekly*, 58 (March 22): 77–8.

Buscombe, E., Gledhill, C., Lovell, A., and Williams C. (1975–6) "Statement: Psychoanalysis and Film," *Screen* 16, 4 (Winter): 119–30.

Butzel, Marcia (1992) *Illuminating Movement: The Choreographic Aspect of Cinema*. Champaign-Urbana: University of Illinois Press.

Byars, Jackie (1991) *All That Hollywood Allows: Re-reading Gender in 1950s Melodrama*. Chapel Hill and London: University of North Carolina Press.

Cahiers du cinéma (collective text) (1969/1972). "Young Mr. Lincoln," *Cahiers du cinéma* 223 (August 1969); English translation in *Screen* 13 (Autumn 1972): 5–44.

Cameron, Gail (1974) "A Breathtaking Visit with Bette Davis," *McCall's* 102 (November): 24, 28, 30, 32, 38, 41.

Carr, C. (1990) "The New Outlaw Art," *The Village Voice*, July 17: 61.

Carroll, Noël (1988) *Mystifying Movies: Fads and Fallacies in Contemporary Film Theory*. New York: Columbia University Press.

Chodorow, Nancy (1978) *The Reproduction of Mothering: Psychoanalysis and the Sociology of Gender*. Berkeley and Los Angeles: University of California Press.

Citron, Michelle, Le Sage, Julia, Mayne, Judith, Rich, B. Ruby, Taylor, Anna Marie, and the editors of *New German Critique* (1978) "Women and Film: A Discussion of Feminist Aesthetics," *New German Critique* 13: 83–107.

Clarke, Jane and Simmonds, Diana (1980) *Move Over Misconceptions: Doris Day Reappraised*. London: British Film Institute.

Collier, Aldore (1990) "Whoopi Goldberg Talks About her Role in *Ghost* and Blasts Critics Over Her Film Choices," *Jet* 78, 18 (August 13): 58–60.

Comolli, Jean-Louis (1971/1986) "Technique and Ideology: Camera, Perspective, Depth of Field [Parts 3 and 4]," in Philip Rosen, ed., *Narrative, Apparatus, Ideology*. New York: Columbia University Press, 421–43.

— and Narboni, Jean (1969/1977) "Cinéma/Idéologie/Critique," *Cahiers du cinéma* (October–November 1969); English Translation in Society for Education in Film and Television, ed., *Screen Reader: Cinema/Ideology/Politics* (1977). London: Society for Education in Film and Television, 2–11.

Considine, Shaun (1989) *Bette and Joan: The Divine Feud*. New York: E.P. Dutton.

Cook, Pam (1978) "Duplicity in *Mildred Pierce*," in E. Ann Kaplan, ed., *Women in Film Noir*. London: British Film Institute, 68–82.

Copjec, Joan (1982) "The Anxiety of the Influencing Machine," *October*, 23: 43–59.

Corliss, Richard (1989) Review of *Field of Dreams*. *Time*, April 24: 78.

— (1990) Review of *Ghost*. *Time*, July 16: 86.

Cowie, Elizabeth (1979) "The Popular Film as Progressive Text – A Discussion of *Coma*," part one, *m/f* 3: 59–81.

— (1980) "Discussion of *Coma*," part two, *m/f* 4: 57–69.

— (1984) "Fantasia," *m/f* 9: 70–105.

Creed, Barbara (1990) "Response," *Camera Obscura* 20–1: 132–6.

Cripps, Thomas (1977) *Slow Fade to Black: The Negro in American Film, 1900–1942*. New York: Oxford University Press.

Davis, Bette (1940) "Code for American Girls," *Photoplay* LIV, 9 (September): 17, 82.

— (1941a) "Don't Be a Draft Bride," *Photoplay* 18, 2 (January): 26–7, 67.

— (1941b) "Uncertain Glory," *Ladies' Home Journal*, 58 (July): 16–17, 107–22.

— (1952) "Could Your Husband Take It?" *Ladies' Home Journal* 59 (June): 18, 140–3.

— (1962; new edition 1990) *The Lonely Life*. New York: G.P. Putnam's Sons.

— with Herskowitz, Michael (1987) *This 'n That*. New York: G.P. Putnam's Sons.

Davis, Curt (1978) "Bette Davis: Getting Under the Skin," *Encore American and Worldwide News*, November 6: 30–1.

Daws, [no first name given] (1990) Review of *Ghost*, *Variety*, July 11: 30.

Debord, Guy (1967; rpt. 1970) *La Société du spectacle*. Paris: Editions champ libre. English translation (1970), Detroit: Black and Red.

De Cordova, Richard (1985) "The Emergence of the Star System in America," *Wide Angle* 6, 4: 4–13.

—— (1990) *Picture Personalities: The Emergence of the Star System in America*. Urbana and Chicago: University of Illinois Press.

de Lauretis, Teresa (1984) *Alice Doesn't: Feminism, Semiotics, Cinema*. Bloomington: Indiana University Press.

—— (1989) "Film and the Visible." Paper presented at the "How Do I Look?" Conference, New York City, October.

Denby, David (1989) Review of *Field of Dreams*, *New York*, April 24: 24.

Diawara, Manthia (1988) "Black Spectatorship: Problems of Identification and Resistance," *Screen* 29, 4 (Autumn): 66–76.

—— ed. (1991) *Wide Angle* (special issue on Black Cinema) 13, 3–4 (July-October).

Doane, Mary Ann (1980) "Misrecognition and Identity," *Ciné-tracts* 3, 3: 25–32.

—— (1982) "Film and the Masquerade: Theorising the Female Spectator," *Screen* 23, 3–4: 74–88.

—— (1984) "The 'Woman's Film': Possession and Address," in Mary Ann Doane, Patricia Mellencamp, and Linda Williams, eds., *Re-vision: Essays in Feminist Film Criticism*. Frederick, Maryland: The American Film Institute/University Publications of America, 67–80.

—— (1987) *The Desire to Desire: The Woman's Film of the 1940s*. Bloomington: Indiana University Press.

—— (1990) "Response," *Camera Obscura* 20–1: 142–7.

Dorenkamp, Monica (1991) "A Sheep in Wolf's Clothing? (*The Silence of the Lambs*)," *Outweek*, March 6: 64–5.

Dubois, W.E.B. (1903; rpt. 1961) *The Souls of Black Folk*. New York: Fawcett World Library.

Dyer, Richard (1977) "Entertainment and Utopia," *Movie* 24, (Spring): 2–13.

—— (1979) *Stars*. London: British Film Institute.

—— (1986) *Heavenly Bodies: Film Stars and Society*. New York: St. Martin's Press.

—— (1988) "White," *Screen* 29, 4 (Autumn): 44–64.

Eckert, Charles (1978) "The Carole Lombard in Macy's Window," *Quarterly Review of Film Studies* 3, 1: 1–21.

Ellmann, Richard (1977) "A Late Victorian Love Affair," in Richard Ellmann and John Espey, eds., *Oscar Wilde: Two Approaches*. Los Angeles: University of California Press, 3–15.

Ellsworth, Elizabeth (1986) "Illicit Pleasures: Feminist Spectators and *Personal Best*," *Wide Angle* 8, 2: 45–56.

Elsaesser, Thomas (1980; rpt. 1986) "Primary Identification and the Historical Subject: Fassbinder and Germany," in Philip Rosen, ed., *Narrative, Apparatus, Ideology*. New York: Columbia University Press, 535–49.

—— (1984) "Film History and Visual Pleasure: Weimar Cinema," in Patricia Mellencamp and Philip Rosen, eds., *Cinema Histories/Cinema Practices*. Frederick, Maryland: University Publications of America/The American Film Institute, 47–84.

Ewen, Elizabeth (1985) *Immigrant Women in the Land of Dollars: Life and Culture on the Lower East Side, 1890–1925*. New York: Monthly Review Press.

176

Fiske, John (1987) "British Cultural Studies and Television," in Robert C. Allen, ed., *Channels of Discourse: Television and Contemporary Criticism*. Chapel Hill, North Carolina: University of North Carolina Press, 254–89.

French, Philip (1989) "On a Fantasy in the spirit of the Sixties," London *Observer*, November 26: 43.

Freud, Sigmund and Breuer, Josef (1893; rpt. and trans. 1974) *Studies on Hysteria*. New York and Harmondsworth: Penguin.

— (1919; rpt. and trans. 1972) ' "A Child is Being Beaten': A Contribution to the Origin of Sexual Perversions," in *Sexuality and the Psychology of Love*. New York: Collier, 107–32.

Friedberg, Anne (1993) *Window Shopping: Cinema and the Postmodern Condition*. Berkeley and Los Angeles: University of California Press.

Friedman, Lester D., ed. (1991) *Unspeakable Images: Ethnicity and the American Cinema*. Urbana and Chicago: University of Illinois Press.

Frye, Marilyn (1990) Lecture at forum on Theories of Sexuality, National Women's Studies Association Conference, Akron, Ohio, June. Printed as "Do You Have To Be a Lesbian To Be a Feminist?" *off our backs* 20, 8: 21–3.

Gaines, Jane (1986) "White Privilege and Looking Relations: Race and Gender in Feminist Film Theory," *Cultural Critique* 4: 59–79.

— (1989) "The Queen Christina Tie-Ups: Convergence of Shop Window and Screen," *Quarterly Review of Film and Video* 11, 1: 35–60.

— and Herzog, Charlotte, eds. (1990) *Fabrications: Costume and the Female Body*. New York and London: Routledge.

Gallagher, Catherine (1989) "Marxism and the New Historicism," in H. Aram Veeser, ed., *The New Historicism*. New York and London: Routledge, 37–48.

Gallop, Jane (1982) *The Daughter's Seduction: Feminism and Psychoanalysis*. London: Macmillan.

Gledhill, Christine (1988) "Pleasurable Negotiations," in E. Deidre Pribram, ed., *Female Spectators*. New York and London: Verso, 12–27.

Goldmann, Lucien (1975) *Towards a Sociology of the Novel*, trans. Alan Sheridan. London: Tavistock.

Gomery, Douglas (1990) "Thinking About Motion Picture Exhibition," *The Velvet Light Trap* 25: 4–11.

Gordon, Linda (1986) "What's New in Women's History," in Teresa de Lauretis, ed., *Feminist Studies/Critical Studies*, Bloomington: Indiana University Press, 20–30.

Greenblatt, Stephen (1989) "Towards a Poetics of Culture," in H. Aram Veeser, ed., *The New Historicism*. New York and London: Routledge, 1–14.

Gretton, Viveca (1990) "'You Could Look it Up': Notes Towards a Reading of Baseball, History and Ideology in the Dominant Cinema," *Cineaction* 21–2: 70–5.

Gronowicz, Antoni (1990) *Garbo: Her Story*. New York: Simon & Schuster.

Hall, Stuart (1980) "Encoding/Decoding," in Stuart Hall, D. Hobson, A. Lowe, and P. Willis, eds., *Culture, Media, Language*. London: Hutchinson, 128–38.

Handel, Leo (1950) *Hollywood Looks at Its Audience*. Urbana: University of Illinois Press.

Hansen, Miriam (1986) "Pleasure, Ambivalence, Identification: Valentino and Female Spectatorship," *Cinema Journal* 25, 4: 6–32.

— (1991) *Babel & Babylon: Spectatorship in American Silent Film*. Cambridge, Mass. and London: Harvard University Press.

Haralovich, Mary Beth (1990) "The proletarian woman's film of the 1930s: contending with censorship and entertainment," *Screen* 31, 2: 15–27.

Hayman, Ronald (1984) *Fassbinder, Film Maker*. London: Weidenfeld and Nicolson.

Heath, Stephen (1975) "Film and System: Terms of Analysis," Part 1: *Screen* 16, 1; Part 2: *Screen* 16, 2: 7–77.

—— (1976; rpt. 1981) "Narrative Space," in *Questions of Cinema*. Bloomington: Indiana University Press, 19–75.

—— (1977) "Film Performance," *Ciné-tracts* 2: 91–113.

—— (1979) "The Turn of the Subject," *Ciné-tracts* 2, 3–4 (Summer–Fall): 32–48.

Hebdige, Dick (1979) *Subculture: The Meaning of Style*. London and New York: Methuen.

Hope, Laura Lee (1914) *The Moving Picture Girls, or First Appearances in Photo Dramas*. New York: Grosset and Dunlap.

Hughes, Holly and Elovich, Richard (1990) "Homophobia at the N.E.A.," *New York Times*, July 28: 14.

Hyman, B.D. (1985) *My Mother's Keeper*. New York: William Morrow.

Jackson, Carlton (1990) *Hattie: The Life of Hattie McDaniel*. Lanham, New York, and London: Madison Books.

Jacobs, Lea (1981) "*Now, Voyager*: Some Problems of Enunciation and Sexual Difference," *Camera Obscura* 7: 88–109.

—— (1987) "Censorship and the Fallen Woman Cycle," in Christine Gledhill, ed., *Home is Where the Heart Is: Studies in Melodrama and the Woman's Film*. London: British Film Institute, 100–12.

—— (1988) "The Censorship of *Blonde Venus*: Textual Analysis and Historical Methods," *Cinema Journal* 27, 3: 21–31.

—— (1991) *The Wages of Sin: Censorship and the Fallen Woman Film, 1928–1942*. Madison: University of Wisconsin Press.

Jacobson, Harlan (1989) "Shot in the Dark: Born Again Baseball," *Film Comment* 25, 3: 78–9.

James, Caryn (1990) "Ghosts Must Catch the Spirit of the Time," *New York Times*, July 29, sec. H: 17.

Jauss, Hans Robert (1982) *Toward an Aesthetic of Reception*, trans. Timothy Bahti. Minneapolis: University of Minnesota Press.

Jet (1962) "Film Actress Bette Davis Wins Negro-Aid Award," Entertainment Column, 21, 26 (April 19): 58.

Jones, Lisa (1991) "The Defiant Ones: A talk with Film Historian Donald Bogle," *The Village Voice*, June 4: 69, 88.

Jowett, Garth (1985) "Giving Them What They Want: Movie Audience Research Before 1950," in Bruce A. Austin, ed., *Current Research in Film: Audiences, Economics, and Law*, vol. 1. Norwood, New Jersey: Ablex, 19–35.

Kaplan, E. Ann (1983a) "The Case of the Missing Mother: Maternal Issues in Vidor's *Stella Dallas*," *Heresies* 16: 81–5.

—— (1983b) *Women and Film: Both Sides of the Camera*. New York and London: Methuen.

Katz, Robert (1987) *Love is Colder Than Death: The Life and Times of Rainer Werner Fassbinder*. New York: Random House.

Kennedy, Lisa et al. (1991) "Writers on the *Lamb*," *The Village Voice*, March 5: 49, 56–9.

Kinsella, W.P. (1982) *Shoeless Joe*. New York: Houghton Mifflin.

Klapp, Orrin E. (1962) *Heroes, Villains and Fools*. Englewood Cliffs, New Jersey: Prentice-Hall.

Klinger, Barbara (1984) " 'Cinema/Ideology/Criticism' Revisited: The Progressive Text," *Screen* 25, 1 (January–February 1984): 30–44.

Krauthammer, Charles (1989) "Sappy Film Captures the Myth of Baseball," *Chicago Sun-Times*, May 13: 19.

Kristeva, Julia (1969) *Semiotikè: Recherches pour une sémanalyse*. Paris: Seuil.

Kuhn, Annette (1982) *Women's Pictures: Feminism and Cinema*. London: Routledge and Kegan Paul.

— (1988) *Cinema, Censorship and Sexuality, 1909–1925*. London and New York: Routledge.

Kuntzel, Thierry (1972/1978) "The Film-Work," *Enclitic* 2, 1: 38–61.

LaPlace, Maria (1985) "Bette Davis and the Ideal of Consumption: A Look at *Now, Voyager*," *Wide Angle* 6, 4: 34–43.

— (1987) "Producing and Consuming the Woman's Film: Discursive Struggle in *Now, Voyager*," in Christine Gledhill, ed., *Home is Where the Heart Is: Studies in Melodrama and the Woman's Film*. London: British Film Institute, 138–66.

Laplanche, Jean, and Pontalis, Jean-Bertrand (1964; trans. 1986) "Fantasy and the Origins of Sexuality," in Victor Burgin, James Donald, and Cora Kaplan, eds., *Formations of Fantasy*. London and New York: Methuen, 5–34.

— (1967; trans. 1973) *The Language of Psychoanalysis*, trans. D. Nicholson-Smith, London: Hogarth Press.

Leab, Daniel J. (1976) *From Sambo to Superspade: The Black Experience in Motion Pictures*. Boston: Houghton Mifflin.

Leinwand, Theodore B. (1990) "Negotiation and New Historicism," *Publications of the Modern Language Association of America* 105, 3: 477–90.

Lentricchia, Frank (1980) *After the New Criticism*. Chicago: University of Chicago Press.

Lesage, Julia (1974) "The Human Subject–You, He, or Me? (Or, The Case of the Missing Penis," *Jump Cut* 4 (November–December): 77–82.

McRobbie, Angela (1980) "Settling Accounts with Subcultures: A Feminist Critique," *Screen Education*, 34: 37–49.

— (1984) "Dance and Social Fantasy," in Angela McRobbie and Mica Nava, eds., *Gender and Generation*. London: Macmillan, 130–61.

Maio, Kathi (1991) *Popcorn and Sexual Politics: Movie Reviews*. Freedom, California: The Crossing Press.

Marchetti, Gina (1986) "Subcultural Studies and the Film Audience: Rethinking the Film Viewing Context," in Bruce A. Austin, ed., *Current Research in Film*, vol. 2. Norwood, New Jersey: Ablex Publishing, 62–79.

Maslin, Janet (1990) "Looking to the Dead for Mirth and Inspiration," *New York Times*, July 13, sec. C: 8.

Maychick, Diana (1989) "More Than a Game: James Earl Jones Sees Baseball as a Metaphor for Living," *New York Post*, April 20: 31–2.

Mayne, Judith (1977) "Fassbinder and Spectatorship," *New German Critique* 12: 61–74.

— (1985) "Review Essay: Feminist Film Theory and Criticism," *Signs* 11, 1 (Autumn): 81–100.

— (1988) *Private Novels, Public Films*. Athens: University of Georgia Press.

— (1990) *The Woman at the Keyhole: Feminism and Women's Cinema*. Bloomington: Indiana University Press.

Mercer, Kobena (1991) "Skin Head Sex Thing: Racial Difference and the Homoerotic Imaginary," in Bad Object-Choices, eds., *How Do I Look? Queer Film and Video*. Seattle: Bay Press, 169–222.

Merritt, Russell (1976) "Nickelodeon Theaters, 1905–1914: Building an

Audience for the Movies," in Tino Balio, ed., *The American Film Industry*. Madison: University of Wisconsin Press, 59–79.

Metz, Christian (1975; English trans. 1982) *The Imaginary Signifier: Psychoanalysis and the Cinema*, trans. Celia Britton, Annwyl Williams, Ben Brewster, and Alfred Guzzetti. Bloomington: Indiana University Press.

Modleski, Tania (1988) *The Women Who Knew Too Much: Hitchcock and Feminist Theory*. New York and London: Methuen.

—— (1989) "Some Functions of Feminist Criticism, or The Scandal of the Mute Body," *October* 49: 3–24.

Montgomery, Kathryn C. (1989) *Target: Prime Time*. New York and Oxford: Oxford University Press.

Montrose, Louis A. (1989) "Professing the Renaissance: The Poetics and Politics of Culture," in H. Aram Veeser, ed., *The New Historicism*. New York and London: Routledge, 15–36.

Morin, Edgar (1956) *Le Cinéma, ou l'Homme imaginaire*. Paris: Editions de Minuit.

—— (1972) *Les Stars*. Paris: Seuil.

Mulvey, Laura (1975) "Visual Pleasure and Narrative Cinema," *Screen* 16, 3 (Autumn): 6–18.

—— (1989) *Visual and Other Pleasures*. Bloomington: Indiana University Press.

Musto, Michael (1990) "La Dolce Musto," *The Village Voice*, September 4: 48.

Naremore, James (1988) *Acting in the Cinema*. Berkeley and Los Angeles: University of California Press.

Nelson, Joyce (1977) "*Mildred Pierce* Reconsidered," *Film Reader*, 2: 65–70.

Nichols, Bill (1989) "Form Wars: The Political Unconscious of Formalist Theory," *The South Atlantic Quarterly* 88, 2: 487–515.

Nochlin, Linda (1983) "The Imaginary Orient," *Art in America*, May: 119–91.

Ohmer, Susan (1990) "Female Spectatorship and Women's Magazines: Hollywood, *Good Housekeeping*, and World War II," *The Velvet Light Trap* 25: 53–68.

Peiss, Kathy (1986) *Cheap Amusements*. Philadelphia: Temple University Press.

Penley, Constance (1985) "Feminism, Film Theory and the Bachelor Machines," *m/f* 10: 39–59.

—— (1988) "Introduction: The Lady Doesn't Vanish: Feminism and Film Theory," in Constance Penley, ed., *Feminism and Film Theory*. New York and London: Routledge, 1–24.

Petro, Patrice (1989) *Joyless Streets: Women and Melodramatic Representation in Weimar Germany*. Princeton: Princeton University Press.

Photoplay (1939) Advertisement, June: 68.

—— (1940) Advertisement for Westmore Cosmetics, May: 87.

Pleynet, Marcelin (1969) "Entretien (avec Gérard Leblanc)," *Cinéthique* 3: 5–13.

Polan, Dana (1986) *Power and Paranoia: History, Narrative and the American Cinema, 1940–1950*. New York: Columbia University Press.

Quirk, Lawrence J. (1990) *Fasten Your Seat Belts: The Passionate Life of Bette Davis*. New York: William Morrow.

Raab, Kurt (1983) "My Life with Rainer," *The Village Voice*, May 3: 43–5.

Radstone, Susannah (1985) " 'Woman' to Women" *Screen* 26, 3–4: 111–15.

Radway, Janice (1984) *Reading the Romance: Women, Patriarchy, and Popular Literature*. Chapel Hill and London: University of North Carolina Press.

Rancière, Jacques (1974). *Les Leçons d'Althusser*. Paris: Gallimard.

Reid, Mark (1991) "The U.S. Black Family Film," *Jump Cut* 36: 81–8.

Renov, Michael (1988) *Hollywood's Wartime Woman: Representation and Ideology*. Ann Arbor: UMI Research Press.

—— (1989) "Advertising/Photojournalism/Cinema: The Shifting Rhetoric of Forties Female Representation," *Quarterly Review of Film and Video* 11: 1–21.
Rentschler, Eric (1981) "Expanding Film Historical Discourse: Reception The-
ory's Use Value for Cinema Studies," *Ciné-tracts* 4, 1: 57–68.
Rodowick, D.N. (1982) "The Difficulty of Difference" *Wide Angle* 5, 1: 4–15.
—— (1988) *The Crisis of Political Modernism: Criticism and Ideology in Contemporary
Film Theory*. Urbana and Chicago: University of Illinois Press.
—— (1991) *The Difficulty of Difference*. New York and London: Routledge.
Rose, Jacqueline (1980) "The Cinematic Apparatus: Problems in Current
Theory," in Teresa de Lauretis and Stephen Heath, eds., *The Cinematic
Apparatus*. New York: St. Martin's Press, 172–86.
—— (1986) *Sexuality in the Field of Vision*. London: Verso.
—— (1990) "Response," *Camera Obscura* 20–1: 274–9.
Rosen, Philip (1984) "Securing the Historical: Historiography and the Classical
Cinema," in Patricia Mellencamp and Philip Rosen, eds., *Cinema Histories,
Cinema Practices*. Frederick, Maryland: University Publications of America/
The American Film Institute.
Rosenbaum, Jonathan (1980) *Moving Places: A Life at the Movies*. New York:
Harper & Row.
Screen Editorial Board, "Editorial," *Screen* 16, 2 (Summer 1975): 4–6.
Signorile, Michelangelo (1990) "The Secret Gay Life of Malcolm Forbes,"
Outweek 38 (March 18) 40–5.
—— (1991a) "Gossip Watch," *Outweek* 87 (February 27): 44–5, 60.
—— (1991b) "Gossip Watch," *Outweek* 96 (May 1): 54–5, 66.
Silverman, Kaja (1983) *The Subject of Semiotics*. New York: Oxford University
Press.
—— (1988) *The Acoustic Mirror: The Female Voice in Psychoanalysis and Cinema*.
Bloomington: Indiana University Press.
Smith, Paul (1988) *Discerning the Subject*. Minneapolis: University of Minnesota
Press.
Stack, Peter (1989) "Corn Grows High in *Field of Dreams*," *San Francisco Chron-
icle*, April 21, sec. E: 1.
Staiger, Janet (1986) " 'The Handmaiden of Villainy': Methods and Problems
in Studying the Historical Reception of a Film," *Wide Angle* 8, 1: 19–27.
—— (1992) *Interpreting Films: Studies in the Historical Reception of American
Cinema*. Princeton, New Jersey: Princeton University Press.
Steinem, Gloria (1986) *Marilyn*. Photographs by George Barris. New York:
Holt.
Stine, Whitney, with Bette Davis (1974; rpt. 1984) *Mother Goddam*. New York:
Hawthorn; rpt. New York: Berkley.
Stuart, Otis (1990) "Alone at Last (Greta Garbo, 1905–1990)," *Outweek* 46 (May
16): 60–1, 71–2.
Studlar, Gaylyn (1988) *In the Realm of Pleasure: Von Sternberg, Dietrich and the
Masochistic Aesthetic*. Urbana: University of Illinois Press.
Taubin, Amy (1991) "Demme's Monde," *The Village Voice*, February 19: 64,
76–7.
Thomson, David (1981) *A Biographical Dictionary of Film*, second edition. New
York: Morrow Quill.
Thompson, E.P. (1978) *The Poverty of Theory*. London: Merlin.
Turner, Graeme (1988) *Film As Social Practice*. London and New York: Rout-
ledge.
Variety (1942a), Poll Results, August 5: 3.

—— (1942b), "Letter," August 12: 12.

Veeser, H. Aram, ed. (1989) *The New Historicism*. New York and London: Routledge.

Waldman, Diane (1982) "The Childish, the Insane and the Ugly: The Representation of Modern Art in Popular Films and Fiction of the Forties," *Wide Angle* 5, 2: 52–65.

—— (1988) "Film Theory and the Gendered Spectator: The Female or the Feminist Reader?" *Camera Obscura* 18: 80–94.

Walkerdine, Valerie (1986) "Video Replay: Families, Films, and Fantasies," in Victor Burgin, James Donald, and Cora Kaplan, eds., *Formations of Fantasy*. London and New York: Methuen, 167–99.

Weiss, Andrea (1991) "A queer feeling when I look at you: Hollywood stars and lesbian spectatorship in the 1930s," in Christine Gledhill, ed., *Stardom: Industry of Desire*. London and New York: Routledge, 283–99.

Wiegman, Robyn (1989) "Negotiating AMERICA: Gender, Race, and the Ideology of the Interracial Male Bond," *Cultural Critique* 13, 89–117.

—— (1991) "Black Bodies/American Commodities: Gender, Race, and the Bourgeois Ideal in Contemporary Film," in Lester D. Friedman, ed., *Unspeakable Images*. Champaign and Chicago: University of Illinois Press, 308–28.

Wilde, Oscar (1891; rpt. 1962) *The Picture of Dorian Gray*. New York: New American Library.

Williams, Linda (1984) " 'Something Else Besides a Mother': *Stella Dallas* and the Maternal Melodrama," *Cinema Journal* 24, 1: 2–27.

Williams, Raymond (1977) *Marxism and Literature*. New York and Oxford: Oxford University Press.

Wilson, Alexander (1981) "Friedkin's *Cruising*, Ghetto Politics, and Gay Sexuality," *Social Text* 4: 98–109.

"With Brickbats and Bouquets [Fan letters page]" (1933a) Letter from Lee Norquest, Lafayette, Indiana. *Photoplay* XLIII 2 (January): 7.

"With Brickbats and Bouquets [Fan letters page]" (1933b) Letter from L.T. Roemer, Galveston, Texas. *Photoplay* XLIII, 2 (January): 7.

Wood, Robin (1982) "Fear of Spying," *American Film*, November: 28–35.

Yearwood, Gladstone L., ed. (1982) *Black Cinema Aesthetics*. Athens, Ohio: Center for Afro-American Studies.

INDEX

cultural studies 43, 54–5, 81, 98, 100

Davis, Bette 8, 65, 127–41
Day, Doris 163
De Cordova, Richard 127–8
de Lauretis, Teresa 57, 58, 70–1, 73, 90
Debord, Guy 5, 28, 35
Dee, Sandra 125, 126
Defiant Ones, The (1958) 155
desire 22–4, 88–90
Devil Finds Work, The 155
Diawara, Manthia 143
Dietrich, Marlene 65, 128; and von Sternberg, Josef 128
Disappearance of Aimee, The 136
Doane, Mary Ann 25, 33, 50, 53, 63–4, 74
Driving Miss Daisy 21
Dry Kisses Only (1990) 135
dualism 4, 29–30, 38, 39, 68, 73, 83, 125, 138, 159
Dubois, W.E.B. 155
Dunaway, Faye 136
Dyer, Richard 65, 96, 124–7, 145–6

Eckert, Charles 51–2
Eco, Umberto 57
Eisenstein, Sergei 34
Ellmann, Richard 109–10
Ellsworth, Elizabeth 67
Elsaesser, Thomas 69
empirical models 53–62
encoding and decoding 57, 92
Enemy Mine (1984) 144
ethnography 42, 54, 59–62, 84, 85, 157
exhibition 65–6

Fame 94–5
fantasy 79, 86–91
Fassbinder, Rainer 167–71
Fatal Attraction 21
female rivalry 132–41
female spectatorship 8, 24, 43, 49, 53, 60, 70–6, 77, 130, 145, 159
feminism 19, 23, 32, 43, 63, 99
feminist film theory 29, 51, 70–6, 100, 105, 128–41, 144
Field of Dreams (1989) 142–3, 145–9, 150, 151–4
film impressionism 6
Fiske, John 94
Flashdance 81, 94–5

Fonda, Jane 124
Forbes, Malcolm 160
Forty-Eight Hours 143
Foucault, Michel 45, 100
Fox and His Friends 170
French, Philip 147
Freud, Sigmund 13, 22–3, 24, 27, 28, 33, 41, 46, 70, 86, 107
Friedberg, Anne 51
Frye, Marilyn 145

Gallagher, Catherine 100
Gallop, Jane 101
Garbo, Greta 160–5, 167
Garland, Judy 65
Gay Community News 162
gay and lesbian audiences 8, 97, 99, 108, 145, 157–72
gaze 22, 32
genre 142–56
Gentlemen Prefer Blondes (1953) 74
Germany in Autumn 170
Ghost (1990) 142–3, 145, 149–54
Ghost Dad 152
Gledhill, Christine 100
Godard, Jean-Luc 4
Goldberg, Whoopi 142, 149, 151, 152, 153, 170–1
Goldmann, Lucien 49–50
Gomery, Douglas 66
Gone with the Wind 139, 142
Gordon, Linda 75, 78
Gossett, Louis, Jr. 144
Grand Hotel 163
Grandma's Reading Glass (1900) 2
Grant, Cary 123
Great Lie, The (1941) 136, 138–9, 142
Greenblatt, Stephen 99
Gronowicz, Antoni 164

Hall, Stuart 59, 81, 92
Hansen, Miriam 67, 71
Haralovich, Mary Beth 108
Harris, Thomas 165
Heath, Stephen 6, 14, 18, 25, 44, 106, 111–12
Hepburn, Katharine 65; and Tracy, Spencer 128
Here Comes Mr. Jordan 143
heterosexuality 85, 90, 97–8; and homosexuality 97, 107–22, 128, 156, 166
His Girl Friday (1940) 57